KUZMINO CHRONICLES

Memoirs of Teenage Holocaust Survival

NARRATED BY LEIB AND GITTEL MOSKOWITZ

Edited by: Nathan C. Moskowitz MD, PhD

Copyright © 2014 Nathan C. Moskowitz MD, PhD
All rights reserved.

Shoah Forensics Art Institute Publications

ISBN: 0692222707
ISBN 13: 9780692222706

In Memory of:

Yehuda Leib (Leba/Leopold) Salomon, Chaye Salomon nee Moskovicova,
Lea (Lenka) Moskowitz nee Salomon, Chaym Hersh Salomon, Golde Ackerman nee Salomon (and six offspring), Dvora nee Salomon, Henach (Chanoch) Moskowitz, Ida (Yetta) Moskowitz nee Niederman, Nathan (Nusen) Moskowitz, Chaya nee Moskowitz (and offspring Shprintza and Mechal), Rizel Farkos nee Moskowitz (and her son Henach Farkos and multiple Farkos offspring), Chaym Hersh (Herman) Moskowitz, Shmiel Moishe Itzcovitz, Sara Itzcovitz, Moishe Wolf Moskowitz, Liba Moskowitz, Michal Moskowitz, Yankel Moskowitz (son of Moishe Wolf and Liba), Shloyme Moskowitz, Yisrael Bear (Berko) Moskowitz, Chana Moskowitz nee Itzcovitz, Ruchel Haberman nee Itzcovitz (and seven offspring), Shmuel Itzcovitz, Shea Itzcovitz, Yankel Itzcovitz (and multiple offspring),
Feiga Itzcovitz, Aaron Itzcovitz (and daughter), Devora nee Itzcovitz (and multiple

offspring) Leah Moskowitz (daughter of Yisrael Bear and Chana), Shoshana Moskowitz, Raizel Moskowitz, Pearel (Pearl) Moskowitz, Wolf Moskowitz, Herschie Moskowitz, and Yankel Moskowitz (son of Yisrael Bear and Chana).

Aleihem HaShalom

Foreword

Perhaps the single most often expressed concern about Holocaust education is whether it will be possible to effectively transmit knowledge of the Shoah once no more survivors are on hand to provide eyewitness testimony. The inevitable march of time makes that question legitimate. This book provides the answer.

The testimony of Leib and Gittel Moskowitz tells, in their own words, the harrowing story of two teenagers swept up in the maelstrom of the German death machine and who, against all odds, managed to survive. They are not historians talking about something that happened to other people. They are not literary craftsmen trying to evoke emotions in audiences that can only imagine what it might have been like in Auschwitz, Mauthausen and Ravensbruck. Leib and Gittel were there. They know what happened. They experienced it. What they are sharing are not reminiscences, but eternal truths.

When Leib recalls facing the "selections" by the infamous war criminal Dr. Josef Mengele, or when Gittel describes her work as a slave laborer in a German ammunitions plant, where even the slightest inadvertent increase in temperature could cause the bullets to explode in her hands, it is the voice of authenticity, ringing out across the generations.

The Moskowitzes' story is unique. While Holocaust memoirs have much in common with each other, ultimately each of them is different. Their experiences were theirs alone. This book, too, is unique. Their son, Dr. Nathan Moskowitz, is the editor of their testimony but he has deliberately refrained from the temptation to polish his parents' English or reorganize their narrative. He lets their words speak for themselves, even when they are rough around the edges or do not flow with perfect smoothness. It is the genuineness of his parents' account that is most important to him, and that is to his credit.

FOREWORD

What Dr. Moskowitz has done, and what makes this book all the more significant, is to insert helpful historical background information, culled from the data bases of major Holocaust institutions. By interspersing these explanations throughout the text, he ably addresses a shortcoming of many Holocaust memoirs. Survivors often casually refer to people, places, and events with which their audience may not be familiar. Readers are forced to search the endnotes buried in the back of the book, or hunt for information in other books or on the internet. In Kuzmino Chronicles, by contrast, the reader is provided with the background as the story moves along, thus preserving the integrity of the narrative.

Ultimately, of course, it is the words of Leib and Gittel that tell us what we really need to know--and what future generations will need to know. Their gripping, powerful testimony transports us back to that blackest of nights. It documents for all time what happened to them and millions of other Jews. And maybe, just maybe, it offers a tiny shred of hope that if the next generation learns the Moskowitzes' story, tomorrow's leaders will work to ensure that it will never be repeated.

> Dr. Rafael Medoff, Founding Director,
> The David S. Wyman Institute for
> Holocaust Studies

Acknowledgements

It would not have been possible to obtain the vast majority of the documentation in this book without the assistance of the Holocaust Survivors and Victims Resource Center of the United States Holocaust Memorial Museum, 100 Raoul Wallenberg Place, S.W. Washington D.C. 20024. In particular we thank Mr. Rene Staedtler of this organization, who upon requests for information and documentation related to - Lipot (Leib) Moskowitz, Gizella (Gittel) Moskowitz, Herman Moskowitz, Nathan Moskowitz and Lea (Lenke) Moskowitz - searched the International Tracing Service (ITS) collection held by the United States Holocaust Memorial Museum, and located and then transmitted the following relevant information: Mauthausen concentration camp records, lists of Jewish Holocaust survivors of Bohemia and Moravia, lists of survivors who arrived in Budapest in 1945, multiple versions of A.E.F.D.P. (Allied

KUZMINO CHRONICLES

Expeditionary Forces Displaced Persons) registration records, registration records of Gabersee bei Wasserburg, Bavaria, Germany, documentation of Bremerhaven, the passenger list of the USAT General Muir, transcript of the Benjamin and Vladka Meed Registry of Holocaust Survivors, the list of children who arrived in Great Britain (Feb/March 1946), child tracing service documents from 1949, the arrival list of children at Millisle, Belfast on April 10, 1946, Mauthausen individual documents and envelopes, the prisoner number registry at Mauthausen concentration camp, the Arrival book of Mauthausen concentration camp (compiled postwar), transfer lists to Mauthausen subcamp Melk to work related 'Project Quartz', the transfer list from subcamp back to main Mauthausen concentration camp, the Infirmary Arrival book at subcamp Melk of Mauthausen concentration camp, the Death book (Totenbuch) of the Mauthausen infirmary, the list of deceased at the Mauthausen sick camp (Revier), the Death book (Totenbuch) of Mauthausen concentration camp, lists by nationality of the victims of Mauthausen concentration camp, the official

ACKNOWLEDGEMENTS

death certificate issued by the ITS for Herman Moskowitz, lists of transportation of prisoners from Auschwitz to Natzweiler, and transfer lists from Natzweiler to Allach, a Dachau subcamp.

We are grateful to the Neveklarsfeld Foundation for listing information on victims of Hungarian Labor battalions on their website.

We are exceptionally grateful to Judy Horowitz a nationally and internationally acclaimed portrait artist who worked tirelessly with me (NCM) on creating the painting that appears on the front cover of this book: "Shoah Forensics III: Family photograph re-illumination". This painting reconstructs a defaced family photograph that appears on the back cover of this book (details of the photograph are outlined in the book). Herman's (Chaym Hersch's) face which was entirely damaged to the point of invisibility, is reconstructed using forensic techniques, and is masterfully illuminated and hauntingly portrayed with the assistance of Judy Horowitz' enormous and superhuman input. Her love and dedication to the project of bringing a vanished, forgotten face back to life, is greatly acknowledged and appreciated. The museum quality, fine art, oil painting of Judy Horowitz employs the classical techniques of under painting and glazing to achieve the *luce di sotto* (interior luminosity, light from within) attributed to the Flemish, Dutch and Italian Masters of the sixteenth and seventeenth centuries, the Golden Age of painting. Her work is represented in numerous private and public collections in the United States and abroad, including Israel, and is notable for its rich psychological insight and realistic attention to detail, attributes which are very evident in the painting on the cover of this book.

We are extremely grateful to Dr. Rafael Medoff for his extensive editorial suggestions, and for the Foreword he so kindly provided for this book. Dr. Medoff is the Founding Director of The David S. Wyman Institute for Holocaust Studies, and is the author of over sixteen books and hundreds of articles related to the Holocaust.

Contents

FOREWORD v
ACKNOWLEDGEMENTS ix
INTRODUCTION xv

BOOK I: KUZMINO CHRONICLES OF LEIB MOSKOWITZ 1
    Chapter 1 My Family Background 3
    Chapter 2 Childhood in Kuzmino before the war 29
    Chapter 3 Life after my father was conscripted into the Hungarian Army 40
    Chapter 4 Deportation: Pesach 1944 50
    Chapter 5 Auschwitz 59
    Chapter 6 Mauthausen 65
    Chapter 7 Melk and Ebensee 84
    Chapter 8 Return to my house in Kuzmino after liberation 159
    Chapter 9 Journeying from Kuzmino to Czechoslovakia 169

Chapter 10 Journeying from Czechoslovakia to
          Germany 185
Chapter 11 Arrival at Germany: American
          DP camp........................ 190
Chapter 12 En Route to America 236

BOOK II: KUZMINO CHRONICLES OF GITTEL MOSKOWITZ............................263

Chapter 1 Childhood in Kuzmino............. 265
Chapter 2 Roundup by Hungarian Police 277
Chapter 3 Auschwitz........................ 280
Chapter 4 Ravensbruck 294
Chapter 5 Malchow......................... 298
Chapter 6 Liberation 304
Chapter 7 Return to Kuzmino 308
Chapter 8 Kindertransport to United Kingdom
          and Arrival to United States 314

POSTSCRIPT................................341
ABOUT THE EDITOR.......................345

Introduction

It's been seventy years since my parents Leib and Gittel Moskowitz survived the Shoah. They were both born and raised in the same small town of Kuzmino located in what was then Czechoslovakia. They were both fifteen years old when the Hungarian police (Gendarmerie) came one sunny Sunday morning in April 1944 and gave them and their families one hour to pack their belongings, after which they were transported to a ghetto in Munkatch, a neighboring town. From there they were hand-delivered into the hating hands of the SS black shirts who herded them into cattle cars destined for Auschwitz.

Both my parents just turned eighty five this year (2014), an age when it is imperative for them to document their experiences before they are lost to the collective historical consciousness of the Jewish people. Despite the passage of seventy years, the memories of what happened to them, their families, their neighbors and friends are as vivid and clear to them today as they were on the dark days and nights when they transpired. As my father says "these things are burned into your brain. I can never forget them".

Despite the fact that countless Holocaust books have been written by historians, and innumerable memoirs and recollections have been penned by survivors including the elegiac and elegant Elie Wiesel and Primo Levi, my parents, ordinary Jews (puhshitta Yeedin) have their stories to tell, and they must be told. It is a matter of testimony, a matter of historical recollection, the need to document and record, and a matter of honoring all the people who they personally remember, many of whose lives may never have been recorded, registered or inscribed anywhere else other than within the reverberating memory circuits still echoing inside my parents' agile yet aging brains.

In this book my parents' memoirs are recorded as told in their own words with their authentic voices. Their words appear in italicized print. When appropriate, historical documentation from Yad Vashem, Mauthausen Museum, and other

INTRODUCTION

predominantly internet sources confirming their recollections are included and appear in non-italicized form. Also included are corroboratory documents obtained from the International Tracing Services (ITS) collection held by the United States Holocaust Memorial Museum (USHMM). These documents include concentration camp arrival and transfer logs, liberation papers, Displaced Person (DP) and other records. Other documentation such as birth certificates, passports, DP Agudath Israel membership cards and photos are included to flesh out and further corroborate my parents' very clear and precise recollections.

I hope this book honors the many victims they still recollect, and testifies to their near forgotten existence and, to the ordeals suffered by the millions of martyred Jews, and of those fortunate enough to have survived.

In Daniel Goldhagen's book "Hitler's Willing Executioners: Ordinary Germans and the Holocaust" (1997) he hypothesizes that the vast majority of ordinary Germans were "willing executioners" in the Holocaust because of a unique and virulent "eliminationist anti-Semitism" and a secularization of theological anti-Semitism which has its origins and roots in medieval times.

According to my parents' accounts, the Germans were not the only willing European executioners. It was the local Hungarian police, not the German SS who collected them. Their neighbors watched as they were rounded up. What they uttered were not words of protest but requests for their possessions. When my parents returned to their town after their liberation they found their homes either totally ransacked or occupied by their neighbors. My father's attempt to resettle in his home was met by death threats from the local populace.

Fortunately, after a long wait, my parents came to the United States of America, the 'Goldena Medina' (Golden Land), the land of opportunity, undeniably the greatest country on earth which radiates democracy along with a heartfelt respect for peoples of all races and religions. It is in these environs where Leib and Gittel recovered from their trauma, flourished and thrived as they lived to raise children, grandchildren and great grandchildren.

BOOK I

KUZMINO CHRONICLES OF LEIB MOSKOWITZ

1

My Family Background

I was born on November 11, 1928 in Kuzmino, Czechoslovakia. My birth was registered in Kalnik, a nearby town which recorded my birth certificate on November 13. I still have this birth certificate (See Figures 1, 2, and 3)

My grandparents weren't alive when I was born. People didn't live very long back then. My mother Lea (Lenka) Moskowitz nee Lea Salomon was, like me, a survivor of Auschwitz and many other camps (See Photo 1). *Her concentration camp number was 20684* (See Figures 4A, B, C, D and E).

She lived until the age of 73. My mother was born in St. Davitkovo C.S.R. on June 6, 1897.

Her father's name was Yehuda Leib (Leba/ Leopold) Salomon. That's who I was named after. My mother's mother's name was Chaye Salomon nee Moskovicova. I also have her birth certificate (See Figure 5).

My mother had two brothers and two sisters. One brother, Chaym Hersh Salomon, died in St. Davidkovo in 1941. He had two daughters that survived, Dvora and Judith. They both immigrated to Israel in 1948 from Czechoslovakia. Dvora Mermelstein nee Salomon died in 2012. Judith Joses nee Salomon still lives in Israel.

My mother's other brother, Shloymo Salomon, survived and lived in the USA. He died in 1977. He had one daughter that survived, Ruth Abramsky.

My mother's sister, Golde Ackerman nee Salamon, along with her husband Nathan Ackerman and their six children perished in the Holocaust as did Golde's other sister Dvora. Dvora had one daughter that survived, Chana Weiss, who lives in Detroit Michigan.

MY FAMILY BACKGROUND

My father's name was Nathan (Nusen) Moskowitz (See Photo 2). He was born on January 11, 1901 in Kuzmino C.S.R. He perished in World War II someplace in the Ukraine. He was drafted by the Hungarians in 1939. He was in Unit # 108/60 TMS2. He was captured in the Ukranian/Russian city Konotovka. He was listed as missing on January 14, 1943 (See Figure 6).

My father's father's name was Henach (Chanoch) Moskowitz. My father's mother's name was Ida (Yetta) Niederman. I also had an older brother, Chaym Hersh (Herman) Moskowitz born in St. Davitkovo C.S.R. on May 16, 1927. He died (actually murdered) in Mauthausen on April 19, 1944. He was 17 years old when he died. His concentration camp number was 68621 (More details and documentation later).

My father had five sisters. Three immigrated to the USA before the war, and two perished in the Holocaust. The two that perished were Chaya and Rizel.

Chaya had a daughter who survived. Her name was Gizela (Gittel) Hershkowitz. Chaya's son Mechal and her other daughter Shprintza perished.

Rizel Farkos perished in the Holocaust. One of her sons Morris (Moishe) Farkos survived. Her son Henoch perished in Ebensee. She had other children who also perished. I don't know how many, or their names.

The three sisters who immigrated to the USA were Feiga, Golda and Shifre. Feiga Einczig lived at 511 East 79th street, NY, NY, USA. She sent me an affidavit to come to the USA (more documents and details later). *Golda Niederman lived in New Brunswick, New Jersey. Shifre lived in New York.*

My first cousin Moishe Farkos told me that my paternal grandfather Henoch was born in Romania. I have no way of knowing if that is or is not true. When my father voted, he wrote down that his political affiliation is Jewish (Zhidofsku in Czech).

MY FAMILY BACKGROUND

Photo 1: Lea (Lenka) Moskowitz, circa 1949.

Photo2: Nathan Moskovitc as a young man probably in his twenties. This photo was sent to his relatives in America and was thus preserved.

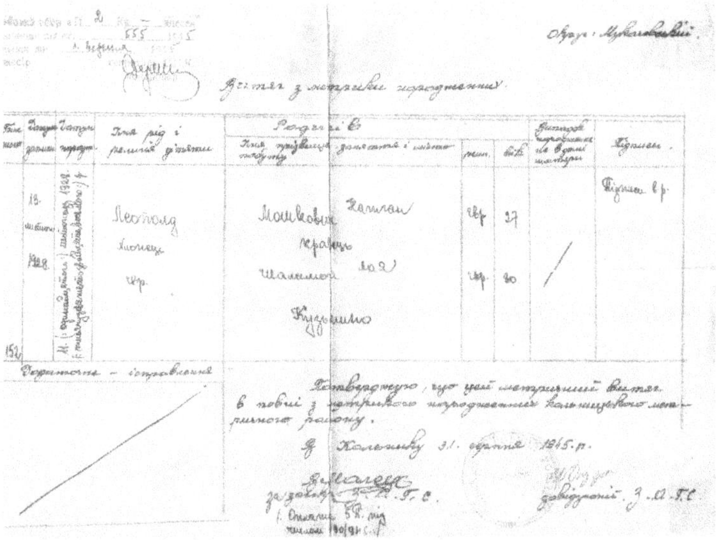

Окр.: Мукачівський

Витяг з метрики народження

152	13. листоп. 1928		Леопольд	Мошкович Кальман / кравець / Шалимон Лея / Кузьмино	євр.	27 / 30	/	Підписи вр.	

Стверджую, що цей метричний витяг в повні з метрики народження ... району.

В Коломику 31. серпня 1945 р.

Figure 1: Copy of Leib's original birth certificate written in Russian. His birth, November 13, 1928 (day of registration) is written in the left column. His name is recorded as Leopold in the fourth column from the left. The names of his father (age 27) and mother (age 30) at the time of birth, and the city of birth (Kuzmino) are recorded. It is stamped 1945 the year it was requested by Leib for identification purposes.

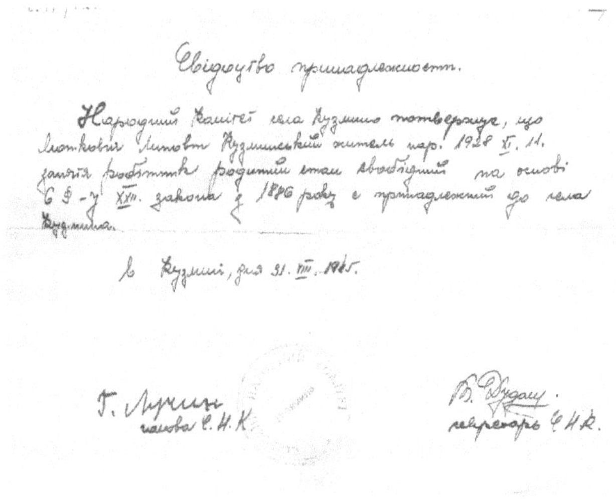

Свідоцтво приналежності.

Народний Комітет села Кузмино потверджує, що [illegible] Кузминський житель нар. 1928 XI. 11. заняття робітник родинний стан свобідний на основі 6 §-у XXII. закона з 1886 року є приналежний до села Кузмина.

в Кузмині, дня 31. VIII. 1945.

Г. [illegible]
голова С. Н. К.

В. [illegible]
писарь С. Н. К.

Figure 2A: A hand written letter documenting Leib's birthplace, and date of birth, November 11, 1928, written in Russian by the mayor of Kuzmino with a Russian stamp (Version 1).

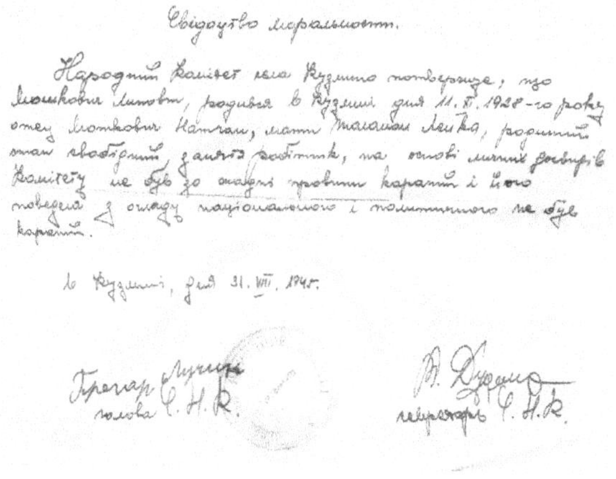

MY FAMILY BACKGROUND

Figure 2B: A hand written letter documenting Leib's birthplace, and date of birth, November 11, 1928, written in Russian by the mayor of Kuzmino with a Russian stamp (Version 2).

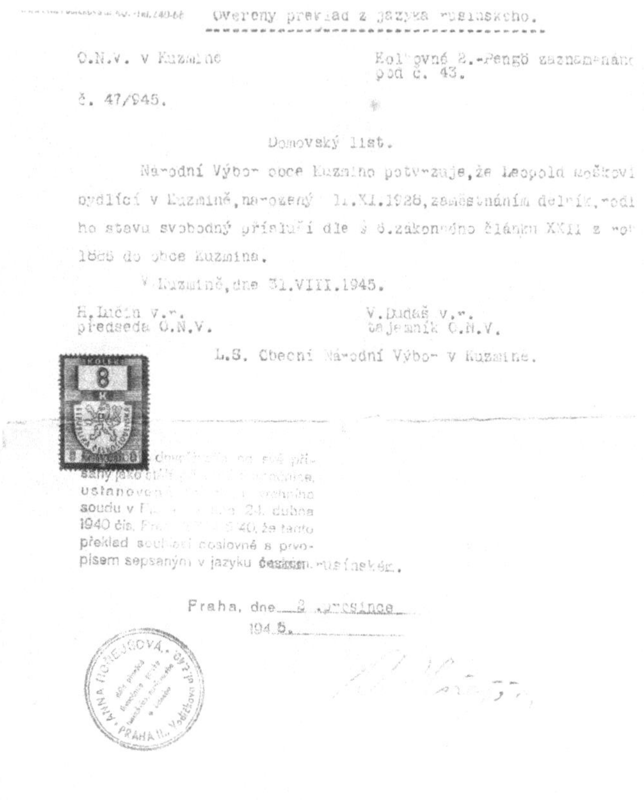

Ověřený překlad z jazyka rusínského.

O.N.V. v Kuzmině   Kolkovné 2.-Pengö zaznamenáno
                                  pod č. 43.
č. 47/945.

Domovský list.

Národní Výbor obce Kuzmino potvrzuje, že Leopold Moškovi
bydlící v Kuzmině, narozený 11.XI.1926, zaměstnáním delník, rodinného stavu svobodný přísluší dle § 6.zakonného článku XXII z roku 1886 do obce Kuzmina.

V Kuzmině, dne 31.VIII.1945.

H.Lucin v.r.   V.Dudaš v.r.
předseda O.N.V.   tajemník O.N.V.

L.S. Obecní Národní Výbor v Kuzmině.

dnešním . . . na mé při-
sahy jako tlumočník . . .
ustanoven . . . vrchního
soudu v P. . . . ze dne 24. dubna
1940 čís. Pr. . . . 40, že tento
překlad souhlasí doslovně a prvo-
pisem sepsaným v jazyku českém rusínském.

Praha, dne 8. července
1945.

Figure 2C: Typed letter documenting Leib's birthplace, and date of birth written by the mayor of Kuzmino in Czech with a Czechoslovakian stamp, specifically the town of Kolek (Version 1).

MY FAMILY BACKGROUND

Figure 2D: *Typed letter documenting Leib's birthplace, and date of birth written by the mayor of Kuzmino in Czech with a Czechoslovakian stamp, specifically the town of Kolek (Version 2).*

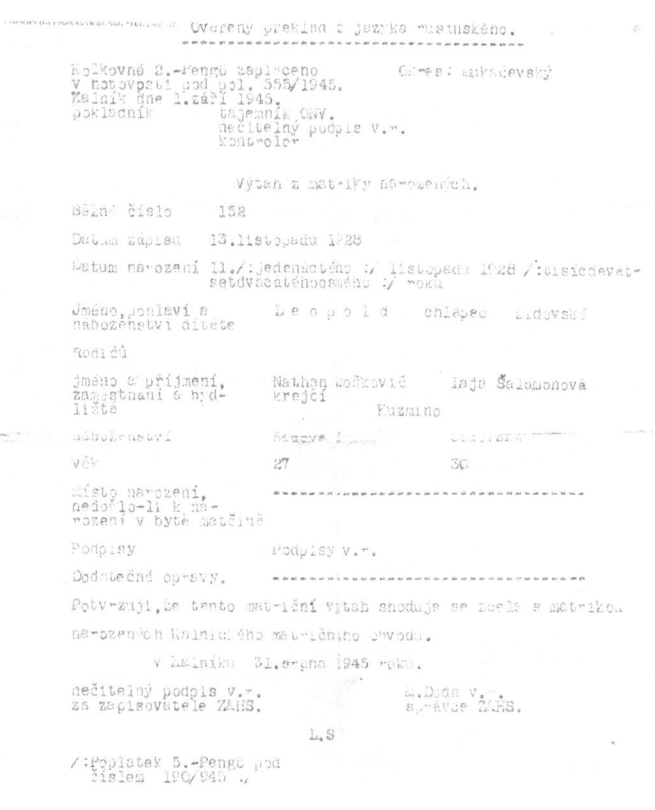

Figure 3: Leib's birth certificate translated into Czech from the original Russian birth certificate. He is registered in Kalnick on 13th of November (Listopadu) 1928. His name is recorded as Leopold, his gender is boy (chlapec), and his religion/nationality is zidovske' (Jew). His parents are Nathan Moskovic (27 year old Jew) and Laja Salomonova' (30 year old Jewess). Place of birth is Kuzmino.

MY FAMILY BACKGROUND

Figures 4A -E are documents obtained from the Holocaust Survivors and Resource Center, United States Holocaust Memorial Museum regarding Lea (Lenke) Moskowitz.

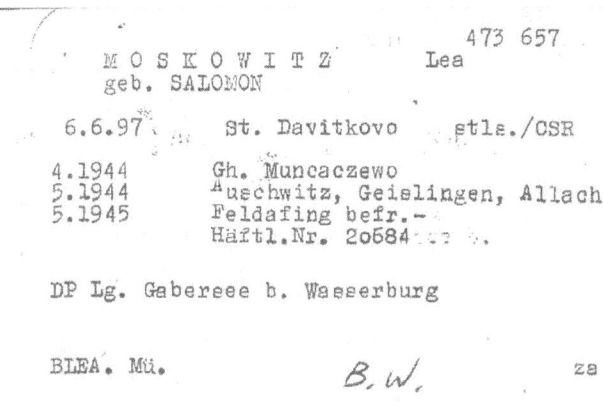

Figure 4A: Summary of Lea (Lenke) Moskowitz' captivity history on an inquiry card recording a request for information and documentation submitted to the ITS. The information was provided by USHMM.

- On 6/6/97 she is born in ST. Davitkovo CSR.

- On 4/1944 she is placed in the Muncaczewo Ghetto

- On 5/1944 she is transported to Auschwitz then to Natzweiler-AL Geislingen where her prisoner number (Haftling number) is 20.684.

- On April 11, 1945 she is transferred to Allach a Dachau subcamp.

- On May 1945 she is liberated. As a displaced person she is registered in DP Lg Gabersee bei Wasserburg in Bavaria Germany.

MY FAMILY BACKGROUND

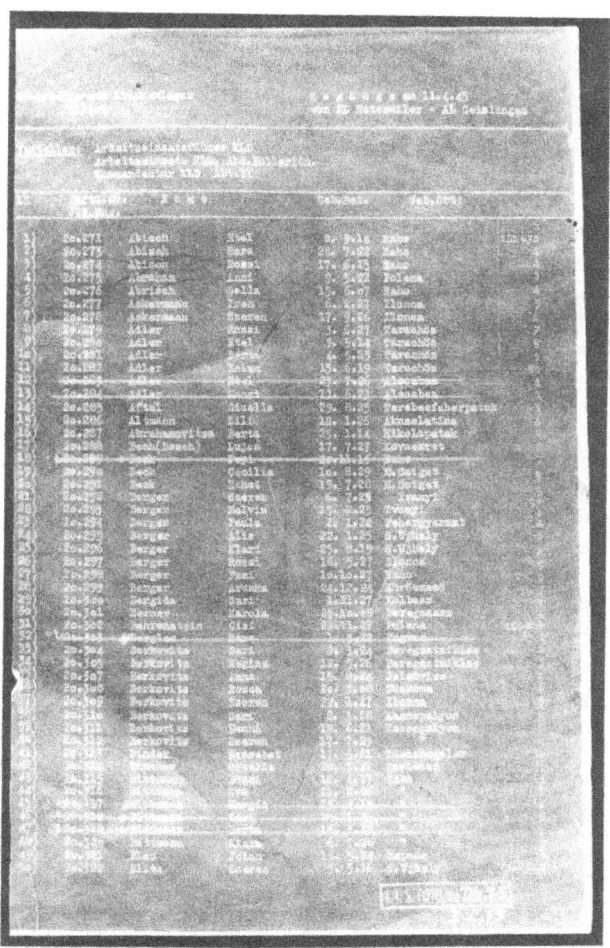

Figure 4B: Record listing prisoner transfers to Allach (a subcamp of Dachau) on April 11, 1945.

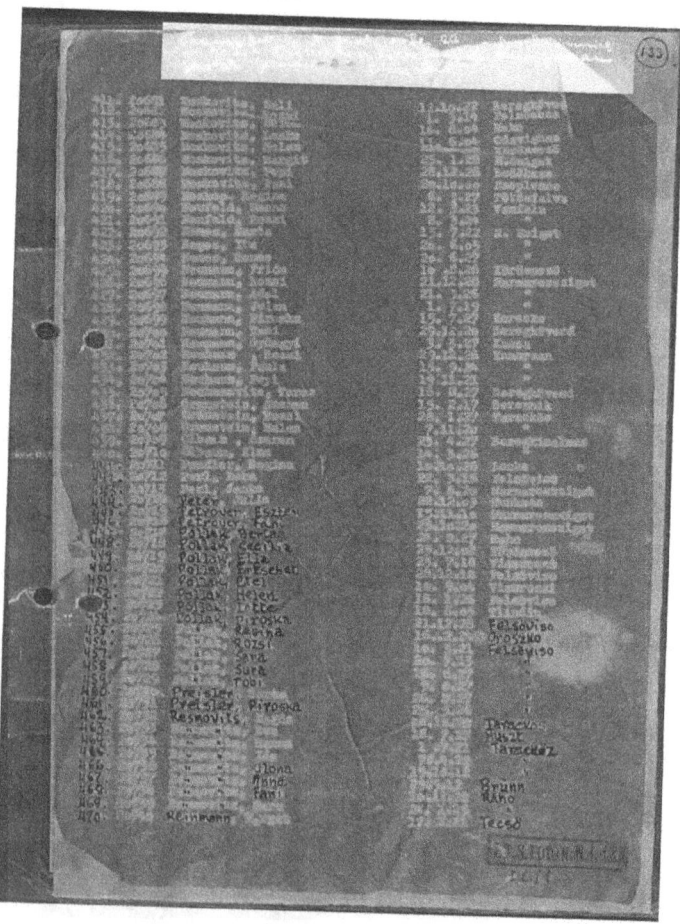

Figure 4C: Records of prisoner transfers to Allach (a subcamp of Dachau) on April 11, 1945 listing Lenke Moskovitz. Lea's Haftling number is 20684. She is listed next to the number 414 (first column, fourth line from the top) as Lenke Moskovits. The second column from the left is her Haftling number (Version 1).

MY FAMILY BACKGROUND

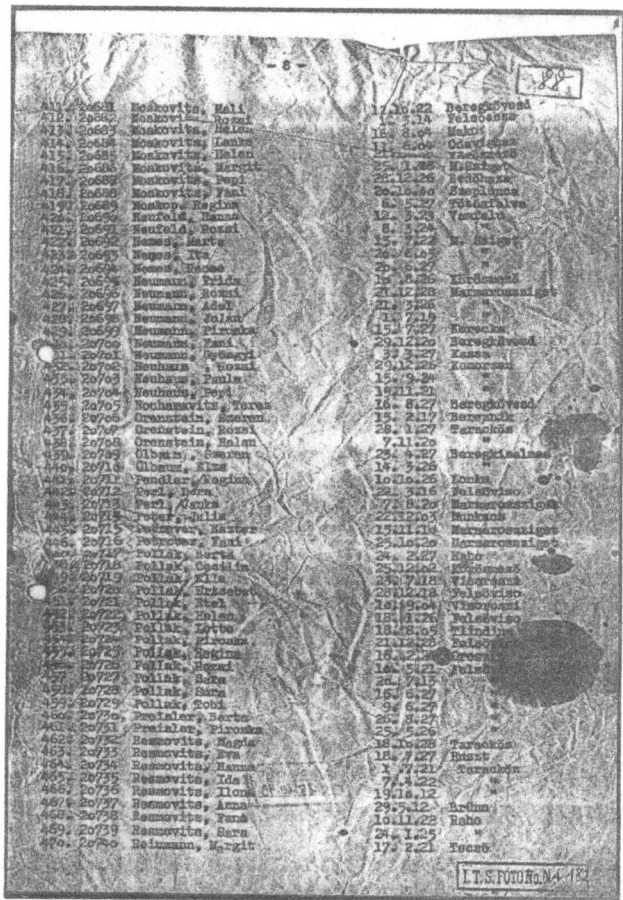

Figure 4D: Records of prisoner transfers to Allach (a subcamp of Dachau) on April 11, 1945 listing Lenke Moskovitz. Lea's Haftling number is 20684. She is listed next to the number 414 (first column, fourth line from the top) as Lenke Moskovits. The second column from the left is her Haftling number (Version 2).

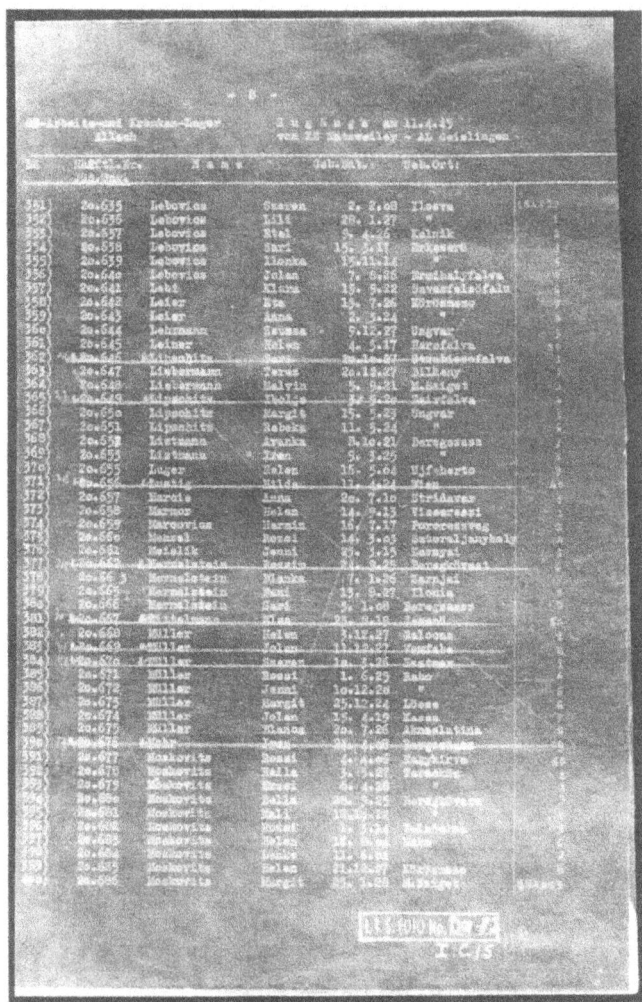

Figure 4E: Records of prisoner transfers to Allach (a subcamp of Dachau) on April 11, 1945. Lea is listed on line #398 as Lenke Moskovits.

Figures 4C and 4D in particular document that Lea's Haftling number is 20684. She is listed next to the number 414 (first column, fourth line from the top) as Lenke Moskovits (the second column is her Haftling number).

Figure 4E has Lea listed after #398 as Lenke Moskovits. In all these documents her birthdate is recorded as June 11, 1904 (Her actual birthdate is 6/6/97). She clearly did not tell the truth about her age. She subtracted seven years for a perceived survival advantage making her 40 not 47 years old at the time of her incarceration.

HISTORY OF DACHAU

"The Dachau camp was a training center for SS concentration camp guards, and the camp's organization and routine became the model for all Nazi concentration camps ... An electrified barbed-wire fence, a ditch, and a wall with seven guard towers surrounded the camp.

In 1942, the crematorium area was constructed next to the main camp. It included the old crematorium and the new crematorium (Barrack X) with a gas chamber...In Dachau, as in other Nazi camps, German physicians performed medical experiments on prisoners, including high-altitude experiments using a decompression chamber, malaria and tuberculosis experiments, hypothermia experiments, and experiments testing new medications. Prisoners were also forced to test methods of making seawater potable and of halting excessive bleeding. Hundreds of prisoners died or were permanently disabled as a result of these experiments.

Dachau prisoners were used as forced laborers. At first, they were employed in the operation of the camp, in various construction projects, and in small handicraft industries established in the camp. Prisoners built roads, worked in gravel pits, and drained marshes. During the war, forced labor utilizing concentration camp prisoners became increasingly important to German armaments production.

DACHAU SUBCAMPS: In the summer and fall of 1944, to increase war production, satellite camps under the administration of Dachau were established near armaments factories throughout southern Germany. Dachau alone had more than 30 large subcamps in which over 30,000 prisoners worked almost exclusively on armaments. Thousands of prisoners were worked to death.

THE LIBERATION OF DACHAU

As Allied forces advanced toward Germany, the Germans began to move prisoners from concentration camps near the front to prevent the liberation of large numbers of prisoners. Transports from the evacuated camps arrived continuously at Dachau, resulting in a dramatic deterioration of conditions. After days of travel, with little or no food or water, the prisoners arrived weak and exhausted, often near death. Typhus epidemics became a serious problem due to overcrowding, poor sanitary conditions, insufficient provisions, and the weakened state of the prisoners.

On April 26, 1945, as American forces approached, there were 67,665 registered prisoners in Dachau and its subcamps; more than half of this number were in the main camp. Of these,

43,350 were categorized as political prisoners, while 22,100 were Jews, with the remainder falling into various other categories. Starting that day, the Germans forced more than 7,000 prisoners, mostly Jews, on a death march from Dachau to Tegernsee far to the south. During the death march, the Germans shot anyone who could no longer continue; many also died of hunger, cold, or exhaustion. On April 29, 1945, American forces liberated Dachau. As they neared the camp, they found more than 30 railroad cars filled with bodies brought to Dachau, all in an advanced state of decomposition. In early May 1945, American forces liberated the prisoners who had been sent on the death march.

The number of prisoners incarcerated in Dachau between 1933 and 1945 exceeded 188,000. The number of prisoners who died in the camp and the sub camps between January 1940 and May 1945 was at least 28,000, to which must be added those who perished there between 1933 and the end of 1939, as well as an uncounted number of unregistered prisoners. It is unlikely that the total number

of victims who died in Dachau will ever be known":
(from: The United States Holocaust Museum:
Holocaust Encyclopedia: http://www.ushmm.org/
wlc/en/article.php?ModuleId=10005214).

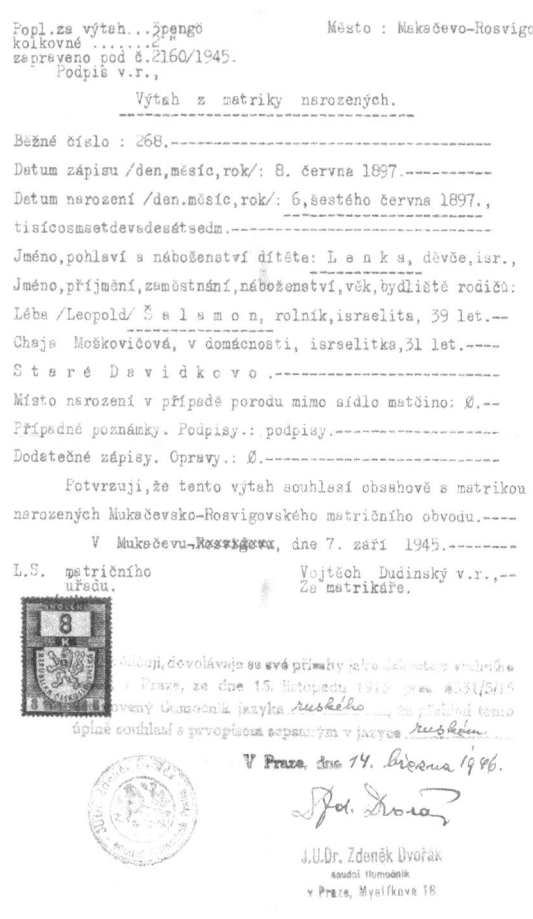

Figure 5A: Czech translation of Lea's birth certificate documenting her birthdate as June 6 (sesteho cervna) 1897. Her name was recorded as Lenka an Israelitka. Her father was Leba (Leopold) Salamon an Israelita aged 39. Her mother was Chaja Moskovicova an Israelitka aged 31. She was born in Saint (Stare') Davidkovo. The document is stamped with a Kolek Czechoslovakia stamp and dated 1946, the time of request (Version 1).

MY FAMILY BACKGROUND

```
Místní národní výbor v Kuzmínu.           Okres: Mukačevo.
Kolkovné 2 pengö pod čís.44.              Číslo : 48/1945.
```

Domovský list
a
vysvědčení zachovalosti.

Místní národní výbor obce Kuzmino potvrzuje, že Lenka M o š k o v i č o v á, rozená Šalamonová,/otec: Léba Šalamon, matka : Chaja r.Moškovičová/,narozená ve Starém Davidkovu, dne 6.června 1897,rodinného stavu provdaná, bydlištěm v Kuzminu, má domovské právo v obci Kuzmino.-- Současně se potvrzuje,že jmenovaná po dobu svého pobytu v naší obci řádně se chovala a dle trestního rejstříku, trestána nebyla.--------------------------

V Kuzminu, dne 31.8. 1945.--------------------
H.Lučín v.r.,   L.S.   Dudaš v.r.,------
předseda m.n.v.,   m.n.v.v Kuzminu. Tajemník m.n.v.,----

Figure 5B: Czech translation of Lea's birth certificate documenting her birthdate as June 6 (sesteho cervna) 1897. Her name was recorded as Lenka an Israelitka. Her father was Leba (Leopold) Salamon an Israelita aged 39. Her mother was Chaja Moskovicova an Israelitka aged 31. She was born in Saint (Stare') Davidkovo The document is stamped with a Kolek Czechoslovakia stamp and dated 1946, the time of request (Version 2).

Record from deportation list

Reference	LABOUR BATTALION
Registrant's Family Name	MOSKOVITS
Registrant's First Name	NATHAN
Gender	M
Date of Birth	1901
Mother's Family Name	NIEDERMANN
Mother's First Name	IDA
Unit	108/60 TMSZ
Draft Notice City	KUZMINA
Captured City	KONOTOVKA
Missing Date	19430114

Figure 6: Nathan Moskovits is listed on this record from a deportation list obtained from the Neve Klarsfeld organization. This documents the year of his birth, that his mother's name is Ida Niedermann, his Unit number, where he was captured and the date that he was declared missing i.e. murdered (Jan 14, 1943).

2

Childhood in Kuzmino before the war

It was a very nice life when I was a kid. We lived in a decent house. My father had a tailor shop in the house. People came to order stuff. He took their measurements. After the measurements he made a pattern. I remember patterns hanging on the wall of all different sizes from size 32 to 44 or 46. He cut out patterns. Each pattern was numbered by the size it was. If he measured you, he pulled off the pattern, cut it and put it on the material. He also made shirts.

In order to become a tailor, my father had to complete an apprenticeship for three years to learn the trade. He had to go to a bigger city for that, probably Munkatch or Seredna. They had a few people, maybe five or six apprentices working in a verkshteib (a work house). *The first and second year of the apprenticeship they used him as an errand boy; whatever the household needed. The third year they actually taught him the trade. I remember my father, he wore suspenders, and his shoulders were already a little stooped after sitting over the sewing machine all day. He also developed a bit of a stomach* (a paunch).

Plus, we had animals: cows, plenty of chickens that laid eggs that we collected on a daily basis, and geese. On Purim (A Jewish Holiday commemorating the salvation of the Jewish People living in the ancient Persian Empire during the reign of Xerxes) *we force-fed the geese for a month. They got fatter, and their weight gain was pure fat. That fat was rendered. We needed to have enough fat (schmaltz) for Passover (Pesach).*

For Pesach, the whole town in one place they baked Matzah. All the women rolled the

CHILDHOOD IN KUZMINO BEFORE THE WAR

matzahs, and one guy was making the holes in the matzahs so that they shouldn't rise. There was another guy sitting by the oven. Every family brought their own flour. You baked enough matzahs that you should have enough for the holidays.

Starting from Purim to Pesach we fermented beets for borsht. We put the beets in a wooden barrel to ferment. We had a very big garden. There were all kinds of fruits: red plums, and Italian plums. Red plums were very plentiful. People came to buy them from us, and they used to make slivovitz (plum brandy) *from them. They came with barrels to fill them up with plums.*

As far as food goes, everything was produced in the fields of our house. We had a garden where we grew vegetables and potatoes.

In the winter we made a big hole in the ground, then put the potatoes in the hole and covered them up with straw. In winter if you needed potatoes, you took them out from the pile as needed, and covered the remainder up with straw. The potatoes stood all winter long until Pesach.

We had apple trees and one walnut tree right by the house. The trees produced walnuts once a year. You grew carrots if you needed them on the side of the house in the garden. We grew cucumbers, scallions, regular onions, *petrishka* (parsley root) ...everything you needed, except tomatoes. We saw wild tomatoes but we were afraid to eat them. We thought they might be poisonous.

We had our own milk; we made our own cheese and butter. First we put the milk on the window sill at night, by morning you skimmed off the top, and made butter out of the top, that was the cream, the remaining bottom was *sauer millich* (sour milk); it had chunks. You put that in a cheese cloth, tied it up and you then you hung it up. You put it into a pail for it to drip off. When all the liquid dripped out, the cheese became chunky like farmer cheese. The *cream that was skimmed off you had like a little wooden barrel, and you kept churning it until it became butter, and then you put it on top of a grape leave. You used it from there; you could use it for cooking. After a while it was put into a dish. Grape leaves were around just during the summer.*

After a rain we went to a little forest and saw the mushrooms coming out. We used to pick them, and prepare them with sour cream- that was delicious.

There were small strawberries on little hills that we saw when we were going through the forest. We used to pick them and sell them to our teachers for a few pennies. We grew our own corn. By corn I mean rye. It had to last a year. Around Tisha B'ov (the ninth day of the Hebrew month Av, an annual fast day which commemorates the destruction of the First and Second Temples in Jerusalem) *we used to cut the sheaves leaving them on the field to dry out. We had a threshing machine which separated out the kernels. The threshing machine was taken from house to house which was used to take out the kernels. If you wanted to make flour you had to go to a mill and grind the flour, bring home the flour and make bread. There was veics from which we made white flour which we used to make bready challas and cakes at a different mill. The rye was dark. You had that for a year. We baked bread on Fridays after that. We put the chulent in the oven so that it was ready for Shabbas after shul.*

We had a stove in a living room; that was used for heating and cooking. If you had to cook or fry something in a pot, then there was an oven in the kitchen. That oven was made out of bricks. There you baked bread and challas, whatever baking you had to do. That was for baking. You couldn't cook in there. First bread and then challas were baked every Friday. After you baked the challa, you put the cholent pot in the oven, and then you sealed the door. Shabbas morning when you came back from shul you opened up the oven door and you had chulent. Then you also had chicken or fish.

CHILDHOOD IN KUZMINO BEFORE THE WAR

There was a non-Jew in town by the name of Yerka. He caught fish and sold them every Friday morning to Jewish people. Some of the fish were still alive when he brought them. That's what he did for a living. My mother made gefilte fish. She skinned the whole fish with a cleaver, and deboned the fish. She then chopped it up and ground it and stuffed it back into the skin. It looked like a live fish. She then put it into a pot with vegetables, cooked it, and when it was finished, she sliced it in two inch slices; and that was gefilte fish, they stuffed it back into the skin. The liquid that the fish was cooked in, they used to dunk the challa in it. That was delicious.

We also had corn on the cob. We used to pick it and from that fed the chickens, the geese and all the animals. We peeled it off from the husks. In the fall we grew cabbage and from every house, the women got together and made sure there were no worms in them. You put it in a barrel with preservative, and that was enough cabbage for the winter. They used to make a soup out of beans and cabbage- enough to last you a year. We grew all kinds of beans. These beans you opened them up dried them up and you had them all year. All the vegetables and fruit grew once a year. Oranges you didn't grow, you bought them in Munkatch. To grow oranges you need a warm climate.

After Sukkos (Feast of Tabernacles) *we collected grapes. We produced a few grapes. In Seredna there were special fields for grapes; there were big vineyards. When I was older they payed you to collect grapes off vineyards. My father used to go make the wine. They used to put grapes in sacks, and they danced and jumped on them, and made wine out of it. We used to take bunches of grapes and hang them in the attic in case someone got sick so they gave them two grapes to feel better. There was a lot of corn in the attic. So we used to put in a couple of apples in the corn near them so they shouldn't freeze, so you had an apple for a refuah* (a medicinal healing). *If you put it in the rye it was preserved.*

A week before Pesach they killed the geese to render the schmaltz. After they killed geese they took off their feathers. The women used to get together to take off the feathers. They used to take the shafts off, and you made pillows and dochenas (blankets) *and covers from them.*

The Shoichet (slaughterer) *came to Kuzmino every Thursday to schect* (slaughter) *chickens or anything else.*

Summer time you couldn't kill a cow or sheep because there was no refrigeration. You could only kill a big animal like a cow, calf or sheep during the winter when it was cold.

We went to two schools. The first school we went to was cheder (Jewish school). *There was not a public building in one place. In Munkatch they hired a melamed* (a teacher). *Whoever had a boy, every week cheder was in a different house where all the kids came of the same grade came, and they taught you aleph beit* (ABCs). *In the morning when you walked to a house there was no light, it was before sunrise and it was dark. I had to walk with a lantern and then we came home, we grabbed a quick bite to eat* (breakfast), *and then we walked to public school.*

Cheder started at 5-6 AM, and public school started at about 8AM until the afternoon. After I finished public school, I came home took a bite (dinner), then walked back to cheder until late at night. Cheder started at age five, before we started to go to public school.

The public school was three houses away from us. It was a beautiful place. The windows were from floor to ceiling. The teacher had a radio; the only one in town. It ran on battery. They had to go to Seredna to buy a battery. There were not too many teachers. You were together with non-Jews. The teachers were so anti-Semitic they used to call you Mushko - Hershko. We all had peyes (sidelocks) and caps. Right away the teachers knew the names of everyone, and they knew who you were. There was a very anti-Semitic geography teacher, every time a Moshku or Hershko (a Jew) went to the black board to identify for example Africa, if you didn't know the answer, he told you to put five fingers together and then he hit you against the board and he hit you with a ruler.

CHILDHOOD IN KUZMINO BEFORE THE WAR

The Melameds (Cheder Jewish school teachers) sometimes pulled your peyes. Every season in Cheder there was a new teacher twice a year. If they liked him they kept them, if not they fired him. There were hundreds of teachers that wanted the job in Munkatch. The town had to put them up and feed them. Going to school in winter was very tough. It was hard to go, you had rubber boots. They used to rip; the water and snow went in.

3

LIFE AFTER MY FATHER WAS CONSCRIPTED INTO THE HUNGARIAN ARMY

My father was taken away in 1939. I was almost eleven. Life was difficult because there was no income. Things got much tougher. We had to fend for ourselves. We didn't have enough wood to heat our house in the winter. The trees had to be cut 3-4 feet long, and they had to be split and dried out during summer. My father used to buy the wood, and cut some trees too.

He was drafted into the Hungarian army. Police came to the door and said you have to report. The Czechs ran away in 1938 when the Hungarians took over. A lot of our teachers were Czech teachers. One teacher by the name of Stupka had epilepsy. My father once saved his life. When Stupka was having a seizure my father put something in his mouth so he shouldn't bite off his tongue. We knew him well. I visited him in 1945 near Praha. His wife was Polish, and they had two children.

When I visited him I wanted a Czech passport. He gave me papers that documented that he knew me from school, and that enabled me to get a Czech passport after the war. (More details below).

After they took my father away, for the first one to one and a half years he was dressed in a full Hungarian (army) uniform. They let him home on furlough for a couple of weeks. He had to go back. Then in approximately 1940 they took away his uniform. He then wore his own civilian clothes, and they gave him a white or yellow arm band - I don't remember. They still let him wear the Hungarian cap from the uniform. They shipped him from city to city to do forced labor.

"**Labor service** (Hungarian: munkaszolgálat) was required of 'politically unreliable' and Jewish men in Hungary during World War II after they were prohibited from serving in the regular armed forces by passage of the Hungarian anti-Jewish laws. In Hungary, Jews comprised over eight percent of the population, and the government imposed an alternative to military service. Labor service was forced labor, performed by labor battalions conscripted by the German-allied Hungarian regime primarily from Hungarian Jewish men during World War II. These units were an outgrowth of World War I units, when Jews served in the Hungarian armed forces along with Christians, as in Germany and other European countries. The Fascist, Nazi-allied Regime commanders treated the Jewish units with extreme cruelty, abuse, and brutality. Men who worked in mine quarries were frequently pushed to their deaths off the man-made cliffs and embankments. These units were stationed all over Hungary, including the Eastern

Front in Ukraine, where most of the men died. The gendarmes and Army men who guarded these "slaves" were mostly members of the Nyilas fascist anti-Semitic political party. The badly fed and poorly clothed units were initially assigned to perform heavy construction work within Hungary. With Germany's attack on Russia, Hungary officials sent most of these units into Ukraine for additional forced labor work. They were subjected to atrocities, such as marching into mine fields to clear the area so that the regular troops could advance, and death by torture of prominent servicemen. Some Munkaszolgálat units were entirely wiped out; others had as few as 5% of their members survive the war." (http://en.wikipedia.org/wiki/Labour_service_(Hungary)

One time my father was near Budapest at a station in Kamarow. He said he went to a shul (synagogue) in Hungary without a talis (Jewish prayer shawl), and they gave him a talis. He was invited for a meal in a Jewish home (in Hungary). He had off time. He was officially in what the Hungarians called Munkotabor: forced labor. He did forced labor. His labor included digging trenches. They had a building like a barracks where they slept. When he finished work he had to go to a barracks. They had one Hungarian policeman to a company of sixty people supervising over them. Those policemen could have been and were bought off. My wife's (Gittel's) father came home also from forced labor in Poland. We were Czech from 1920 until 1939, and then in 1940 we were taken over by Hungary. Germans came in to our area in 1944.

Either at the end of 1942 or 1943 we got a postcard from my father stamped December 24 which said that he was being shipped to the Russian front. He came home twenty four hours before that to get warm clothes. They told him where he was going. That was the last communication we had from him. We know now that he died at the Russian front. Before that we got a postcard from him once every two weeks from whatever city he was at.

"**Hungarian Labor battalions**: The Jews in the labor battalions did not receive weapons, and later on did not even receive soldiers' uniforms. They served in separate units, in battalions and divisions under non-Jewish command. They worked primarily in varied labor for the army, such as laying railroad track and fixing broken track, digging defensive ditches and anti-tank trenches and the like. The Jews were discriminated against and publicly humiliated, and in many cases the commanders' intentions were that the Jews not return from the battlefront. The most chilling example of this is when Jews were forced to clear minefields with their bare hands and no protection. The Jews worked in these battalions both within Hungary and beyond her borders, on the Ukrainian and Serbian fronts, until the Germans conquered Hungary in March 1944. Approximately

42,000 Jews died in these units". (http://www.yadvashem.org/yv/en/exhibitions/this_month/september/07.asp).

When my father was taken away we had nothing to heat the house. We had no money to buy wood. When the non-Jews went to church on Sunday we went to the forest with our saw and axe, cut down a tree and cut it in four or five parts, and tied it up. The trees were government property. We (me and my brother) ran home before anyone could see us. Those trees were fresh. We covered the stump with snow.

You put it in the stove and it didn't burn... but it was the best we could do. We used a sled for transportation of the wood.

When the Hungarians came in, the whole town had levente (youth movement) for Jews and non-Jews. They gave you a shovel and a shield.

"**Levente Associations** (Hungarian: Levente Egyesületek) or simply 'levente' were paramilitary youth organizations in Hungary in the interwar period and during the Second World War. It was established in 1921 with the declared purpose of physical and health training. Since mid-1930s they have de facto become an attempt to circumvent the ban for conscription imposed by the Treaty of Trianon and over the time it had openly become a pre-military organization under the leadership of veterans. Since 1939, by the Act of Defense, all boys of ages 12–21 were required to take part in levente": (http://en.wikipedia.org/wiki/Levente (organization).

When my brother turned sixteen they took him away to forced labor too. He mostly cut trees. He went to forced labor during the day. At night they let him go home.

For my Bar-Mitzvah there was a man named Shlomo Mermelstein who taught me my Haftora.

He was my neighbor. For my Bar Mitzvah I got an aliya (called up to the Torah). *We brought a bottle of slivovitz and a piece of sponge cake. People in shul* (synagogue) *said L'chaim, you're bar- mitzvahed. This was 1941. During this time it was a struggle to survive with everything.*

We had heard certain stories from Chaym Leib, the father of the guy who taught me my Haftora. He was known as a big liar. He came back with stories telling us in shul that people are getting killed and being taken away. Everyone said he lost his mind. He was a liar, and was laughed off. People were being taken away to forced labor, some came back some didn't. In 1941 and 1942 a family that didn't have Hungarian citizenship they, the Suchen (official searchers), *deported them to Poland (Kamenets- Podolsk). They had to dig their own graves then they shot them.*

Hungarian Aliens: "In the summer of 1941 thousands of foreign and undocumented Jews living in the eastern Carpathians were targeted for expulsion by the Hungarian National Central Alien Control Office. In July and August approximately 20,000 of these Jews were rounded up by Hungarian units and deported over the Ukrainian border into the waiting hands of the SS. After being transported to Kolomyia, these Jews were marched in columns to Kamenets-Podolsk...on August 27, SS units, military police, Ukrainian auxiliaries and Hungarian troops gathered in Kamenets-Podolsk. They collected the Jewish deportees along with local Jews and marched them to a point ten miles out of the city. There over a two day period the prisoners were machine-gunned into mass graves prepared from shell craters created during the German invasion of the USSR... the total number shot... was 23,600 the first five figure massacre of Jews to take place on the eastern front". (From the Yad Vashem website: http://www.google.com/culturalinstitute/asset-viewer/hungary-hungarian-jews-without-citizenship-being-transferred-towards-kamenec-podolsk/IgHw3kGnsFoEQw?hl=en)

4

DEPORTATION: PESACH 1944

We just finished celebrating Pesach (Passover) in 1944. The last day of Pesach, (acheron shel pesach in Hebrew) was a Shabbas. The next day, Sunday, early in the morning 8-9 AM the Hungarian police came in and said you have one hour to get ready, you can take your bedding. You could take one package, in an hour we're coming for you. We had to be collected in one house in a courtyard. Everybody took whatever. My brother Chaym Hersch locked the door and took the key with him. We thought we were coming back. They said they were taking us to a farm. Some neighbors standing on the side said:

DEPORTATION: PESACH 1944

"Give me your valuables; wherever you're going you're not going to need it".

We got collected in one place, the whole town. The Hungarian police marched us to Kalnick (three miles away). Whoever couldn't walk they gave you a horse and wagon for elderly people and children. The whole town was cleared out -about thirty families. At Kalnick we slept there one night in a schoolyard then they took us to Munkatch in a ghetto in a big brick factory. There were already people there from all different towns. Our family we were moved in one night to a different ghetto.

In the next town Kutchivo there were two families, and two cousins ran away into the forest. Whoever was closest to that town was taken to a different ghetto. We went to a different town also a brick factory, pot horyan (in Hungarian). We went here and men anyone over sixteen were taken by the Gestapo.

Here there were no more Hungarians, Germans were in charge. They called them the black shirts. They took everyone over sixteen including my brother and put them in a room, and they went to work physically torturing them to get information where the two escapee cousins were.

I later found out that these two cousins ran away to the Partisans. One came home without a leg. His name was Shloyme Feldman. The other cousin didn't make it. His name was Menashe Feldman. He went to cheder with me. We were in the ghetto approximately four and a half weeks. These torture sessions went on every day. They were beating people and breaking bones. My brother was also beaten. He got a broken nose. The Nazis reported that on his Mauthausen Haftling (Prisoner) card (details below)*. The screams were something awful. At the time we didn't know if they ever found those two cousins.*

"The **Munkács Ghetto**: The first ghettos to be established in the occupied areas of Hungary were in Subcarpathian Rus'. The initial deportation orders came from the

DEPORTATION: PESACH 1944

German authorities, and the Hungarian government activated its police forces to carry them out. According to the original plan, the ghettoization of Subcarpathian Rus' was to be completed by 6 April 1944, but the date was postponed because the Hungarian army claimed that too fast a process would complicate its operations in the region.

In the first half of April, staff at the Hungarian Ministry of the Interior, SS officers, gendarmes and police officers met to discuss the fate of Hungarian Jewry. They decided to purify the area of Jews, and detailed how they would achieve this aim: concentration of Jews, robbery of their belongings, and deportation outside of Hungarian borders. László Baky, Hungarian Deputy Minister of the Interior in the political department, summed up the meeting of 4 April in a detailed document. On 15 April, a discussion was held in Munkács in the presence of Dieter Wislieceny, one of Adolf Eichmann's men, on the ghettoization of the

Jews of the town. Eichmann himself came to visit the Munkács ghetto at the end of April, accompanied by László Endre, Hungarian Deputy Minister of the Interior in the organization department.

Immediately following Passover, on 18 April, the Judenrat publicized a Hungarian flyer in the streets of Munkács about the forced entrance of the Jewish population into the ghetto. A few sections of the city were designated for the Jews of the town. They were allowed to take only a few items into the ghetto: two sets of clothing, folding beds, food, and a further load of up to 50 kg. Jews were ordered to lock their apartments and put their keys in an envelope on which they were to write their old address and their new address in the ghetto. They gave the envelopes to the Judenrat. The empty apartments were plundered the day the Jews were expelled. When representatives of the authorities came a month later to create a list of the houses' contents, they found most of them stripped bare"

DEPORTATION: PESACH 1944

From: http://www.yadvashem.org/yv/en/exhibitions/communities/munkacs/ghetto.asp.

During that time men and women slept in the same room. One day they gathered us together, and they put us on a cattle train. There was no room to sit down. There was a tiny window. They packed people in like herring. They put in one pail who ever had to use facilities. There were one hundred people to a car approximately. They close the door and the train starts going. The train is going and going and going. No one knew where we were going.

They said they would take you to a farm to work. One man, our neighbor, Pinchas Abramowitz, lost his mind on the train. He started screaming: "they're killing us, they're shechting us". We were going back and forth, the train stopped, started again, we arrived at Auschwitz.

Evacuation of Munkács ghetto: "A day before the evacuation of the Munkács ghetto, the Germans gathered all the Jews with beards and sidelocks and ordered them to destroy what was left of the famous Yeshiva of Rabbi Shapira, singing while they labored. The Jews carried out their task under a hail of lashes. The deportation of Hungarian Jewry to Auschwitz-Birkenau was meticulously planned. László Ferenczy, a senior gendarme officer, was appointed to command the deportation operation, and he fixed his seat of power in Munkács. In meetings held in the town on 8 and 9 May 1944, all the details of the deportation of Subcarpathian Rus' Jewry were settled, and written orders were sent to the mayors of those towns with ghettos and train stations.

The first deportation train left Munkács on 11 May. The deportation route and number of cars was predetermined: 3,000 people were to be evacuated on each train. The loading of the trains, carried out at a distance from the civilian stations, were overseen by a

DEPORTATION: PESACH 1944

gendarme or German army officer, and the Jews were allowed to take with them just a few belongings.

On the nine transports that left the Munkács brick factories, 28,587 Jews from the town and its surroundings were sent to Auschwitz-Birkenau. According to data of the Hungarian train service in Kassa, the transports from Munkács passed through Kassa on 14, 16, 17, 18, 19 and 20 May, carrying Jews from the area.

After 15 May, Jews from Munkács were brought from the ghetto to the brick factory, a five-kilometer walk away. Their passage was accompanied by abuse and violence: they were urged to walk faster and beaten mercilessly. When they arrived at the factories, the Jews were commanded to undress, and a thorough search of their clothes was conducted in order to rob them of their final possessions. The journey to the factories left many victims dead. The few days spent at the brick factories were marked by unceasing violence. Jews were forced to collect tefillin and talitot and burn them.

The remainder of the Jews of Munkács was sent in three transports that passed through Kassa on 21, 23 and 24 May, to the same destination – Auschwitz-Birkenau. The Jews were forced onto the deportation wagons under a hail of physical and mental abuse. They were pushed into the cattle cars, 70-80 people in each enclosed car, with one bucket of water for a three-day journey and one bucket to use as a toilet, with no fresh air or space to lie down. Some died along the way. Some committed suicide. Others lost their minds" (from: http://www.yadvashem.org/yv/en/exhibitions/communities/munkacs/liquidation.asp).

5

AUSCHWITZ

The train doors opened up, and then the Polish kapos jumped on us... "Raus raus" they hollered as they take us out. "Whatever you brought, leave, you don't need it". They had a leather strap beating the hell out of people. You had to line up and there was Doctor Mengele. He had one hand, the left, stuck into his vest. In the right hand he had a stick. "Link, recht... link, recht (left, right)" he pointed to the people marching in front of him.

Everyone was marching as he was pointing with a stick which way to go. Women with kids went on one side, the men on another side. The Sundercommandos (Jewish workers; more details later) *whispered in Yiddish to the young kids: "Tell them that you're older". We didn't know what they were talking about. We were in a trance.*

"Junge how old?" one of them said to me.

I said "Seventeen" - I was fifteen. So I went 'left' to work. 'Right' went to crematoria. If a woman held a kid they thought she was mother, they were all going 'right'. This selection from a very long train of many train cars, took no more than thirty minutes. The people went. The people on the left they started marching us. They took you to a big room, they cut the hair off, they shaved you and you had to leave your clothes, and they gave you a striped uniform, and after that they marched you again into a very big barracks. Here at Auschwitz-Birkenau, there were beds, twelve people to a bed. In the morning it was cold, at night you could freeze, daytime you could burn to death. You had a cap.

They had a counting (roll call,) 5 people to a row; in 10 rows, there were 50 people. They teach you to mitzen up, and mitzen down, meaning throw your head up or down. Mitzen was the name of the striped cap we wore. They gave you a little black bread and a red bowl of spinach from which five people had to eat from. No matter how hungry you were they didn't eat it. You couldn't go to the bathroom unless escorted. That was Birkenau.

Auschwitz-Birkenau: "Birkenau, like the whole Auschwitz complex, combined two functions in a single place and time: as a concentration camp, that is, a place where various categories of prisoners were imprisoned and slowly exterminated as a result of deliberately created conditions that made long-term survival impossible; and as a direct extermination center, where Jews, above all, were exterminated, although other categories of victims were also murdered on a smaller scale. Prisoners registered in the concentration camp died mainly of starvation; the direct extermination center used the gas chambers above all for this purpose.

Aside from the gas chambers and crematoria, the basic facilities of the extermination center included the unloading ramp and the warehouses used for storing, sorting, and shipping the victims' plundered property. The basic facilities in the concentration camp were living quarters for the prisoners and the SS supervisors, kitchens, storage areas, workshops, offices, and transportation and communication equipment.

These two constituent institutions that made up the Auschwitz camp complex, which went under the name Konzentrationslager Auschwitz, did not exist in parallel; rather, they functioned in mutual symbiosis. Along with the Security Police posts scattered across the Third Reich and the occupied countries, the extermination center supplied the concentration camp with an uninterrupted flow of human labor; from the concentration camp, it took in corpses and people suffering from terminal exhaustion in order to put them to death and burn them. The concentration camp supplied the direct extermination center with the SS and prisoner crews who worked the unloading ramps, the gas chambers, the crematoria, and the open-air pyres; it also provided the transport that brought the victims and their property to the intended destination, and the clerical services required by the direct extermination center.

Birkenau and the other components of the Auschwitz complex combined in a single place and time the functions of concentration camps like Mauthausen or Dachau with those of direct extermination centers like Treblinka or Bełżec. It represented a new category of Nazi camp, intended to carry out the economic and exterminationist tasks of the Nazi state simultaneously and in the most efficient manner possible" (From Memorial and Museum Auscwitz-Birkenau website:

http://en.auschwitz.org/h/index.php?option=com_content&task=view&id=10&Itemid=9&limit=1&limitstart=4).

I was there about ten days. From Birkenau they shipped us to Mauthausen. Two slave labor camps requested 1000 prisoners. They took us on a train, a thousand people. They took us to Mauthausen in a box car which wasn't as squashed as the one that went to Auschwitz.

6

Mauthausen

We arrived at Mauthausen. Someone said "Hant is Shevuous" ("Today is Shavuoth, the Feast of Weeks"). *I didn't care. By the time they marched us up a hill we come there, and there were set up tables with schreibers (secretaries), you had to give them your name, your birthday, where you come from, they made a record* (Mauthausen Haftling card), *and gave you a number from tin and wire (*See Figures 7 and 8*). Your number was also put on the uniform pants, and back of your jacket. From now on you were 68576. From now on when they wanted you at the count (Appelplatz) we had to congregate. Whatever happened when they called out your number you had to say "Yavol". After* *that I was there for about maybe a week, then the same thousand people were split in half. One half went to Ebensee, and the other half went to Melk (Austria). First group, numbers 68000 to 68500 went to Ebensee. The bottom 500 went to Melk. I went to Melk.*

Mauthausen: "Concentration camp located near an unused stone quarry about three miles from the town of Mauthausen in Upper Austria. Mauthausen commenced functioning in August 1938, a few months after the Anschluss (the annexing of Austria by Germany)... Mauthausen was divided into three sections: the prison camp, administrative area and SS housing...The camp complex was guarded by the brutal SS "Death's Head Units." Prisoners held various positions of authority such as; camp elder, the elder's deputies and camp registrar. The work in the camp was overseen by Kapos whilst the camp blocks were handled by the block elder, block registrar, and room elders. All prisoners in positions of authority were given special privilege...

A large number of new prisoners arrived in 1944. Consequently, the German authorities ordered the construction of several satellite camps to control the overflow. Altogether, more than 65,000 new prisoners were recorded, and the maximum population that year was 114,524. In May 1944, Mauthausen admitted large transports of Jews from Auschwitz. The number of Jews who died in Mauthausen that year topped 3,000. Many groups of Poles also arrived in Mauthausen in 1944, after the Warsaw Polish Uprising was suppressed, in October 1944. Many Polish students and underground members were killed soon after they arrived.

Almost 25,000 new prisoners came to Mauthausen in 1945, including a stream of Jewish prisoners from Hungary who had been previously interned in camps along the Austrian-Hungarian border, and forced to build a line of fortifications. As the battlefront drew closer, their camps were emptied out and the prisoners were marched on foot to Mauthausen. Many died en route.

The Jews interned in Mauthausen were treated much worse than the other prisoners. They were forced to dig tunnels at the sub-camps for underground ammunition factories and were expected to do so at an unbearably fast pace. After a month or so, the Jewish workers were so physically broken and exhausted they could hardly move.

On May 3, 1945, a police unit from Vienna took over the camp's security. The next day, all work stopped at the camp and the SS officers left. On May 5, American troops arrived and liberated the camp. Altogether, 199,404 prisoners passed through Mauthausen. Approximately 119,000 of them, including 38,120 Jews, were killed or died from the harsh conditions, exhaustion, malnourishment and overwork. Furthermore, the sick, weak and 'undesirable' prisoners were taken to the nearby Hartheim Castle to be exterminated in the gas chamber during the periods of August 1941 to October 1942 and April to December 1944" (From: *http://www.yadvashem.org/odot_pdf/Microsoft%20 Word%20-%206639.pdf*)

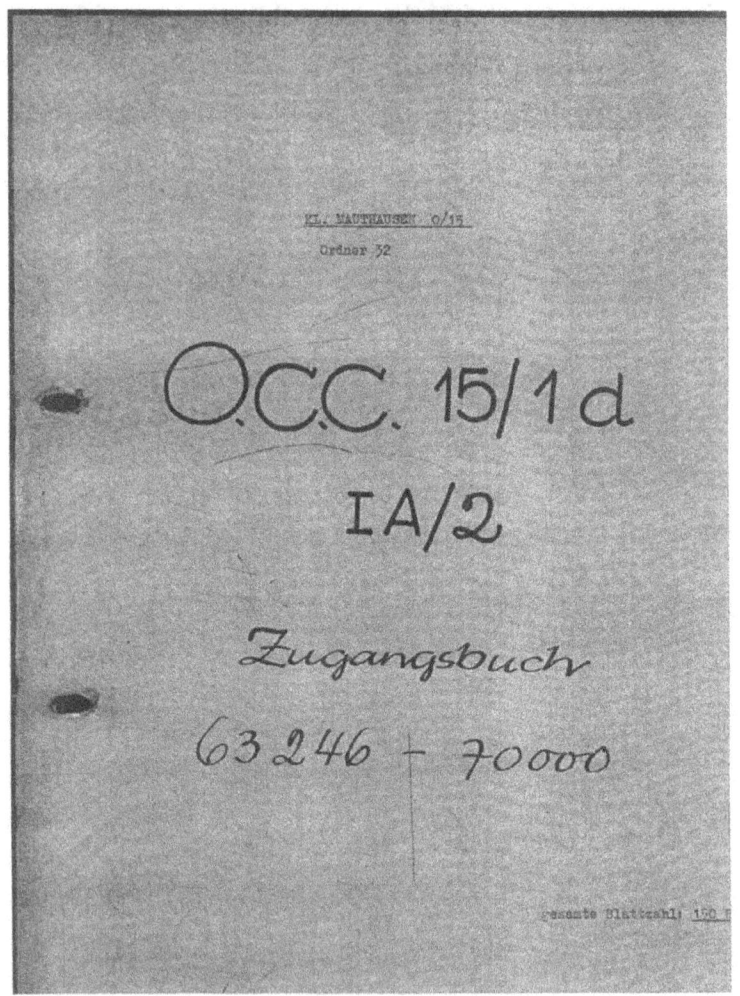

Figure 7A: Archival cover sheet of Mauthausen records documenting Leib's transfer to Mauthausen on May 28, 1944.

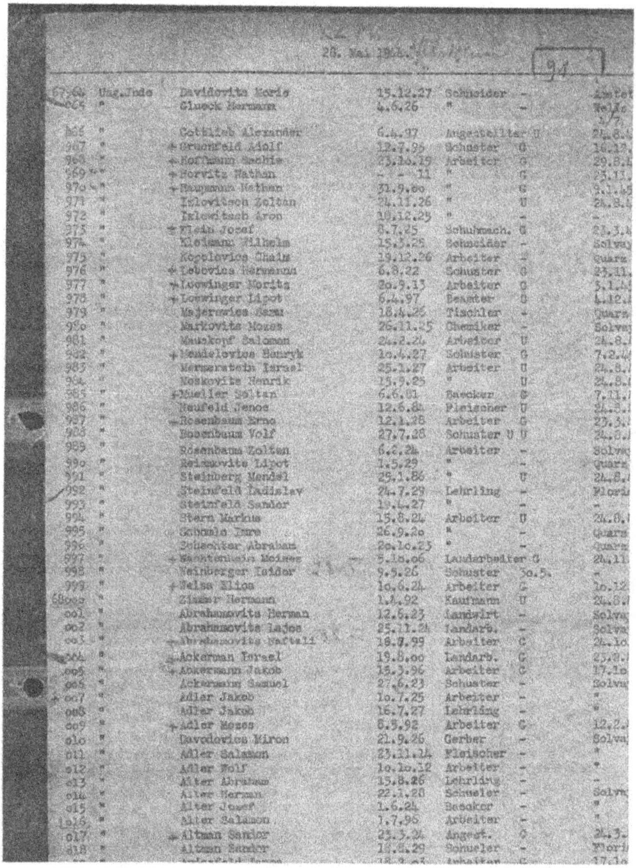

Figure 7B: A page of Mauthausen records listing multiple people, listed numerically by their prisoner number, who were transferred to Mauthausen on May 28, 1944.

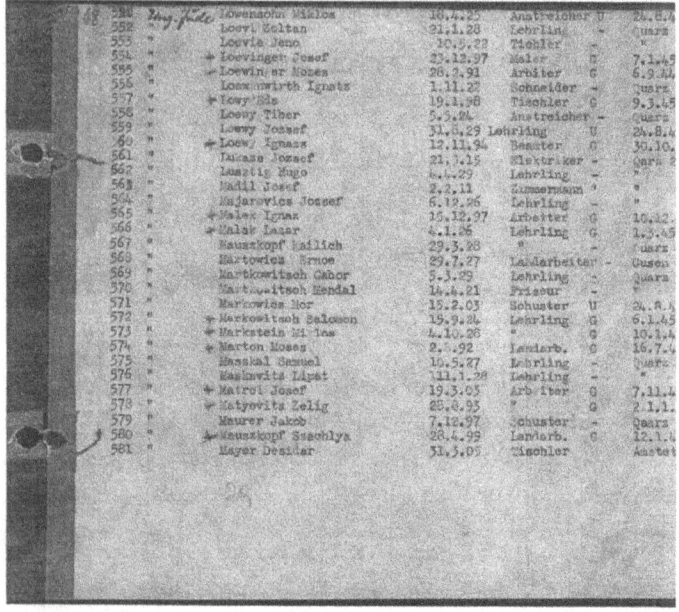

Figure 7C: A page of Mauthausen records documenting Leib's transfer to Mauthausen on May 28, 1944. Leib is listed on line 576 as Lipat Maskavitz born 1, 11, 1928 (a typo which should have read 11, 11, 1928).

MAUTHAUSEN

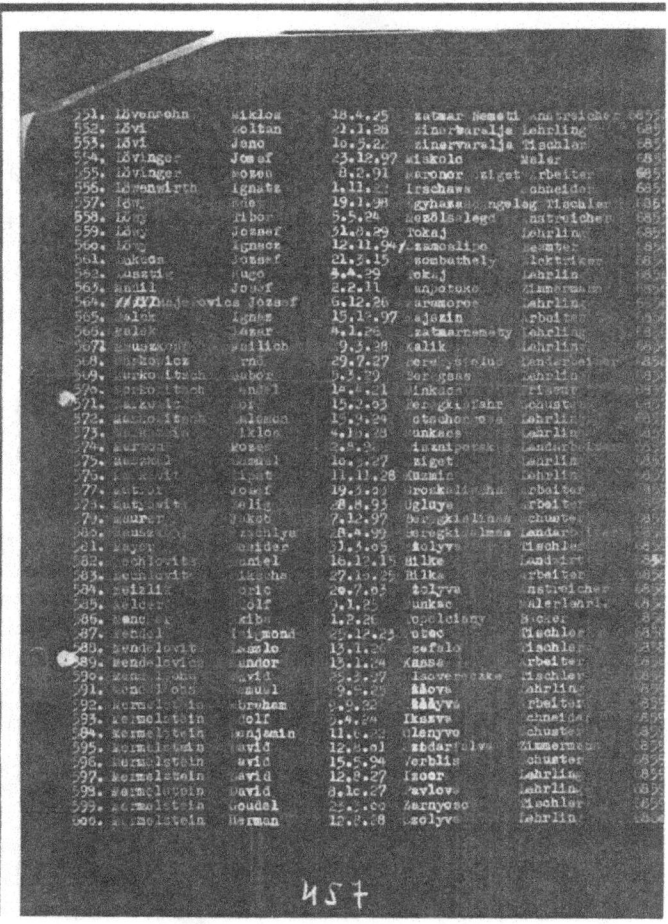

Figure 7D: Another page of Mauthausen records documenting Leib's transfer to Mauthhausen on May 28, 1944. This is a similar record to that in Figure 7C. Line 576 lists Lipat Maskovits with the correct birthdate of 11/11/28.

For confirmation of this transfer date (May 28, 1944), please refer to top of Figure 7B.

In Fig 7C Leib is listed on line 576 as Lipat Maskavitz born 1, 11, 1928 (a typo which should have read 11, 11, 1928). He is a Lehrling (apprentice) and will be involved with project Quarz (refer to explanation in text).

Figure 7D is a similar record. Line 576 lists Lipat Maskovits with the correct birthdate of 11/11/28.

Figure 8A: Archival Cover sheet for Mauthausen prisoner Number Book (Nummerenbuch) listing prisoners with numbers 64881 through 69830.

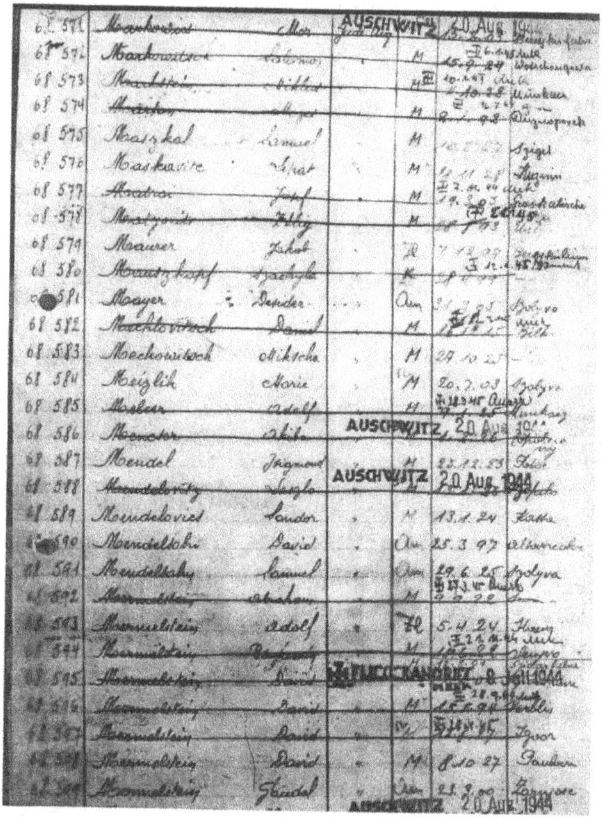

KUZMINO CHRONICLES

Figure 8B: Lipat Maskovitc is listed under number 68576 (presented in numerical order). He is documented as being born on 11 11 28, and is from Kuzmin (Kuzmino).

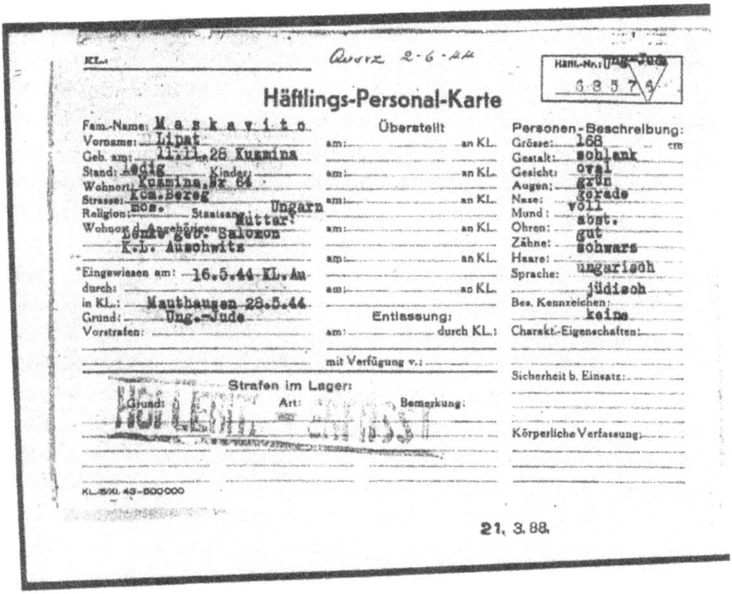

KL.: Quarz 2-6-44

Häftl.-Nr.: Ung-Jude 63574

Häftlings-Personal-Karte

Fam.-Name: Maskavito
Vorname: Lipat
Geb. am: 11.11.28 Kuzmina
Stand: ledig Kinder:
Wohnort: Kuzmina, Nr 64
Strasse: Kom. Bereg
Religion: mos. Staatsang.: Ungarn
Wohnort d. Angehörigen: Mutter: Lenke geb. Salomon K.L. Auschwitz
Eingewiesen am: 16.5.44 KL. Au
durch:
in KL.: Mauthausen 28.5.44
Grund: Ung.-Jude
Vorstrafen:

Überstellt
am: an KL.
am: an KL.
am: an KL.
am: an KL.
am: an KL.
am: an KL.

Entlassung:
am: durch KL.:
mit Verfügung v.:

Personen-Beschreibung:
Grösse: 168 cm
Gestalt: schlank
Gesicht: oval
Augen: grün
Nase: gerade
Mund: voll
Ohren: abst.
Zähne: gut
Haare: schwarz
Sprache: ungarisch jüdisch
Bes. Kennzeichen: keine
Charakt.-Eigenschaften:
Sicherheit b. Einsatz:
Körperliche Verfassung:

Strafen im Lager:
Grund: Art: Bemerkung:

KL./5/XI. 43-500000

21. 3. 88.

*Figure 8C: Leib's Mauthausen Prisoner card (*Front: *See text).*

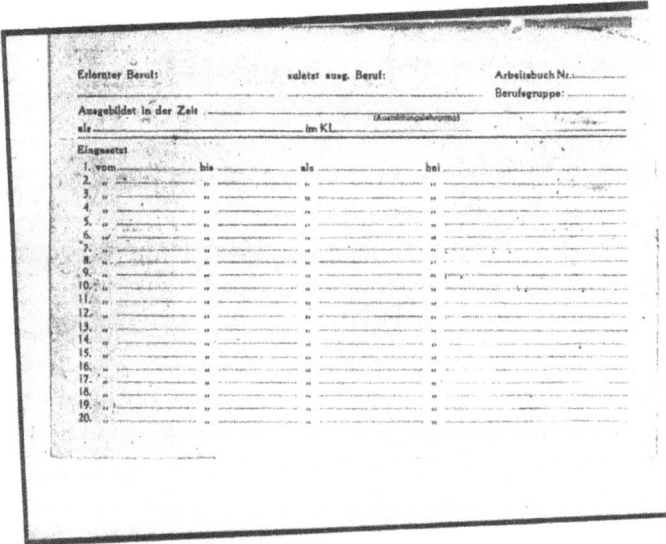

Figure 8C: Leib's Mauthausen Prisoner card (Back: *See text*).

MAUTHAUSEN

Figure 8D: Another Mauthausen record of Lipat Maskavitc's transfer to Mauthausen on May 28, 1944. He is identified by his Prisoner number (See text).

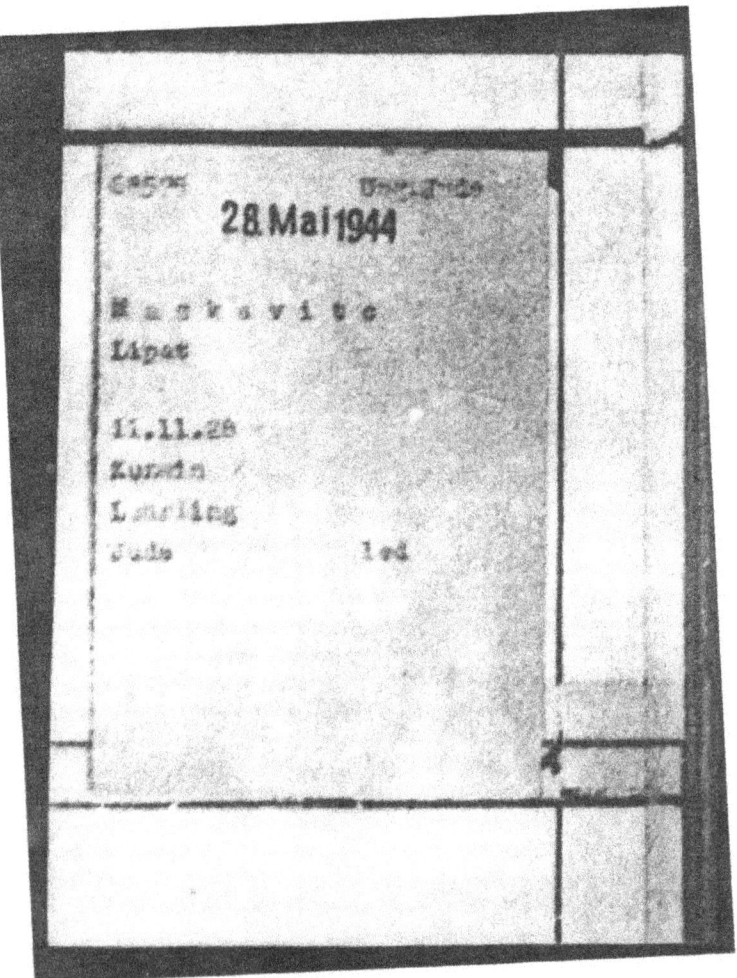

Figure 8D: Another Mauthausen record of Lipat Maskavitc's transfer to Mauthhausen on May 28, 1944 (See text).

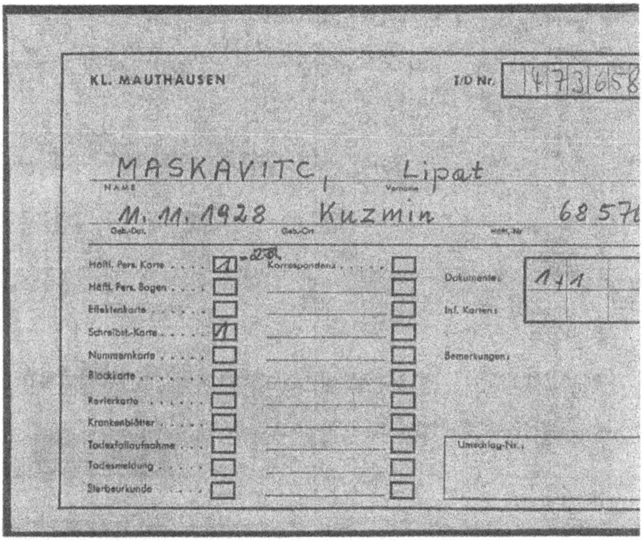

KL. MAUTHAUSEN

I/D Nr. 473658

MASKAVITC, Lipat

NAME Vorname

11.11.1928 Kuzmin 68 57

Geb.-Dat. Geb.-Ort

Häftl. Pers. Karte 1

Häftl. Pers. Bogen

Effektenkarte

Schreibst.-Karte 1

Nummernkarte

Blockkarte

Revierkarte

Krankenblätter

Todesfallaufnahme

Todesmeldung

Sterbeurkunde

Korrespondenz

Dokumente: 1+1

Inf. Karten:

Bemerkungen:

Umschlag-Nr.:

Figure 8E: Copy of an envelope created by the ITS (International Tracing Service) to hold individual documents from Mauthausen for Lipat Maskavitc (See text).

Figures 8C (Front) and 8C (Back) are Leib's Mauthausen Haftling prisoner card (front and back). "Quarz" for "Project Quartz" is hand written on the top of the card. On the top upper right of the card inside a rectangular box is Leib's number and his identification as Hungarian Jew (Ung-Jude). The column on the left documents his name, his birthdate, his marital status (single /leidig) His address is Kuzmina Number 64, the street is Kom. Bereg. His religion is Mosaic. He was living with his mother (Mutter) Lenke who was born Salomon who is in KL Auschwitz. He was brought to Auschwitz on 5/16/44 and transferred to Mauthhausen on 5/28/44. He is a Hungarian Jew. On the right hand column is his personal description recorded by the secretary (The secretaries were also Jewish prisoners). He is 168 centimeters. He is thin (schlank), his face is oval, his eyes are green, his nose is straight (gerade), his mouth is full, his ears stand out, his teeth are good, his hair is black, he speaks Hungarian and Jewish.

Figure 8D-Front and 8D-Back are the front and back covers of another Mauthausen record of Lipat Maskavitc's transfer to Mauthhausen on May 28, 1944. Like his Haftling card it lists his prisoner number, birth town, Nationality, religion, birthdate and profession.

Figure 8E is a copy of an envelope created by the ITS (InternationalTtracing Service) to hold individual documents from Mauthausen for Lipat Maskavitc.

7

Melk and Ebensee

We come in tzellappel (roll call), and they started asking "What's your profession? What do you do? What do you know?"

My brother Herman says he's a schneider (tailor).

"Junge!" they ask me, "What do you do? What do you do?"

"I can make pants", I said nervously as I shivered.

They assigned us to a barrack. I was in a barrack -Block on top of kitchen with no number. We could go in like a garage; there was a ramp on one side, and another ramp. Every block had a blockelderste, the guy in charge of the barracks, and he had a Shtubedeinst; he was in charge when people went to work that everything is in order. If you didn't make your bed right you had to answer for it. You had three tier beds. You had your own bed. There was bottom center top (three tiers). *I was on the top.*

My brother was three to four beds away. I tried to stick with him. But we landed up in different work places. He worked night shift and I worked day shift. We alternated. Right away they took us to work. We had to walk to a train. They made companies of 60 people. From the 60 people they asked 'who speaks German?'

There was a man, a wealthy man, Weinberg, he volunteered. He was very educated he spoke Deitch (German). *They gave him a strap, a whip, and told him: "You're the kapo, you're in charge, whatever orders we give you, you translate it and tell them what to do."*

Our first job was to put wood in railroad tracks and lifted the tracks. There were gereman meisters (foremen) mechanics telling you how to do it, where to place the wood and tracks. The kapo Weinberg was a very nice gentle man. They told him "if someone doesn't lift off the tracks shmeise (whip) *them". He couldn't do it, he couldn't hurt anyone. So they showed him how to do it. They whipped him to death killing him with the whip they had given him. That was on Tisha Bov* (a fast day commemorating the destruction of both Jewish Temples). *In the meantime there were sixty people in our company, and it had to stay at about sixty. We had to line up at an appelplatz where the counting was going on. If one number (person) was missing (unaccounted) you would stay there for up to 48 hours until they found the missing one: dead or alive.*

There was tzellappel (roll call) *every morning and night. We worked for 12 hours at a time. We were marched to a train, and then transported by a train. The SS was on the train. Another place I worked they built underground factories that they were digging. They had little lorries taking out the dirt. Melvin Mousekopf was a shpitzentrager at the end of machine. He had to put the machine you make the holes with. You had to shove dirt in the little lorrie, kept digging until they made a factory. It was probably an arms factory.*

They were building buildings for the fleictlinging (German civilians running away from the Russian front). These were living quarters built for them for them because the Russians were closing in. I remember working there. The building was four or five stories. I had a wheelbarrow bringing bricks or cement. They made a plank, and I had to run up the bricks on third floor bring it up, fill in the cement bring it up come back down. Trainloads of cement used to come. You had to unload the cement. Two people were on the train, and they threw down cement. I couldn't carry that cement, they threw it on your shoulder and you had to run with it.

One night it was dark, between day and night I don't know where I was going I was walking, and there was fresh cement. I accidentally stepped into fresh cement. A Nazi walked by and gave me a setz (a thunderous clap) on the right side of my face, on the cheek with an open hand. I spat out a tooth. I was lucky he didn't shoot me.

In Melk the Russians bombed the camp. There were a lot of casualties when I worked the night shift. During the day there used to be flugel (literally horn in German) *alarm every day at 11AM. There were hundreds of English planes. They chased us to Shutzengraben (trenches).*

"**History of Melk satellite camp**: As the Allied air raids on the armaments production centers increased, the Armaments Ministry under Albert Speer and the armaments industry decided to transfer production underground. After production had been decentralized and facilities moved to the Ostmark, which had until then escaped bombing, this was the only way of keeping up the supply of armaments on anything like the required scale. Concentration camp inmates were to be used to build the underground facilities and produce the arms. Steyr-Daimler-Puch AG, the largest armaments concern in Austria with turnover of RM 456 million and 50,000 employees in 1944 (compared with RM 57 million and 7,000 employees in 1938) had become the third largest roller bearing manufacturer in the German Reich. The most important customer was the aircraft industry, and roller bearings were also required for tanks and vehicles. Steyr-Daimler-Puch AG had a roller bearing plant in Steyr-Münichholz, which was to be transferred to an underground facility in Melk to protect it from air raids.

Work started under the code name "**Project Quartz**" in March 1944. At the same time, a satellite camp of Mauthausen was established in Freiherr von Birago military barracks in Melk. On 21 April 1944 the first 500 inmates arrived from the main camp around 70 kilometers away. They were accommodated in 18 housing blocks and employed in the tunneling work. The inmates were divided into work commandos led by SS men and supervised by civilian workers and kapos. The tunneling site in Roggendorf was around four and a half kilometers from the camp in Melk. Every day after morning roll call the inmates were driven into goods wagons and transported by train to the site. They worked three shifts of eight hours [Leib Moskowitz testifies that this was false. There were two twelve hour shifts]. In December 1944 production started in the new roller bearing plant (code name "Erle") in the completed tunnels. By 15 March 1945 a production area of 7,880 m² had been completed. By the time the tunneling work was discontinued, two thirds of the planned tunnels had been dug and one third lined with concrete. There was no adequate medical care in the infirmary for sick and weak inmates and the conditions were dire because of the increasing overcrowding in the second half of 1944. Many of the seriously ill were killed by the medical orderly Gottlieb Muzikant by injection into the heart. The camp doctor in Melk was Dr. Josef Sora, a member of the air force, who unlike Muzikant had a very human approach to the inmates. Survivor reports describe how he saved inmates from death and cooperated with illegal inmate organizations in the camp. Of the 15,000 inmates interned in Melk, almost 5,000 died either as a result of the inhuman working conditions, absence of safety provisions in the tunnels, inadequate food, mistreatment or deliberate killing. The death rate in Melk peaked at the end of 1944 and beginning of 1945. More than 1,000 inmates died in January 1945 alone. Between 11 and 15 April 1945 the inmates were evacuated from Melk to Ebensee, with the sick being sent to Mauthausen" (from Mauthausen memorial website: http://en.mauthausen-memorial.at/db/admin/de/index_main.php?aufl=1&pgCPage=10&stext=&sort=&sortdir=&status=&search=&char=&carticle=258&fromlist=).

I used to see my brother once a week on Sundays. We were off Sunday. They used to check you for lice. We met up once a week to see what's what.

One of them had to go to night shift, you had to go to the bathroom, they chased you to showers. Sometimes they took away clothes for delousing, they steamed them. In the meantime you were naked waiting for them to bring back. You covered yourself with a blanket in the barracks. It took two hours and they brought it back.

We were given a little piece of black bread, sometimes margarine in the morning. For lunch they brought a kessel (pot in German) *to the work place with black coffee. The kapo was in charge of giving out soup. You carried your own red plate and spoon which was on you at all times. I had a piece of wire it was tied to my pants that was my property. I called the soup water. If there were two potato peels in there you were very lucky. Most of the time you got water.*

There was a kapo by the name of Velvel Moskowitz (no relationship). He came from Svaleve and he had an uncle there, and the uncle asked him: "Tee mer a tova geb mier a bisel zip from the bottom" ("Do me a favor and give me a little soup from the bottom"). He gave him a fist in his stomach.

MELK AND EBENSEE

I met him in the US many years later at a wedding. He was a mechuten (in-law) to a family of my cousin. He lived in Borough Park. He came late to the USA from Russia. I wanted to have it out with him, but my wife said I shouldn't say anything. His uncle didn't make it, he didn't survive.

One Sunday I didn't meet up with my brother like we always did every Sunday. I asked people "where is he?"

"He's in the Revier (hospital)".

That was March of 1945 (ten weeks before liberation). The hospital had barbed wire. In there you couldn't walk in. Someone was outside the hospital; I asked him 'can you do me a favor and see if you can locate 68621? That man walked in, and so he Herman came out of building.

"Voose tiest dee?" I asked him.

He said he had a growth on his chest. To me he looked like he was delirious. He asked: "Give me a pair of shoes!"

"Where am I going to get shoes?" I asked myself.

On Christmas they gave every prisoner two cigarettes. I said to him "I'll give you cigarettes". I kept cigarettes because I thought I was going to be able to barter cigarettes for bread.

"No! geb mich schiech!"

That's all he said. He looked like he was dying any minute. He couldn't stand on his feet barely. I had to leave, and he went back in. Supposedly a couple days later the whole hospital was shipped back to Mauthausen. Whoever was in there the whole hospital was evacuated to Mauthausen. He lived until April 19th. That was the last time I seen him.

[Figures 9-18 document Herman's transfer to Mauthausen from Auschwitz, his transfer to Melk, his arrival at the hospital, his transfer back to main Mauthausen, and documentation of his death. Figures 7-8 (previous chapter) document Leib's transfer to Mauthausen from Auschwitz. Photos 3 and 4

MELK AND EBENSEE

are forensic paintings of Herman (by Nathan C. Moskowitz) reconstructing him based on his Mauthausen Prisoner card. These paintings can be found both on the websites *www.nahumhalevi.com* and *www.shoahforensicsartinstitute.com*)].

One day after night shift, I was walking, and I hear the sounds of people crying or coming out of one block. I thought somebody was hurt or being killed. When I got closer, I could hear that a group of people were singing 'unesana tokef' (a High Holiday dirge). It must have been Rosh Hashanah or Yom Kippur. I had to move on.

We were still going out to work. One day during the day there was a flugel alarm. I went to work by day, and when I came back, a few blocks were bombed. Around the camps were barracks. The Russians thought they were army barracks; quite a few people were killed. The word was out that the Russians were coming. They kept records of who was killed during that flugel alarm. The word was out that the Russians are closing in.

Every day at about 11 AM we had to run into the bunkers. I looked up in the sky and saw there were hundreds of English aircraft. They looked like so many tiny like birds. I was hoping they would bomb us and finish us. We heard we were getting evacuated. The Germans started to evacuate the camp. Some people were evacuated by boat.

I was evacuated by train to Ebensee four to six weeks before liberation. We come to Ebensee. It's a big camp. They counted you. I didn't work much there. Once they took us out, there was a field and I remember finding a snail near a brook, so I picked it up. I bit it and swallowed it up. That snail was delicious; better than a steak. If I ever saw a piece of coal I ate that too, your stomach grumbled so much. The food was minimal. In that camp they had steingruben, factories under stone mountains. A lot of people died there where you were worked to death, it was tougher than Melk. We had countless countings. Corpses were piled so high the crematoria couldn't burn them fast enough. There was less and less food. One day they called a tzellappel

MELK AND EBENSEE

(roll count). They asked would you like to go underground in the stone quarry to be saved because the factory is going to get bombed. The kapos found out that the Germans had dynamite in the entrance, and once herded in they were going to ignite the dynamite and kill you. The kapos said: "Say, no you're not going, let them bomb us. We will die here".

"**History of Ebensee:** The construction of the Ebensee subcamp began late in 1943, and the first 1,000 prisoners arrived on November 18, 1943, from the main camp of Mauthausen and its subcamps. The main purpose of Ebensee was to provide slave labor for the construction of enormous underground tunnels in which armament works were to be housed. These tunnels were planned for the evacuated Peenemünde V-2 rocket development but, on July 6, 1944, Hitler ordered the complex converted to a tank-gear factory.

Approximately 20,000 inmates were worked to death constructing giant tunnels in the surrounding mountains. Together with the Mauthausen subcamp of Gusen, Ebensee is considered one of the most horrific Nazi concentration camps.

Jews formed about one-third of the inmates, the percentage increasing to 40% by the end of the war, and were the worst treated, though all inmates suffered great hardships. The other inmates included Russians, Poles, Czechoslovaks, and Gypsies, as well as German and Austrian political prisoners and criminals.

Prisoners arose at 4:30 a.m. and worked until 6:00 p.m., constructing and expanding the tunnels. After some months the work was done in shifts covering 24 hours a day. There was almost no accommodation to protect the first batch of prisoners from the cold Austrian winter and deaths increased greatly. Bodies were piled in heaps and taken every three or four days to the Mauthausen crematorium to be burned, as Ebensee did not then have its own crematorium. The bodies of the

MELK AND EBENSEE

dead were also piled inside the few huts that existed. The smell of the dead combined with the stenches of sickness, phlegm, urine, and feces was said to be unbearable.

Prisoners wore wooden clogs, and went barefoot when the clogs fell apart. Lice infested the camp. In the morning, food rations consisted of half a liter of ersatz coffee; at noon, three quarters of a liter of hot water containing potato peelings; and, in the evening, 150 grams of bread. Due to such inadequate rations and the inhuman living conditions, beatings, and the onerous demands of the hard labor, the death toll continued to rise" (From: http://en.wikipedia.org/wiki/Ebensee_concentration_camp).

I could hardly walk. All of a sudden there was a different SS, they looked like civilians. They looked like civilians with white arm bands; people went out and didn't see SS. All of a sudden I'm in the block and somebody came in saying "We are free we are free" (in Yiddish).

I remember I don't know how I got there I saw two very big tanks with black soldiers. They started throwing down chewing gum and other foods. Everyone said the gates were open. There were 20,000 people when we were liberated. The Americans came in. When the Germans left; they cut off water and electricity. After three days the Americans started giving out food like gravy. They gave a nice piece of bread and soup. People started eating. They gave you all you wanted, so I saved the bread they gave me, and ate soup. A day or two later I fell down. Someone grabbed me, took me on his shoulder, and took me to an American field hospital. I had tremendous fever. I think I had typhus. I had blood transfusions and an IV with glucose. I couldn't eat. I was there for four weeks. There was a guy Yankle Lebovitch who visited me.

"Kimt aheime" ("Come home") he said to me.

"I can't".

He said "I'll carry you".

I went out and collapsed, I asked the doctor "How long will I live?"

They kept writing and writing (American army doctors). "When am I dying? When?"

I must have had tremendous temperatures. Then a guy came in who spoke Slavic so I told him where I come from, and how I would like to go home. I had no clothes. They burned my uniform, it was full of lice. I had a hospital gown I begged him for clothes. "Where is home?" He asked me. We communicated in Russian or Czech. He gave me a Nazi pair of green pants, and some kind of shmatta (rag) *shirt. When I went to tzellappel, whoever wants to go home had to register. I walked out of hospital. I registered. They asked your name and birthday, where you come from. They told me: "Be here tomorrow at 11 there will be 3 trucks and they will take you home". They gave me liberation papers* (See Figures 19 A, Front and Back. Also refer to Figures 19 B-I for lists documenting Leib's Liberation from Ebensee).

Liberation at Ebensee: "As the Second World War in Europe came to an end, mass evacuations from other camps put tremendous pressure on the Mauthausen complex, the last remaining concentration camp in the area still controlled by the Nazis. The 25 Ebensee barracks had been designed to hold 100 prisoners each, but they eventually held as many as 750 each. To this number must be added the prisoners being kept in the tunnels or outdoors under the open sky.

The crematorium was unable to keep pace with the deaths and naked bodies were stacked outside the barrack blocks and the crematorium itself. In the closing weeks of the war, the death rate exceeded 350 a day. To reduce congestion, a ditch was dug outside the camp and bodies were flung into quicklime. On a single day in April 1945, a record 80 bodies were removed from Block 23 alone; in this pile, feet were seen to be twitching. During this period, the inmate strength reached a high of 18,000.

In May 1945, shooting in the distance could be heard from inside the camp and there was a sense among prisoners that American and

MELK AND EBENSEE

British forces were close at hand. On May 4, 1945, the commandant of the camp informed prisoners that they had been sold to the Americans and that they should seek shelter in the camp's underground tunnels for protection. Prisoners refused and remained in their barracks; hours later some of the tunnels exploded, reputedly due to the detonation of mines. On May 5, 1945, prisoners awoke to find that the SS had deserted Ebensee and that only elderly Germans armed with rifles were guarding the camp.

American troops of the US 80th Infantry Division arrived at the camp on May 6, 1945 - though for many inmates liberation came too late and they died of hunger, disease and exhaustion despite the efforts of American doctors to save them" (from: http://en.wikipedia.org/wiki/Ebensee_concentration_camp).

On the trucks they gave you a whole round bread, and two cans of spam. In the hospital they gave me chocolate pudding. In the beginning I couldn't eat anything.

We went on the truck it was a nice sunny day. It was the end of June. It was nice and warm, the air was so fresh, I ate the bread and spam. It was delicious. We were going there; there were three seats on a bench. These were open trucks, the weather was beautiful.

The next day in the morning we arrive in Czechoslovakia. The Budejovice people (from the town Ceske Budejovice) *took us to a restaurant from the truck. This was the first time I ever saw white table cloths. They gave us a beautiful breakfast; whatever we wanted. After we ate we took a bath, we then went to sleep to rest. We were there for one day. Then they took us to the train, and our destination was Bratislava. We were separated on the train, and we were called katzetniks* (prisoners). *We weren't with other people we were in our compartment. On the way I met Moishe Farkos, my father's sister's son (first cousin). He asked me "Vilst essen zip und fleisch?" ("Would you like to eat soup and meat?")*

MELK AND EBENSEE

"Nein ich vil fleish" ("No I want meat") I told him. I was getting sick (mentally).

I said to him "If you don't give me fleish I will kill you!" We were on the train on the way to Bratislava. We were by the German border. I got violently sick. I was screaming and yelling.

They stopped the train in Berno, and brought me to a tiny hospital (there were ten to twelve people there). They tried to treat me. I was screaming bloody murder. I was out of it. They took blood from my veins. After 6-7 days they kicked me out in the street. I'm walking in the street. I still have SS pants so somebody passes me and says: "Who are you?"

"What do you want?" I asked him. He recognized me. I had long hair which grew back. You could still see two or three fingers wide the head was shaved. He recognized me. "You have papers?" He asked.

"What are you talking about?" I answered.

He reached into my pants pockets and found my liberation papers.

"I will take you to a committee they'll give you regular clothes". We start talking, and they gave me a suit, underwear, and 500 Cronin (Czech) and a piece of paper, and the guy is talking to me, it feels like I'm coming back to myself (mentally). I still have the paper from that 500 Cronin (See Figure 20).

They took me to a place where I can stay for 3 days and then leave. Then I went to the train to continue to go to Bratislava. I came to the train and people are hanging from the roof. They can't get on. Someone gets off the train, and says to me "I come from Seredna come back".

He got off the train, and I told him I have nowhere to stay.

"Just come with us".

I went with them, two brothers, and they took me in, and after a few days took me to the train. Somehow he got me on the train, and took me to Bratislava, and there I met Devora and Judy (two cousins), and they told me "The mamma leibt" ("Your mother lives").

"How do you know?"

"She's either in Davidkov or Kuzmino".

I was in Bratislava for three days. I went from there to Budapest by train. I was in Budapest another three days, then I took a train to Munkatch. In Ebensee after 20,000 people were liberated within one week ten thousand were dead. They brought in Germans to build mass grave, and threw them in. They died from the food. Their stomachs couldn't take it and they were weak. If the war was going to last another day or two, everyone would have been dead. You didn't have food.

In Munkatch I found a gentile from our town, it was almost night, after sunset.

"Are you going home? Can I get a ride?" *I asked him.*

I hopped a ride, I went to Kuzmino. I went to the mayor's house. I'm talking to him and my mother comes outside. She asked me where Chaym Hersch (Herman) my brother was. I told her the truth.

The truth of the matter is that I don't remember what I ate yesterday but these memories are burnt in the brain. I'll never forget. We never wanted to talk about it. We were ashamed, people didn't want to talk. The only time we felt like human beings was in 1967 after the Six Day war, then we started feeling human. Otherwise we had very little contact with Americans. We refugees kept to ourselves. Everyone kept to their own. No one, even relatives who were in America before us, didn't want to mix with you. They thought you were sick people.

In the DP camp I had to register, so I registered both myself and my mother with Aguda (more details and documentation below).

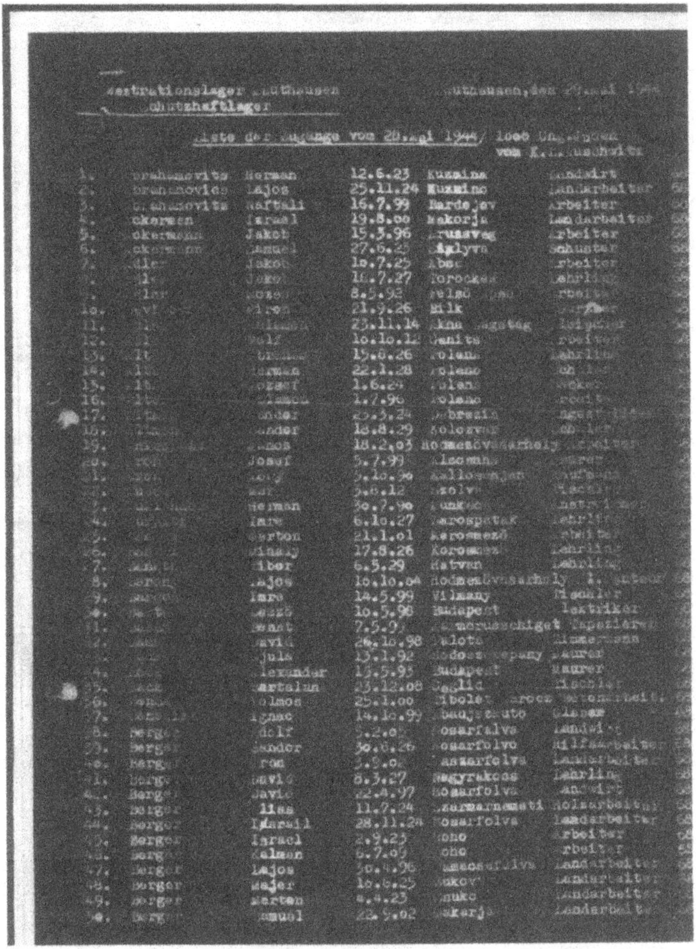

MELK AND EBENSEE

Figure 9A: A page listing prisoners transferred to Mauthausen on Mai (May) 28, 1944, in alphabetical order.

KUZMINO CHRONICLES

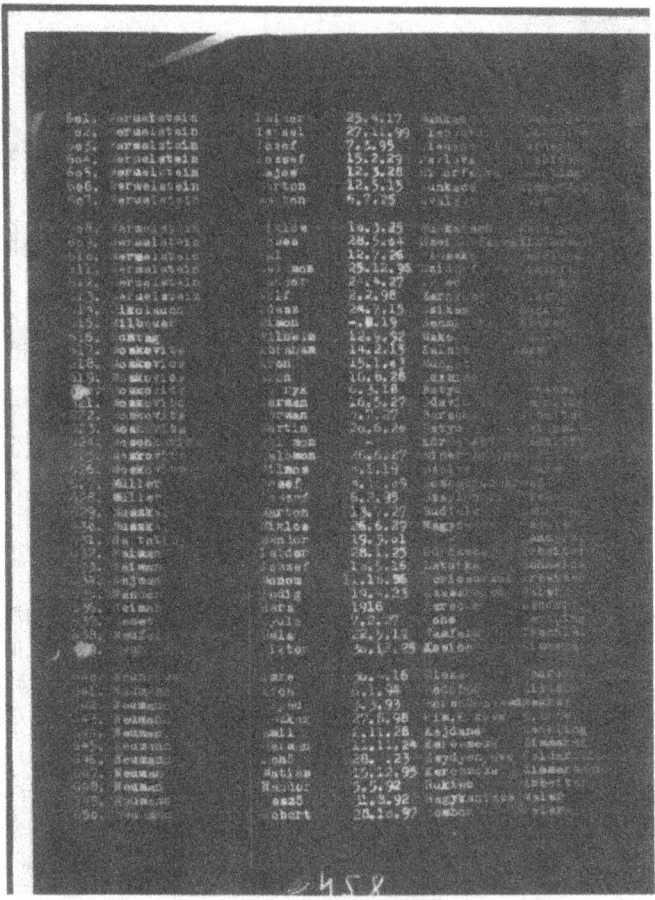

Figure 9B: A page listing prisoners transferred to Mauthausen on Mai (May) 28, 1944, in alphabetical order. Herman Moskovitc is listed on line 621. He was born on 5/16/27 in Davidkov. His profession is listed as Lehrling (barely visible).

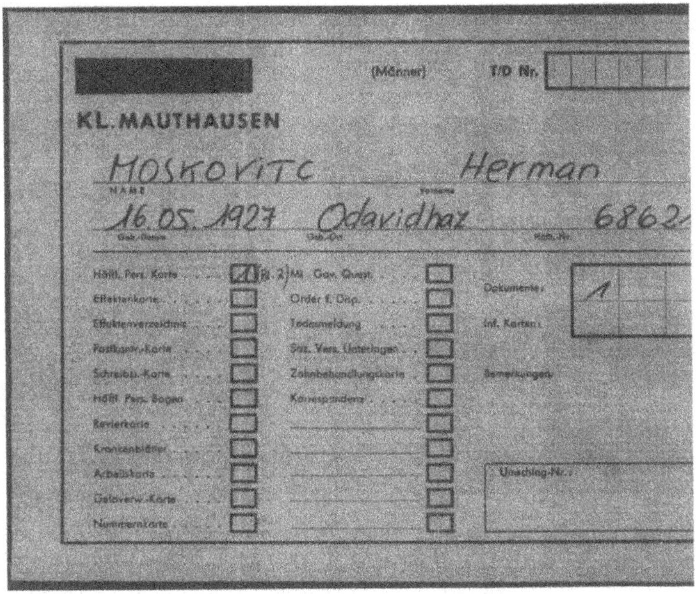

MELK AND EBENSEE

Figure 9C Front: Envelope created by the ITS (International Tracing Service) to hold individual documents from Mauthausen for Herman Moskovitc.

Figure 9C -Back: Envelope created by the ITS (International Tracing Service) to hold individual documents from Mauthausen for Herman Moskovitc.

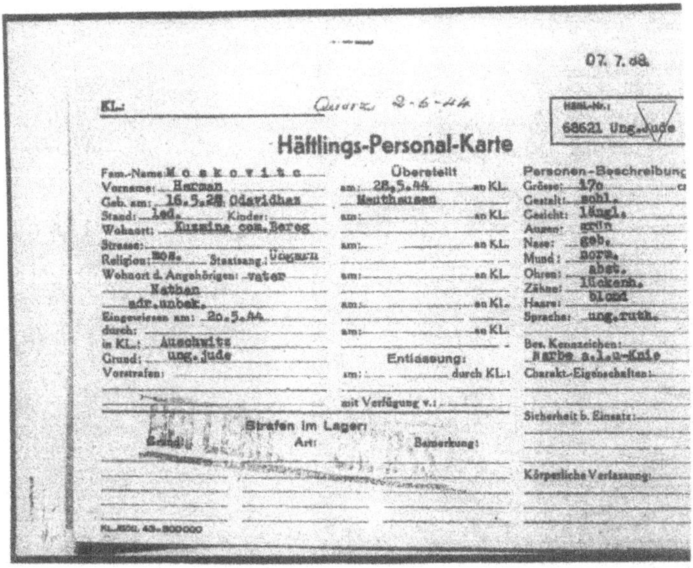

07. 7. 08

KL.: Quarz 2-6-44

Häftl.-Nr.: 68521 Ung. Jude

Häftlings-Personal-Karte

Fam.-Name: M o s k o v i t s
Vorname: Herman
Geb. am: 16.5.28 Odavidhaz
Stand: led. Kinder:
Wohnort: Kuzmina com. Bereg
Strasse:
Religion: mos. Staatsang.: Ungarn
Wohnort d. Angehörigen: vater Nathan adr. unbek.
Eingewiesen am: 20.5.44
durch:
in KL.: Auschwitz
Grund: ung. jude
Vorstrafen:

Überstellt
am: 28.5.44 an KL. Mauthausen
am: an KL.
am: an KL.
am: an KL.
am: an KL.
am: an KL.

Entlassung:
am: durch KL.:
mit Verfügung v.:

Personen-Beschreibung
Grösse: 170 cm
Gestalt: schl.
Gesicht: längl.
Augen: grün
Nase: geb.
Mund: norm.
Ohren: abst.
Zähne: lückenh.
Haare: blond
Sprache: ung. ruth.
Bes. Kennzeichen: Narbe a. l. u-Knie
Charakt.-Eigenschaften:
Sicherheit b. Einsatz:
Körperliche Verfassung:

Strafen im Lager:
Grund: Art: Bemerkung:

KL. 2/0. 43. 300000

Figure 9D: Front of Herman's Mauthausen prisoner card. On the top of the card is the hand written word 'Quarz' designating his work assignment on "Project Quartz" (See text).

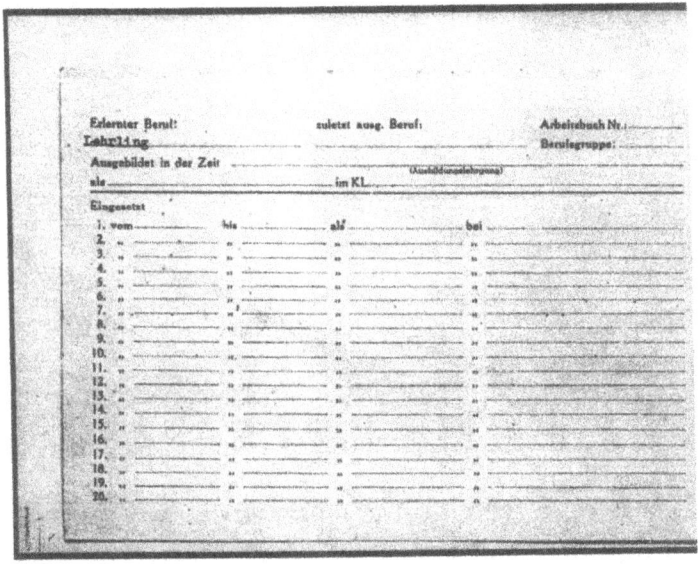

Figure 9E: Back of Herman's Mauthausen prisoner car.

MELK AND EBENSEE

The column on the left of Herman's Prisoner card designates his demographics: his name and birthdate, his birth town (Odavidhas), that he is single, he comes from Kusmina com. Bereg. His religion is Mosaic. His father is Nathan whose address is unknown. He arrived at Auschwitz on May 20, 1944. He is a Hungarian Jew. The middle column records that he was transferred to Mauthausen of May 28 1944. On the upper right column is his prisoner number 68621, and his national identity-Hungarian Jew.

The column on the right documents his personal characteristics: He is 170 cm, he is slender (schlank), his face is long, his eyes are green, his mouth is normal, his ears stand out, he has spaces between his teeth, his hair is blond, he speaks Hungarian and Ruthenian. Identifying marks include a scar (Narbe) under his left knee (a.l.u.-knie).

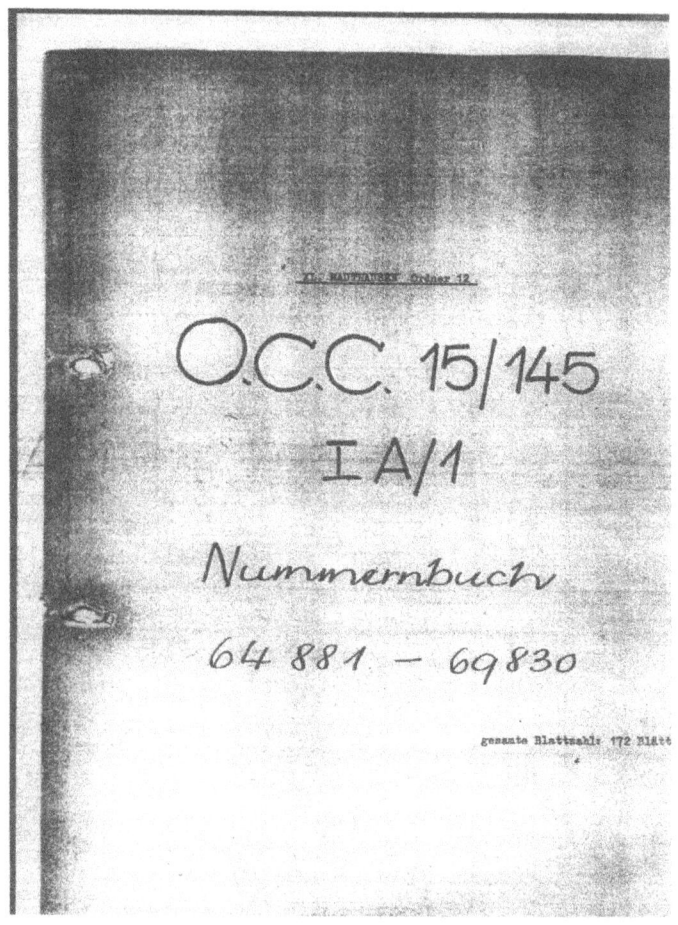

Figure 10A: Archival cover sheet from the Mauthausen concentration Number Book (Nummerenbuch) 64881-69830 which was compiled post war.

MELK AND EBENSEE

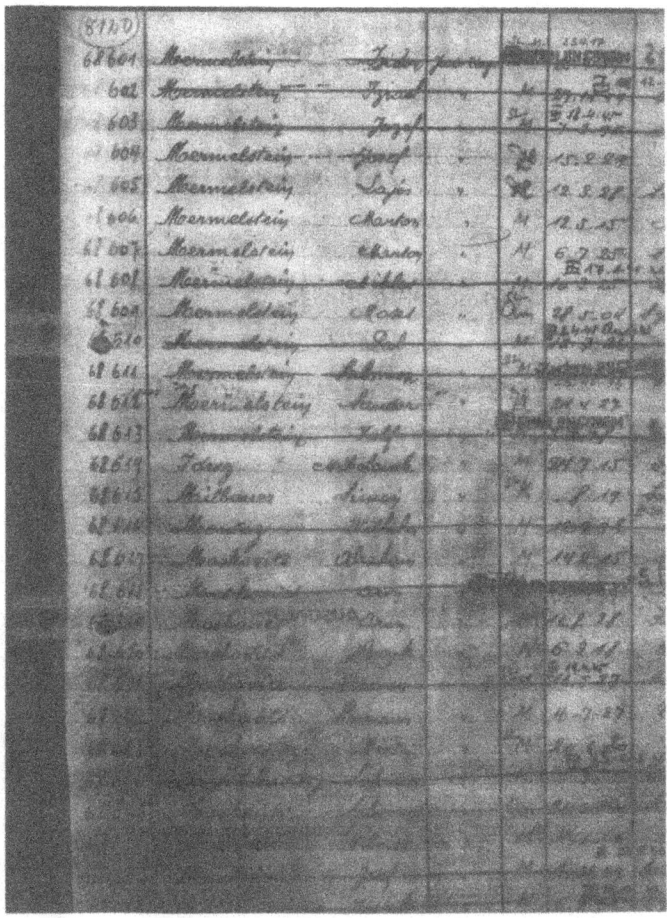

Figure 10B: Herman's name appears on this page of the Mauthausen Number Book under the number 68621.

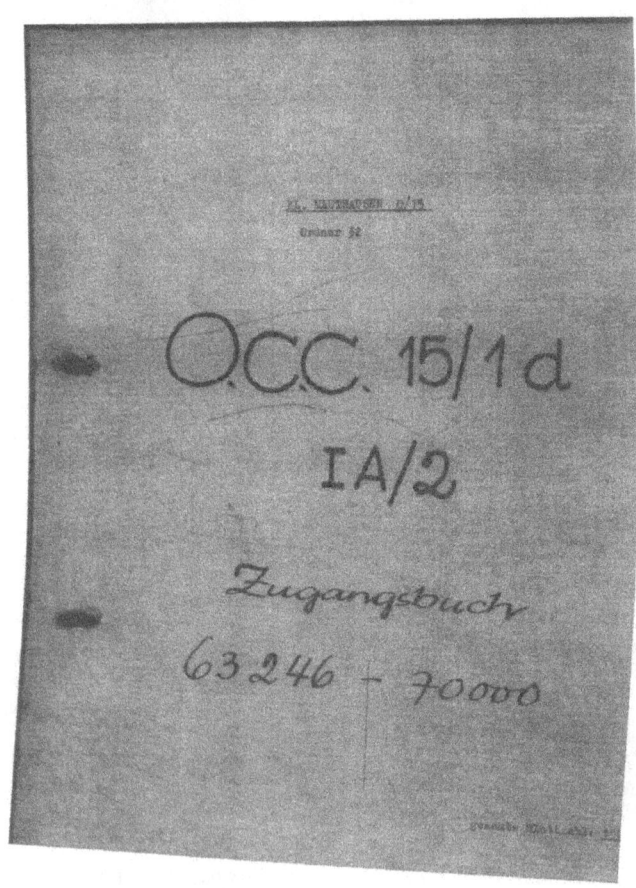

Figure 10C: Archival Front sheet of Arrival Book (Zugangsbuch) for numbers 63246- 70000.

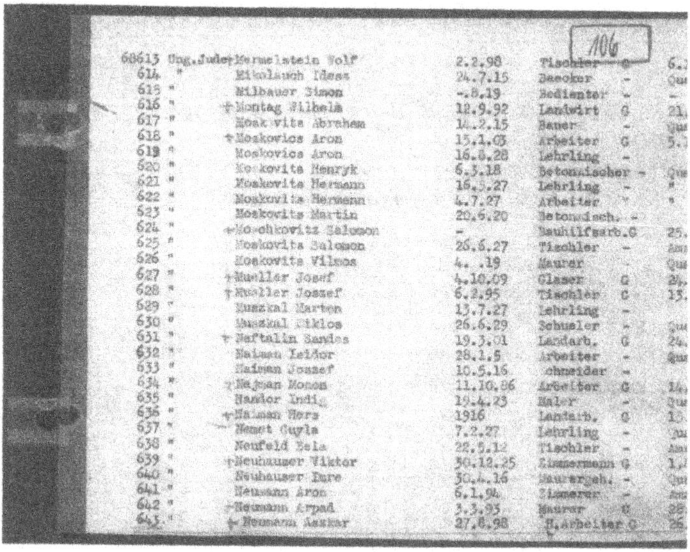

106

68613	Ung.Jude	†Hermelstein Wolf	2.2.98	Tischler	G	6.
614	"	Mikolauch Idess	24.7.15	Baecker	-	Qu
615	"	Milbauer Simon	-.8.19	Bedienter	-	-
616	"	†Montag Wilhelm	12.9.92	Landwirt	G	21.
617	"	Moskovits Abraham	14.2.15	Bauer	-	Qu
618	"	†Moskovics Aron	15.1.03	Arbeiter	G	5.
619	"	Moskovics Aron	16.8.28	Lehrling	-	
620	"	Moskovits Henryk	6.3.18	Betonmischer	-	Qu
621	"	Moskovits Hermann	16.5.27	Lehrling	-	"
622	"	Moskovits Hermann	4.7.27	Arbeiter	-	"
623	"	Moskovits Martin	20.6.20	Betonmisch.	-	
624	"	†Moschkovitz Salomon	-	Bauhilfsarb.	G	25.
625	"	Moskovits Salomon	26.6.27	Tischler	-	Am
626	"	Moskovits Vilmos	4. .19	Maurer	-	Qu
627	"	†Mueller Josef	4.10.09	Glaser	G	24.
628	"	†Mueller Jozsef	6.2.95	Tischler	G	15.
629	"	Muszkal Marton	13.7.27	Lehrling	-	
630	"	Muszkal Miklos	26.6.29	Schueler	-	Qu
631	"	†Naftalin Sandor	19.3.01	Landarb.	G	24.
632	"	Naiman Leidor	28.1.5	Arbeiter	-	Qu
633	"	Naiman Jozsef	10.5.16	Schneider	-	
634	"	†Najman Monos	11.10.86	Arbeiter	G	14.
635	"	Nandor Indig	19.4.23	Maler	-	Qu
636	"	†Naiman Hers	1916	Landarb.	G	1
637	"	Nemet Gyula	7.2.27	Lehrling	-	Qu
638	"	Neufeld Bela	22.5.12	Tischler	-	Am
639	"	†Neuhauser Viktor	30.12.25	Zimmermann	G	1.
640	"	Neuhauser Imre	30.4.16	Maurergeh.	-	Qu
641	"	Neumann Aron	6.1.94	Zimmerer	-	Am
642	"	†Neumann Arpad	3.3.93	Maurer	G	28.
643	"	†Neumann Aszkar	27.8.98	H.Arbeiter	G	26.

Figure 10D: Record indicating Herman's transfer to the sub concentration camp Melk to work on Project Quarz on June 2, 1944. See line 621 (68621) listing his name, birthdate, profession and work designation on project Quarz (last column on the far right). There are quotation marks underneath the line above with the first three letters of the word 'Quarz' (Qua).

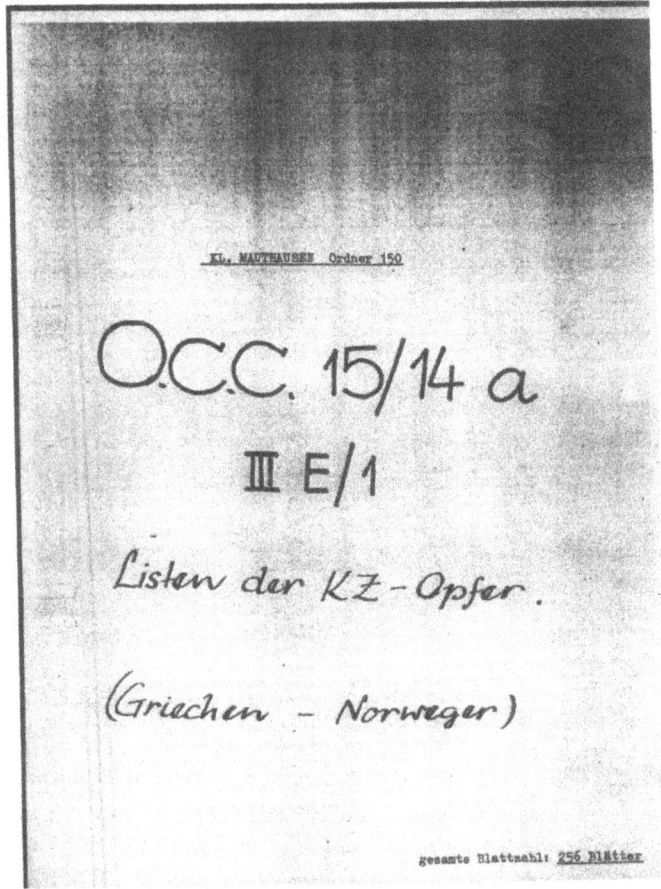

Figure 10E: Archival cover sheet of records documenting prisoners with the names Kz to Opfer that were transferred from the sub-camp back to the main Mauthausen concentration camp on April 11, 1945.

MELK AND EBENSEE

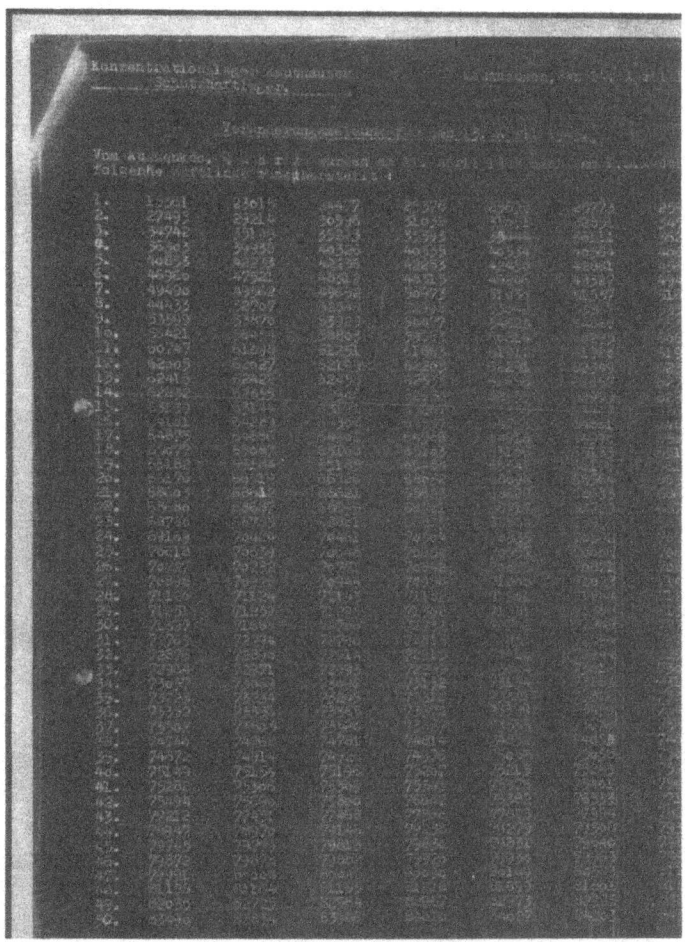

Figure 10F: List documenting that on April 11, 1945 Herman was transferred from the sub camp back to the main Mauthausen concentration camp. He is only listed under his assigned prisoner number 68621 (Line 21, Column 3).

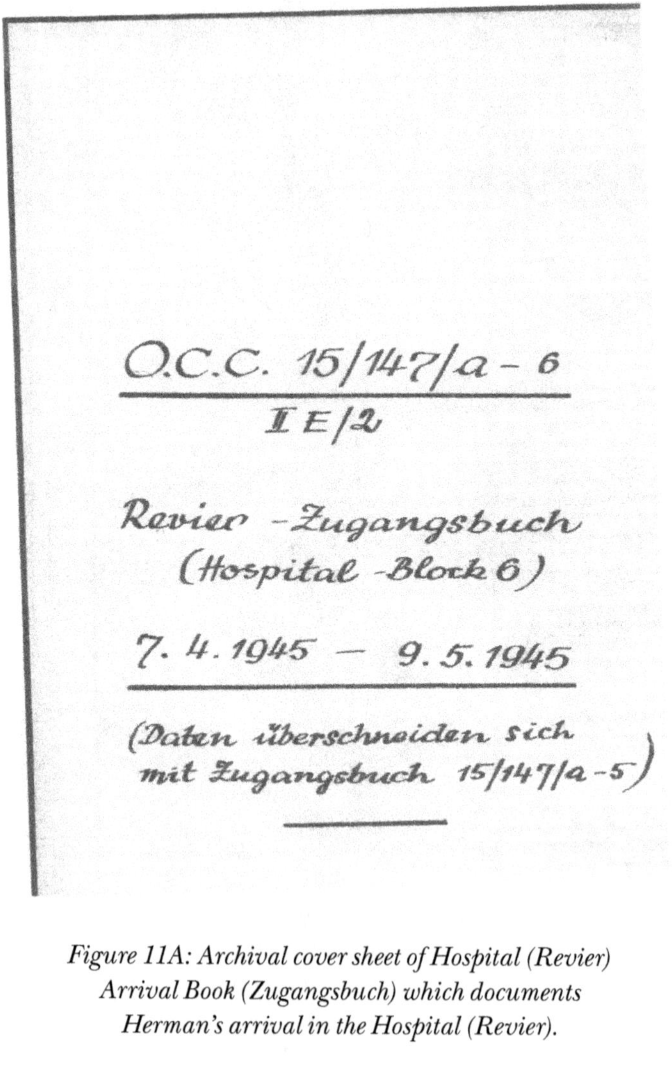

O.C.C. 15/147/a - 6
―――――――――――
I E/2

Revier -Zugangsbuch
(Hospital -Block 6)

7. 4. 1945 — 9. 5. 1945

(Daten überschneiden sich
mit Zugangsbuch 15/147/a-5)

Figure 11A: Archival cover sheet of Hospital (Revier) Arrival Book (Zugangsbuch) which documents Herman's arrival in the Hospital (Revier).

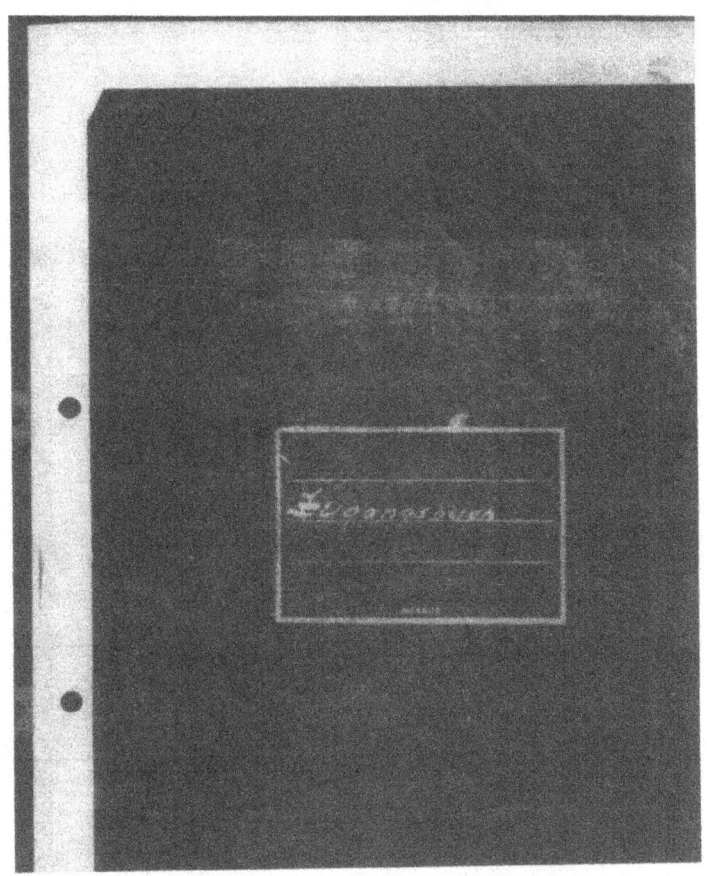

Figure 11B: Title page of Arrival Book (Zugangsbuch).

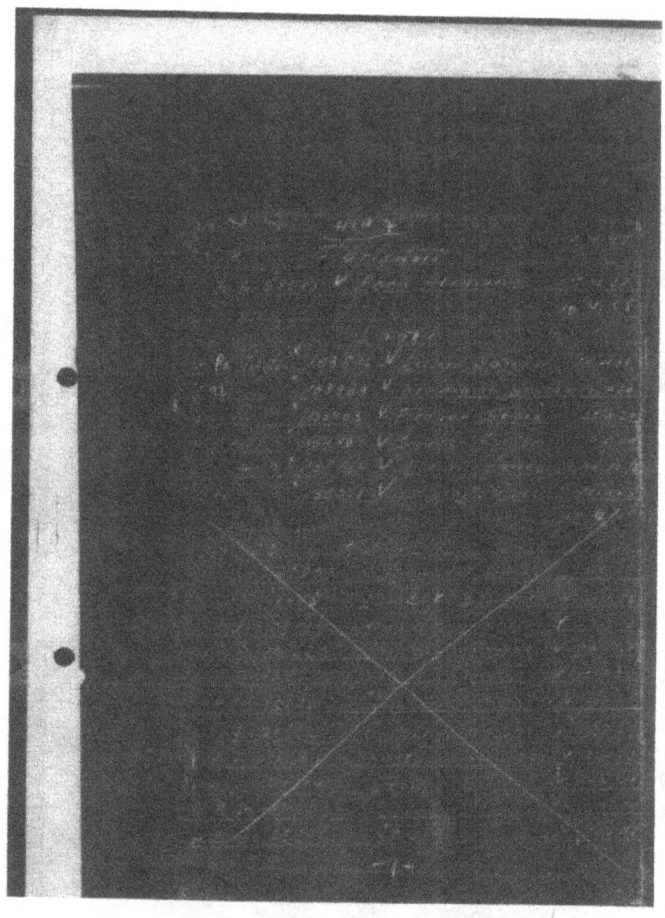

Figure 11C: Page of the Arrival Book with prisoner' names preceding the page documenting Herman's presence.

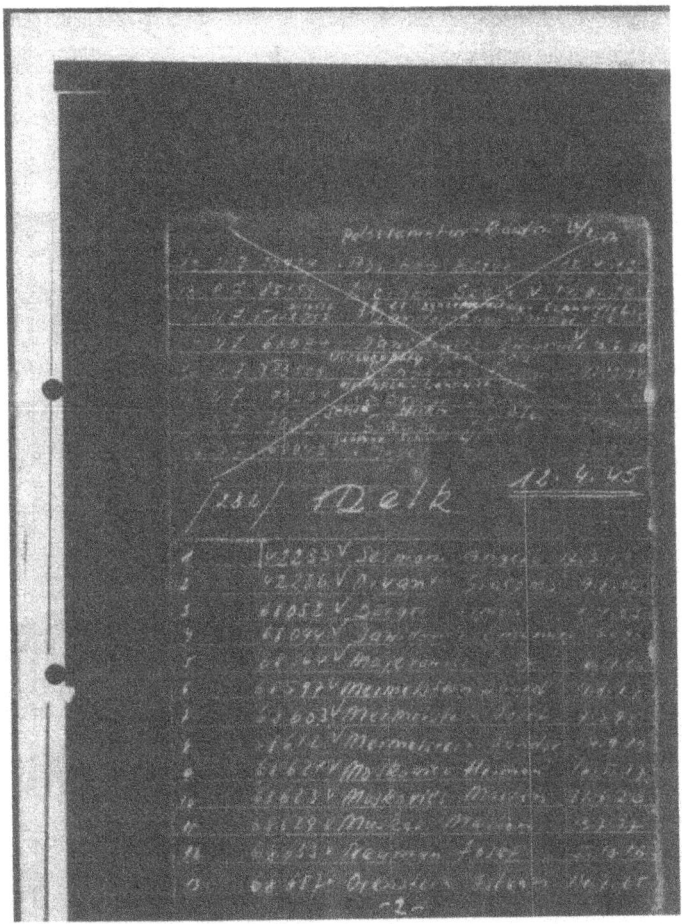

Figure 11D: Page of the Arrival Book which specifically records that Herman arrived from Melk on 4/11/45. He is listed on line 9 and identified by his prisoner number and name.

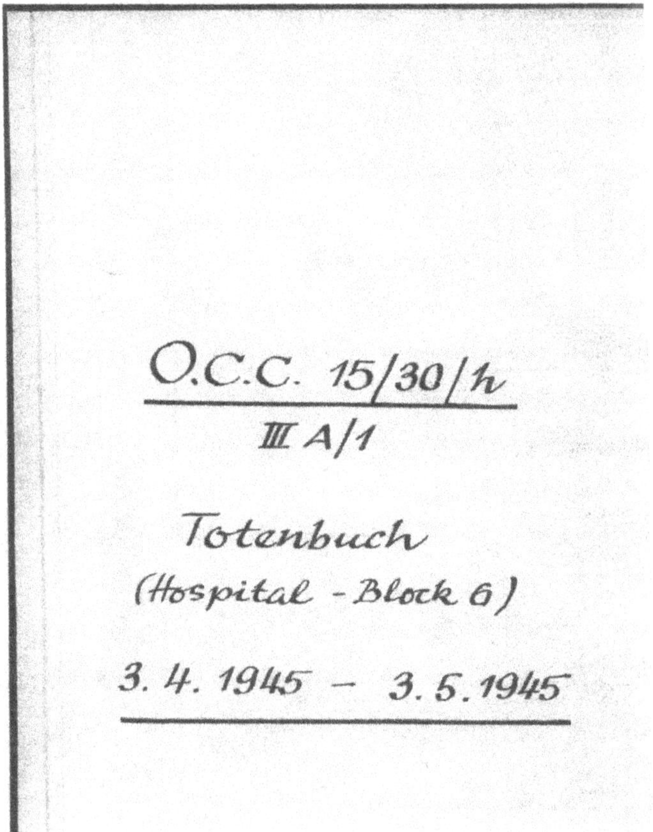

O.C.C. 15/30/h
III A/1

Totenbuch
(Hospital - Block 6)

3. 4. 1945 — 3. 5. 1945

Figure 12A: Archival cover sheet of documents from the Death Book (Totenbuch) of the Mauthausen Infirmary (Hospital Block-6).

Figure 12B: Title page of the Death Book (Totenbuch).

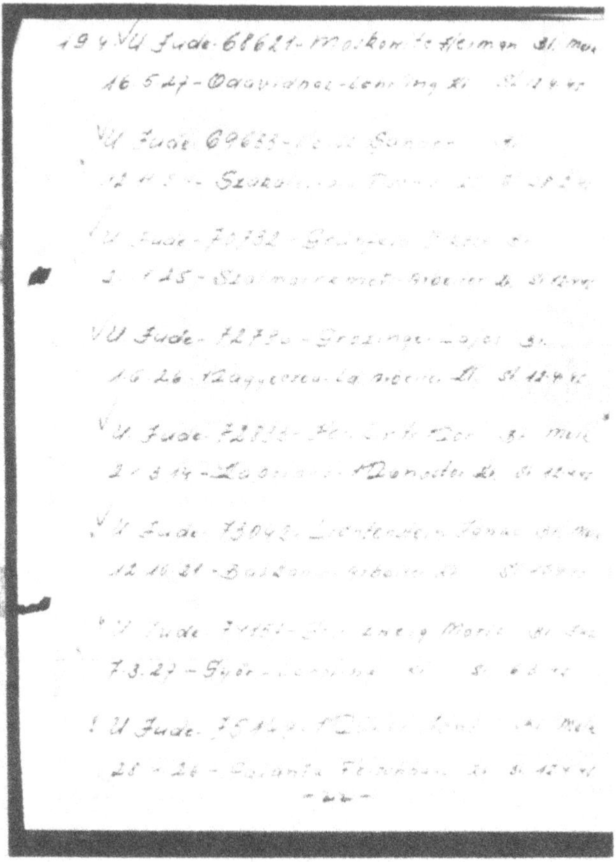

KUZMINO CHRONICLES

Figure 12C: Page from the Death Book documenting that Herman perished on April 19, 1945. He is listed on the top line of the page identified as 19.4 (April 19, 1945), Jude (Jew) 68621- Moskowitc Herman, 31 Melk, 16.5.27 (birthday) – Odavidhaz (birthplace) – Lehrling (apprentice) KL (concentration camp), SL 12.4.45 (date of arrival).

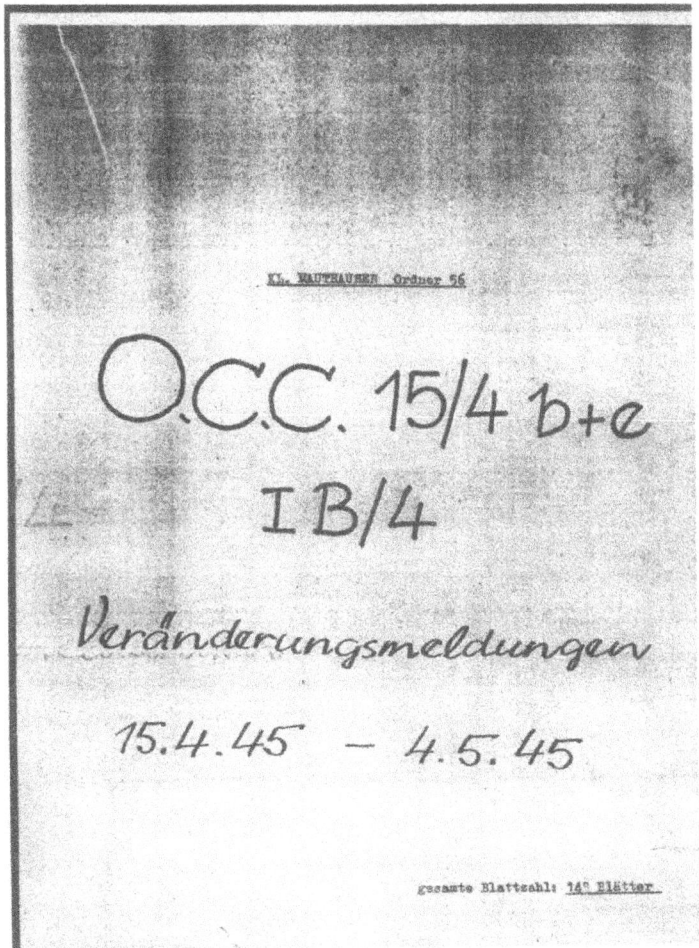

Figure 13A: Archival cover sheet for documents recording a list of Mauthausen Concentration Camp prisoners who died (Abgang/ verstorben) between April 15, 1945 and March 4, 1945.

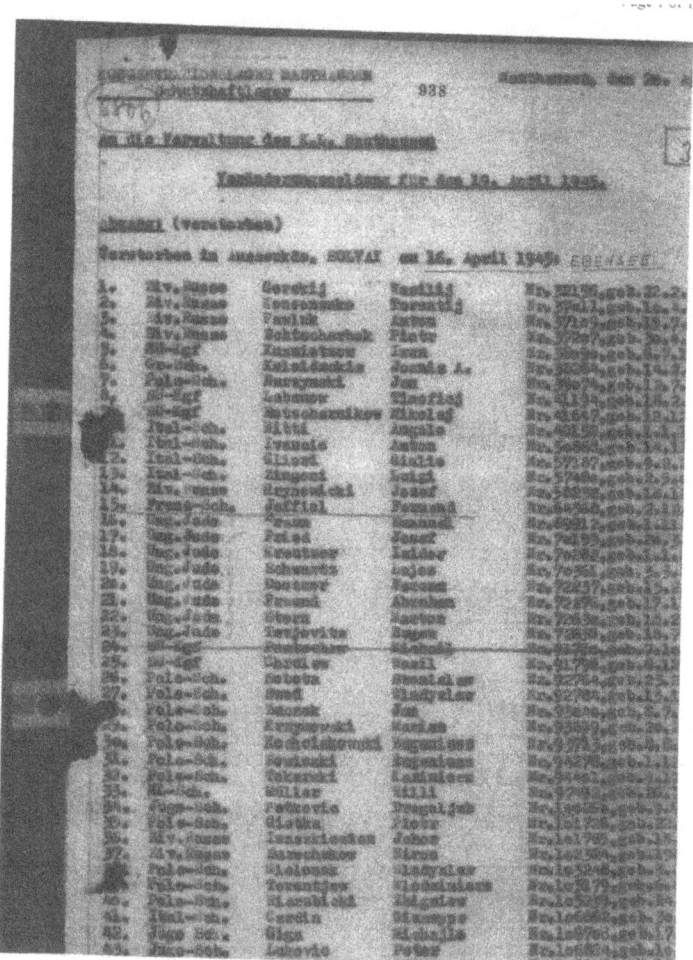

Figure 13B: Page of Mauthausen Concentration Camp prisoners who died (Abgang/ verstorben) on April 19, 1945, preceding the page that lists Herman.

Figure 13C: Page of Mauthausen Concentration Camp prisoners who died (Abgang/ verstorben) on April 19, 1945. Herman is listed on line 205, and is described as being a Hungarian Jew, and further identified by his prisoner number and birthdate.

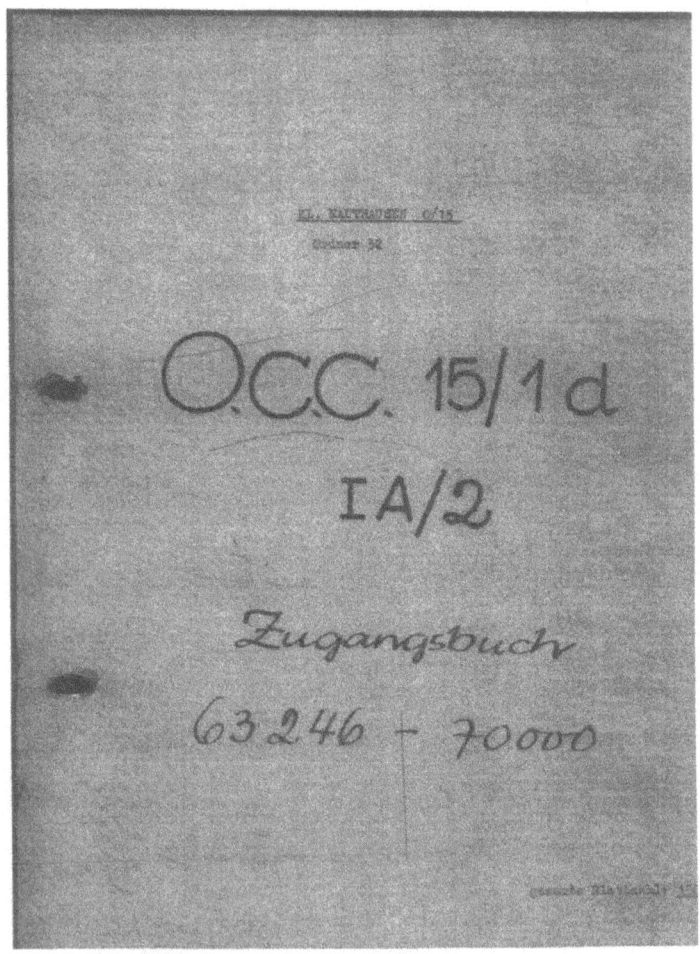

Figure 14A: Archival Cover sheet of documents listing prisoners 63246-70000 in the Mauthausen Arrival Book (Zugangsbuch).

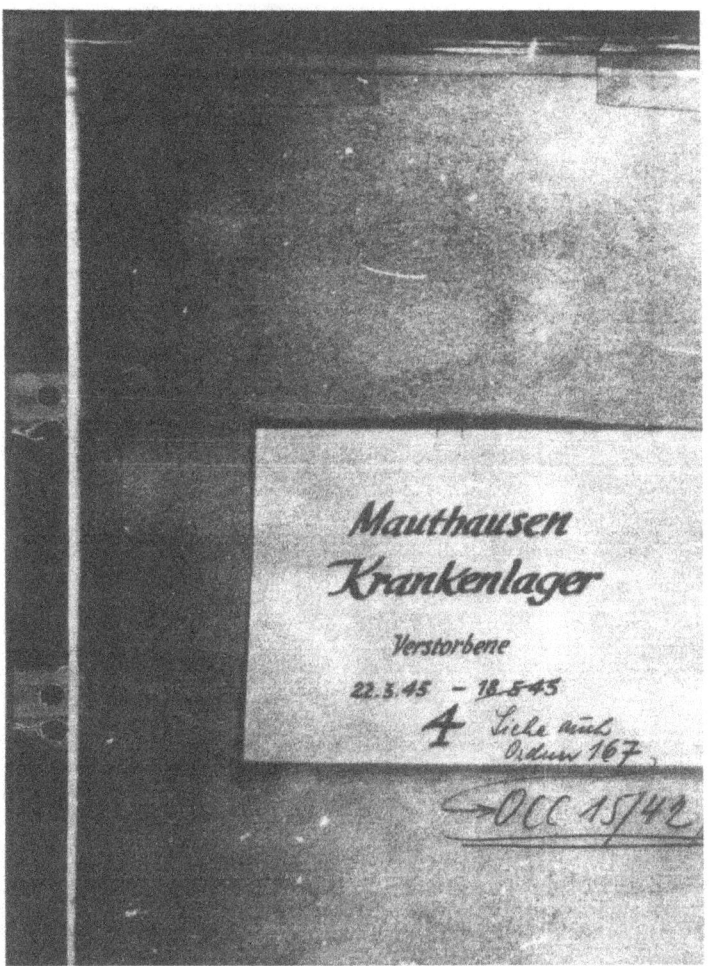

Figure 14B: Title page of Mauthausen Krankenlager (sick-camp).

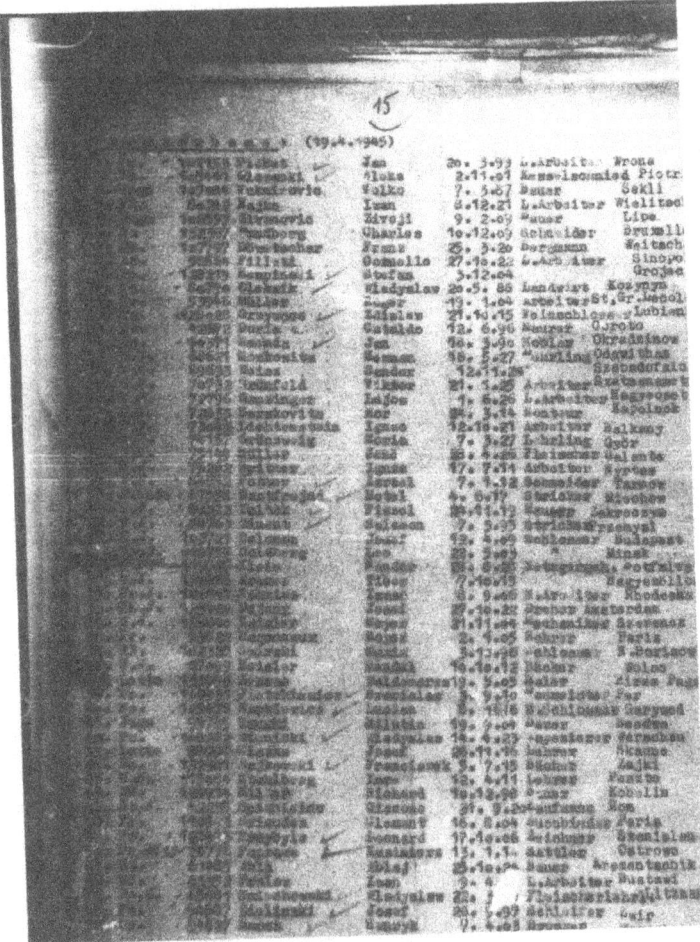

Figure 14C: List of prisoners that died (verstorbene) in the "Mauthausen sick-camp (Krankenlager)".
Herman's name appears on the 15th line from the top. The heading of the page is dated April 19, 1945, the day he died in the sick camp.

MELK AND EBENSEE

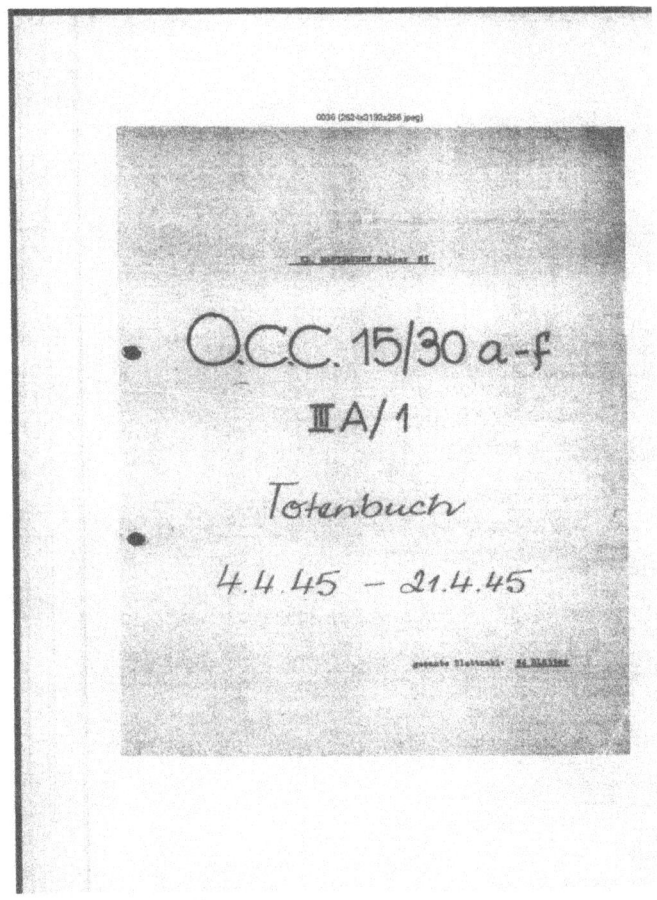

Figure 15A: Archival Cover sheet of documents from the Death Book (Totenbuch) of Mauthausen concentration camp from April 4, 1945-April 21, 1945.

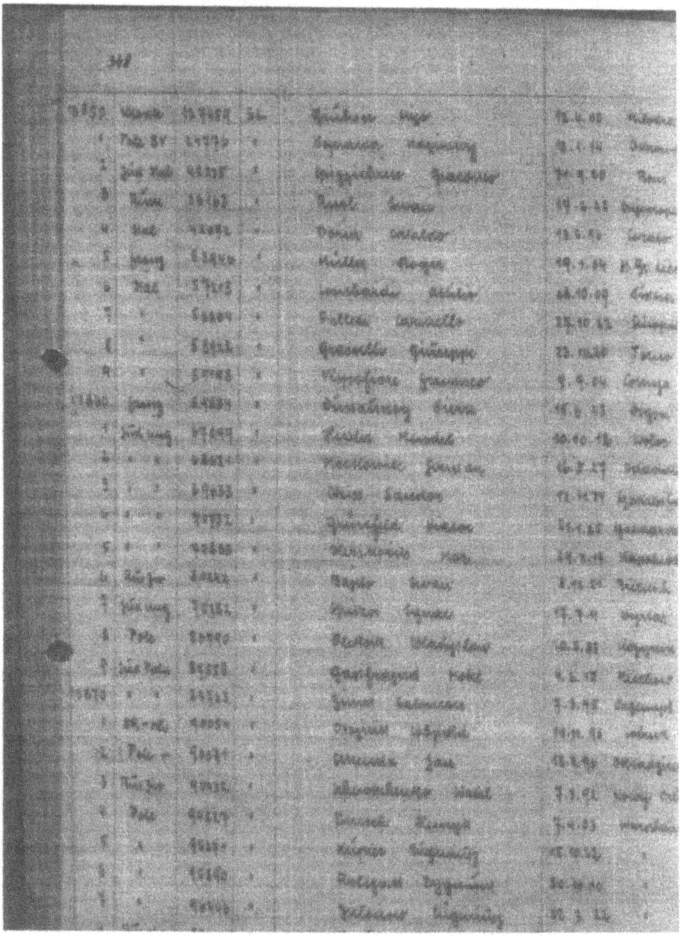

KUZMINO CHRONICLES

Figure 15B: Page from the Death Book (Totenbuch) of Mauthausen concentration camp listing Herman on 13th line from the top. He is listed as number 13862.

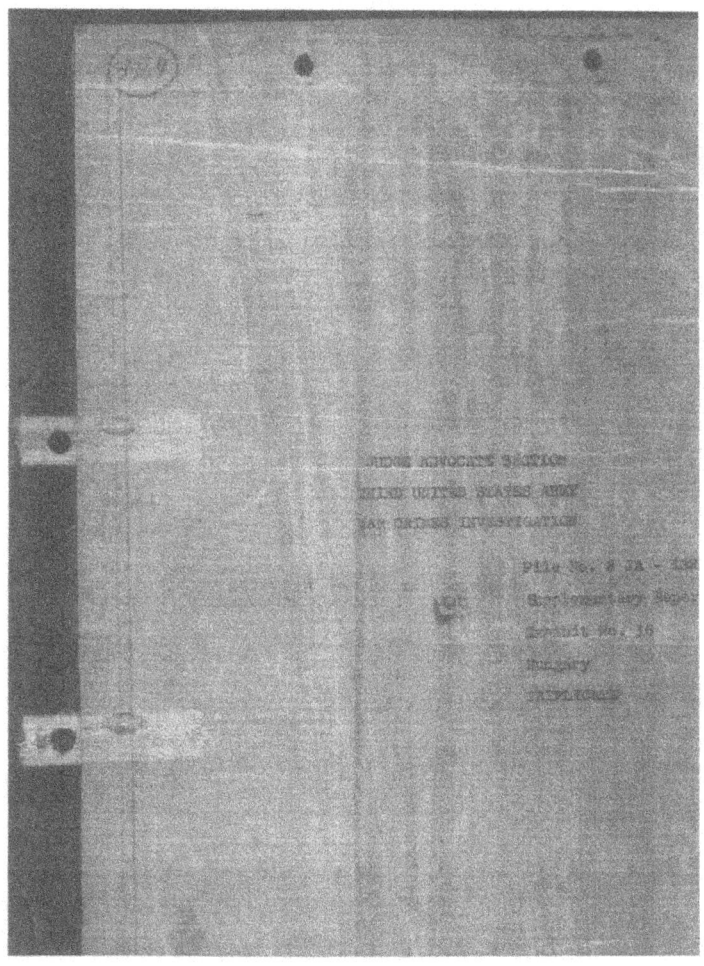

Figure 16A: Cover page of "Judge Advocate Section Third United States Army War Crimes Investigation" which includes a list by nationality (Hungarya) of the victims of Mauthausen concentration camp.

KUZMINO CHRONICLES

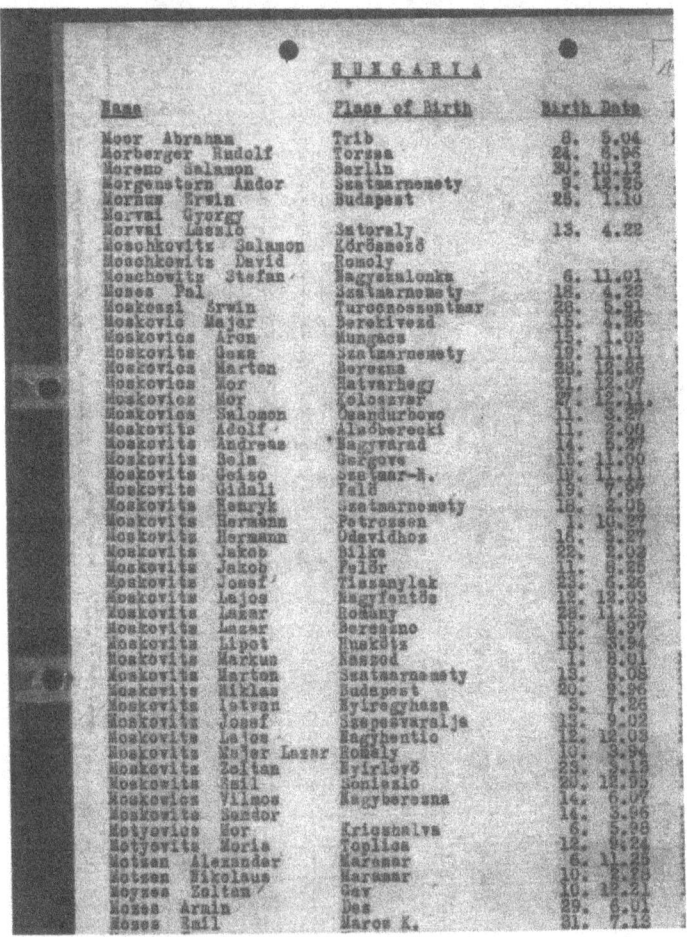

Figure 16B: Alphabetical list by nationality (Hungarya) of the victims of Mauthausen concentration camp from the "Judge Advocate Section Third United States Army War Crimes Investigation" where Herman is listed as Moskovits Hermann from Odavidhoz, born on 5/ 16 /1927.

```
DEM SONDERSTANDESAMT VORGELEGT          Datum: ............
Name: ....MOSKOVITC, Herman      Mai 68621
geboren am 16.5.1947 in Odávidház    Nat. Ung. Jude
gestorben am 19.4.1945, 0ʰ40 in Mauthausen
Todesursache ....Kreislaufschwäche
beerdigt am ................................ in ..........................
─────────────────────────────────────────
STERBEURKUNDE Nr. 4/06, Abt. M (Stempel)    Da. 15. Juli 1957
ausgestellt aufgrund folgender Dokumente:
                                    Sonderstandesamt
                                    Arolsen, Kreis Waldeck
                                              bitte wenden
```

Figure 17A: Front side of official death certificate issued for Herman by the ITS. The cause of death is recorded as circulatory insufficiency (Kreislaufschnache).

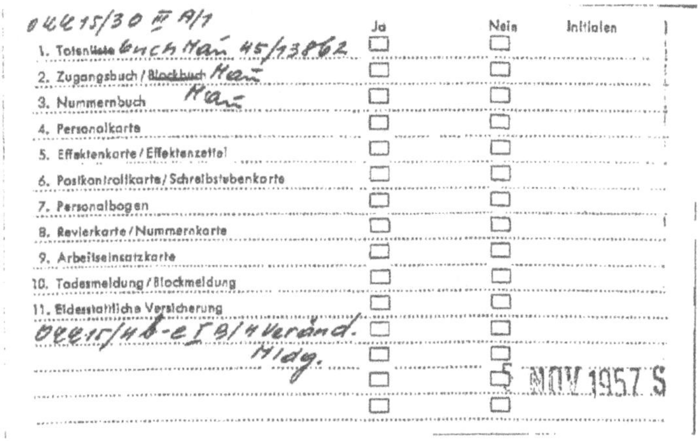

0 44 15/30 III A/1

	Ja	Nein	Initialen
1. Totenliste buch Mau 45/13862	☐	☐	
2. Zugangsbuch / ~~Blockbuch~~ Mau	☐	☐	
3. Nummernbuch Mau	☐	☐	
4. Personalkarte	☐	☐	
5. Effektenkarte / Effektenzettel	☐	☐	
6. Postkontrollkarte / Schreibstubenkarte	☐	☐	
7. Personalbogen	☐	☐	
8. Revierkarte / Nummernkarte	☐	☐	
9. Arbeitseinsatzkarte	☐	☐	
10. Todesmeldung / Blockmeldung	☐	☐	
11. Eidesstattliche Versicherung	☐	☐	
0 44 15/4 b-e I 8/4 Veränd.	☐	☐	
Mldg.	☐	☐	
	☐	☐ 5 NOV 1957 S	
	☐	☐	

Figure 17B: Back side of official death certificate issued for Herman by the ITS. The cause of death is recorded as circulatory insufficiency (Kreislaufschnache).

List from
Yad Vashem
Archives

Scanned copy will
be available shortly

Hermann Moskovits was born in Odavidhaza, Czechoslovakia in 1927. He was a child. During the war he was in Mauthausen, Austria. Hermann was murdered/perished in 1945 in Mauthausen, Austria. This information is based on a List of murdered persons found in Card File of Hungarian Jews who perished prepared by the Hungarian branch of the World Jewish Congress, 1945-1946.

Original Record No.:	V 27 c-162
Last Name:	Moskovits
First Name:	Hermann
Gender:	Male
Date of Birth:	16/05/1927
Place of Birth:	Odavidhaza,Mukacevo,Carpathian Ruthenia,Czechoslovakia
Marital Status:	CHILD
Place during the war:	Mauthausen,Camp,Austria
Place of Death:	Mauthausen,Camp,Austria
Date of Death:	19/04/1945
Status victim at creation of list:	murdered/perished
Related item:	Card File of Hungarian Jews who perished prepared by the Hungarian branch of the World Jewish Congress, 1945-1946
Source:	Card File of Hungarian Jews who perished prepared by the Hungarian branch of the World Jewish Congress, 1945-1946
Type of material:	List of murdered persons
Item ID:	7320929

Herman Moskowitc

Figure 18: Record of Herman Moskowitc obtained from the Yad Vashem Central data base of Shoah victims' names.

KUZMINO CHRONICLES

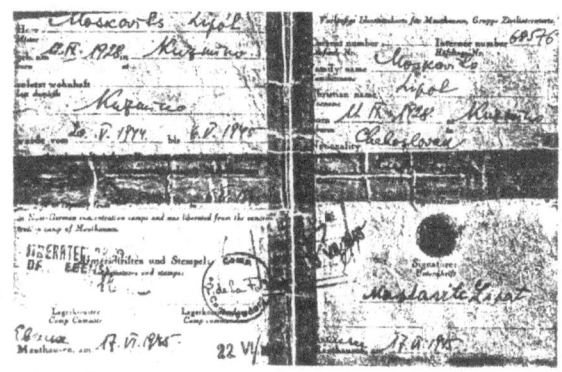

Figure 19A -Front: Liberation document for Leib (See Text).

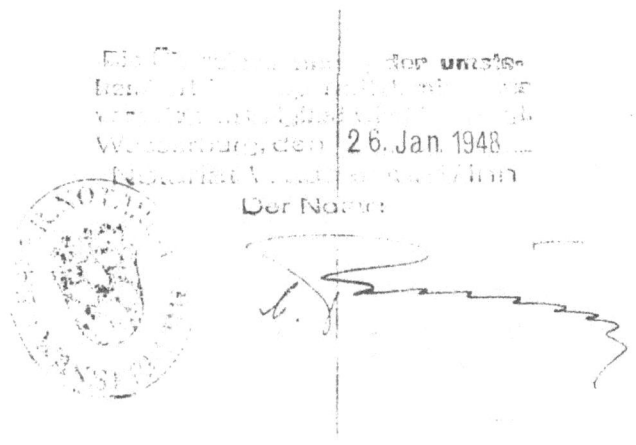

Figure 19A -Back: Liberation document for Leib (See Text).

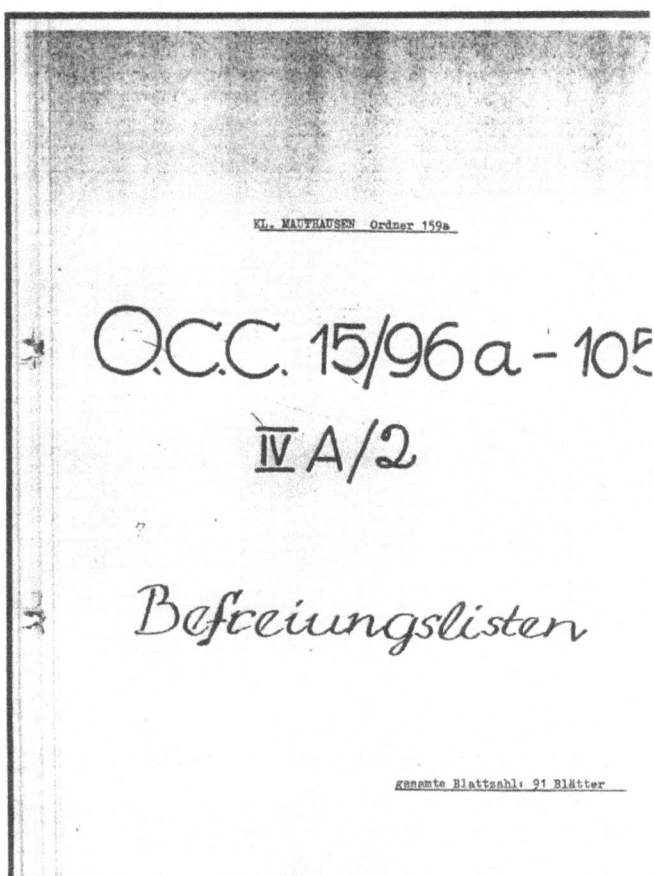

Figure 19B: Archival cover sheet of the list of those liberated (Befreiungslisten) from Ebensee.

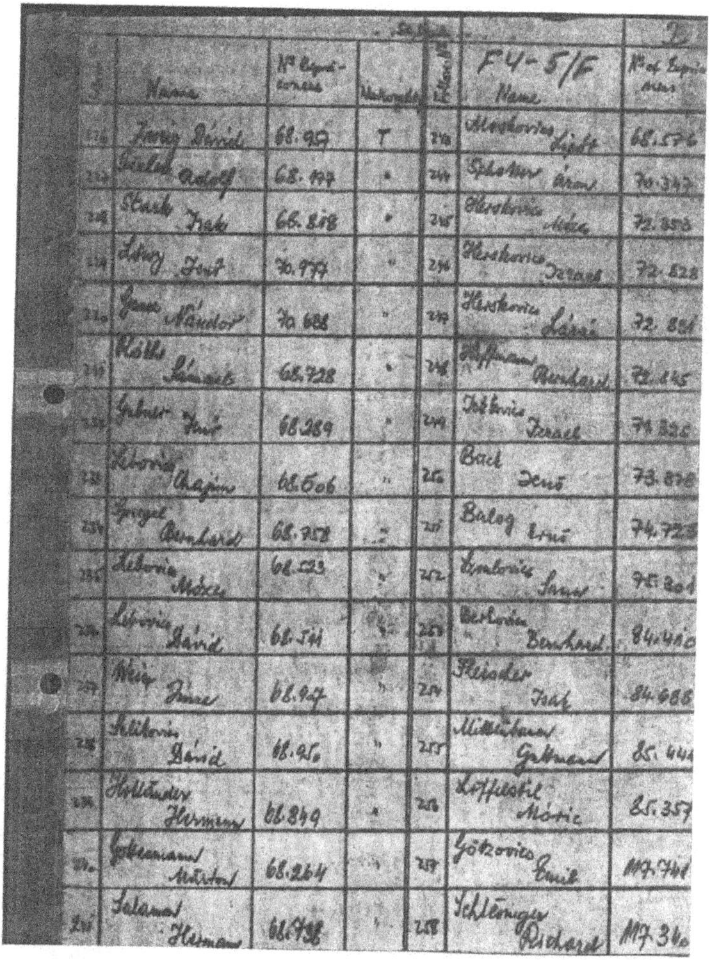

Figure 19C: List which records Lipot Moskovics 68.576 on the top line. He is identified by his prisoner number 68.576.

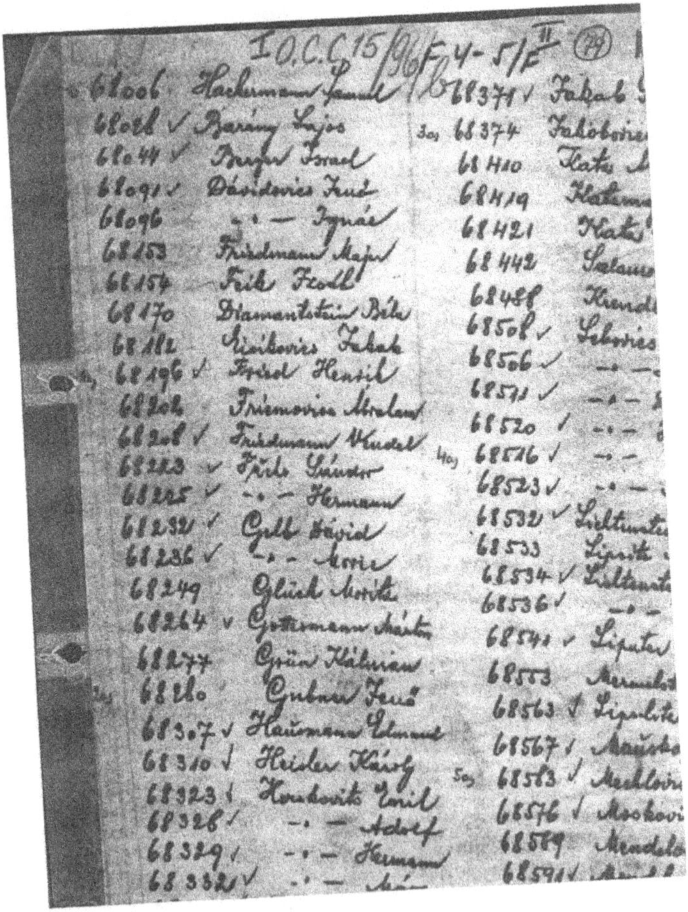
I.O.C.C. 15/196 F 4-5/F II

68006 Hackermann Samuel
68028 ✓ Baráry Lajos
68044 ✓ Berger Israel
68091 ✓ Dávidovics Jenő
68096 —"— Ignác
68153 Friedmann Majer
68154 [illegible]
68170 Diamantstein Béla
68182 [illegible] Jakab
68196 ✓ Fried Hersil
68204 Friemovics Abraham
68208 ✓ Friedmann Vendel
68223 ✓ Fried Sándor
68225 ✓ —"— Hermann
68232 ✓ Gold Dávid
68236 ✓ —"— Móric
68249 Glück Mórits
68264 ✓ Gottesmann Márton
68277 Grün Kálmán
68280 Gubner Jenő
68307 ✓ Hausmann [illegible]
68310 ✓ Heisler Károly
68323 ✓ Horowitz Emil
68328 ✓ —"— Adolf
68329 ✓ —"— Hermann
68332 ✓ —"— [illegible]

68371 ✓ Jakab [illegible]
68374 Jakobovics [illegible]
68410 [illegible]
68419 [illegible]
68421 [illegible]
68442 [illegible]
68488 [illegible]
68508 ✓ [illegible]
68506 ✓ —"—
68511 ✓ —"—
68520 ✓ —"—
68516 ✓ —"—
68523 ✓ —"—
68532 ✓ [illegible]
68533 [illegible]
68534 ✓ [illegible]
68536 ✓ —"—
68541 ✓ [illegible]
68553 [illegible]
68563 ✓ [illegible]
68567 ✓ [illegible]
68583 ✓ [illegible]
68576 ✓ Moskovi[illegible]
68589 [illegible]
68591 ✓ [illegible]

Figure 19D: List which records Lipot by his number 68576 on the second column, third line from the bottom (Moskovi...).

MELK AND EBENSEE

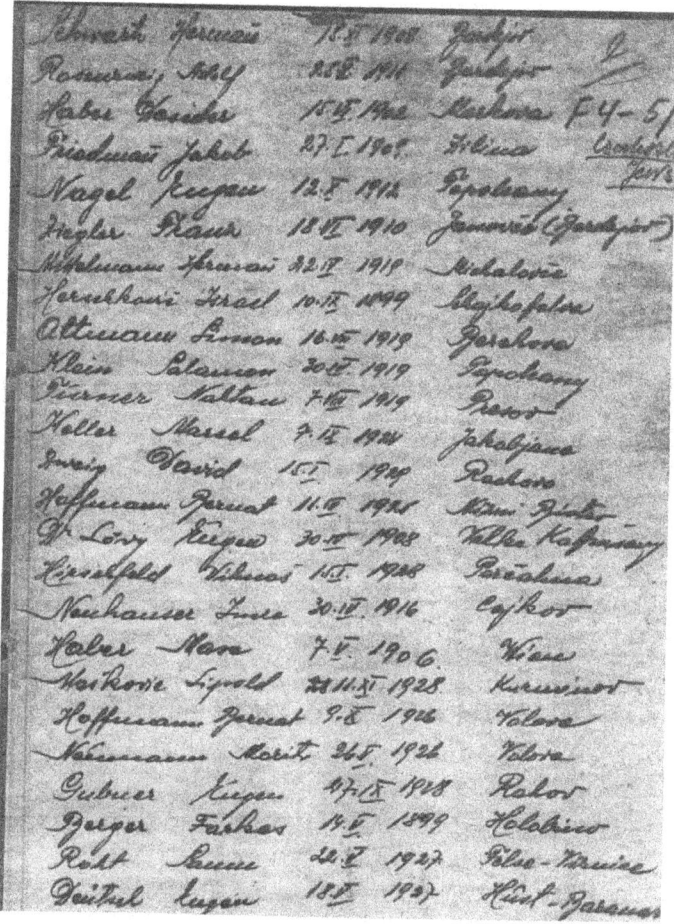

Figure 19E: List which records on the seventh line from the bottom, Leib's name and identification which are written in script as Moskovic Lipold, 11 XI 1928, Kusminov.

```
                                -7-                              Record
LIST OF CZECHO-SLOVAK PRISONERS IN EBENSEE CONCENTRATION         15 May
CAMP
                        Conc.
                        Camp                          13
Name                    No.    Age    Place of Birth
                                                                 ALL RE
Weissberger Menyhert    68928   40    Podhorany              CS
Path  Georg            119171   43    Zlate Morovce           "
Simon Menyhert         137240   36    Fanciko                 "
Brunfeld Erno          135734   21    Felsokarasze            "
Weinberger Tibor       136355   28    Batov                   "
Neumann Aron            63641   51    Podoc                   "
Neumann Samuel          73131   37    Podoc                   "
Neumann Mozes           73130   20    Podoc                   "
Alt Robert             113514   24    Uhersky Brod            "
Mermelstein Godel       63599   45    Zadnia                  "
Mermelstein Josef       67650   18    Bozec                   "
Turner Nathan          113334   26    Presov                  "
Altmann Simon          118515   26    Berehovo                "
Zwecker Koloman         68956   18    Haho                    "
Bolog Ernest            74723   18    Komarom SV.Peter        "
Haber Dezider          119801   43    Malacky                 "
Fesaler Ignac          118723   19    Trnava                  "
Klein Salamon          118912   26    Topolcany               "
Barkovine Bernat        84410   17    N. Neresnice            "
Berskovics Mor         117830   36    Cingdevo                "
Neumann Erno           119123   26    Mukacevo                "
Czik Chajim            119619   37    Barove u/T              "
Schatten Juraj         124327   39    Jasina                  "
Notlieb Doni            69652   30    Berehovo                "
Kats Schije             61423   45    Hukliva                 "
Buchbinder Zoltan       85417   19    Trneva                  "
Goldstein Miklos       107005   19    Uzhorod                 "
Goldstein Vojnech      108977   18    Uzhorod                 "
Fried Henrich           68196   24    Felsevise               "
Friedmann Henrik        68201   19    Bilke                   "
Salamon Blek           137216   16    Sirma                   "
Diamantstein Mor       136572   21    Kuzmina                 "
Diamantstein Major     136571   19    Kuzmina                 "
Diamantstein Beni      136570   17    Kuzmina                 "
Salamon Herman          88738   19    Kuzmina                 "
Goldberger Mor          72747   47    Berehovo                "
Moskowits Lipot         68576   17    Kuzmina                 "
Koskowits Aron          63619   16    Kuzmina                 "
Mauskopf Majer          68567   17    Kalnik                  "
Weinberger Bernat       68937   17    Fedelesovo              "
Rot Samuel              68728   18    V. Visnica              "
Berskovits Adolf        63328   21    Kajdanovo               "
Berskovits Vojtech      74950   20    Savljus                 "
Ottesmann Martin        68264   17    Fedelesovo              "
Fixler Adolf            68177   15    Iska                    "
Zoltan David           103380   20    Bicka                   "
Weinberger Jakab       137357   18    Mukacevo                "
Salamon Tibor          137277   17    "                       "
```

Figure 19F: List which records Leib on the 12th line from the bottom. He is listed as Moskowits Lipot 68576, age 17, Kuzmina.

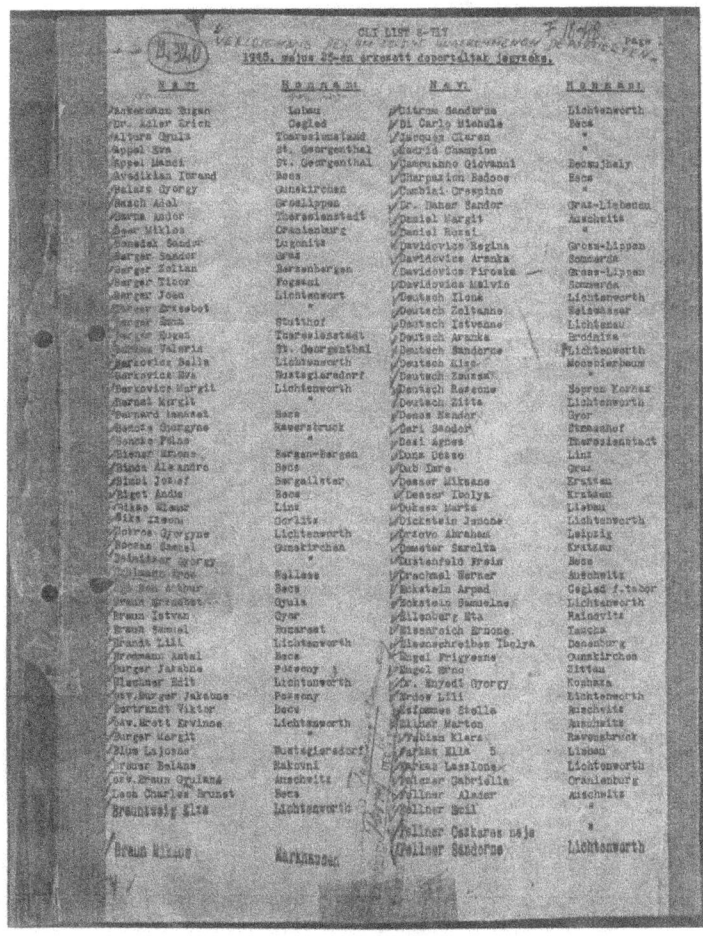

Figure 19G: Alphabetical list of other liberated prisoners.

KUZMINO CHRONICLES

```
                MILITARY GOVERNMENT OF GERMANY           Records a
                Concentration Camp Processing Docket     18 May 194
Ebensee Concentration Camp - Ebensee, Austria
CZECHO-SLOVAK MALE PRISONERS
                              Conc.
                              Camp                                    Date
Name                          No.      Age   Place of Birth           Entry
                                                                ALL RELE
Salamon Zelman                68742    52    Klacanova        CS   20.4.
Lichtenstein Salamon          68532    51    Podmanaster      "    18.4.
Lichtenstein Max              68533    20    Podmanaster      "    23.4.
Lichtenstein Bernard          68534    18    Podmanaster      "     9.4.
Schwarz Mor                   68813    44    Brod             "    20.4.
Schwarz Herman                68809    18    "                "    20.4.
Redlich / Georg / Jirka       117201   22    Praha XII        "    16.4.
Kahan Vilem                   75001    19    Selehee          "    13.4.
Weiss Aron                    68898    17    Karecks          "    18.4.
Weiss Vilmos                  68926    21    "                "    16.9.
Glencik Peter                 119788   47    Krustenko        "    28.3.
Spielmann Sandor              68765    19    Bosegova         "    17.4.
Roth Arnold                   68720    17    Novy Klenovec    "    18.7.
Frommer David                 68219    22    Karecks          "    17.4.
Rusek Frantisek               117248   19    Praha VII        "     3.5.
Knaver Simek                  118891   47    Vrany            "    20.4.
Neumann Moses                 137036   16    Voluva           "    18.4.
Grunwald Juda                 136757   15    Sucha Branka     "    18.4.
Mendelsohn Samuel             68591    20    Bvelva           "    19.2.
Fabian Otto                   118711   31    Bransouce        "    18.2.
Seuxmann Majer                72519    34    Vysny Studeny    "     7.3.
Friedmann Ignats              72290    27    "     "          "    20.4.
Mandel Svzen                  119046   18    Mukacevo         "    20.4.
Spiegel Zoltan                136200   17    Velky Lucky      "    19.4.
Schwimmer Henrik              137204   42    Mukacevo         "    17.4.
Bleckstein Samuel             136511   21    Selos            "    19.11.
Rosner Salamon                68718    17    Velky Lucky      "    10.9.
Sternbach Tobias              68845    48    Holubine         "    18. 4.
Weiser Vilmos                 67974    17    Makasovo         "    27.4.
Abo Arnold                    118551   44    Toboleany        "    24.3.
Wertheim Mor                  68943    19    Mukacevo         "    10.9.
Jakubovic Josef               136580   43    Herase Zdara     "    20.4.
Roemer Miksa                  68733    20    Volky Lucky      "    15.3.
Weingarten Jeno               68896    5(?)  Varsoky          "    20.4.
Weingarten Moses              68587    21    "                "    25.3.
Weingarten Aron               68385    20    "                "    18.4.
Grunzweig David               68274    28    Lipschi Poliens  "    20.4.
Lein Bela                     116904   27    Ilosuva          "    25.3.
Leatovic Lipot                67990    16    Rachov           "    18.4.
Huss Izrael                   68357    50    Patrova          "    20.4.
Schwarcz Herman               121353   37    Bardejov         "    20.4.
Siegler Frentisek             120487   35    Bardejov         "    20.4.
Haber Desider                 119809   43    Markova          "    20.4.
Wassermann Arnost             71312    42    Presov           "    20.4.
Salamen Tibor                 137227   17    Mukacevo         "     5.5.
Ganz Herman                   70637    20    Vonheva          "    20.4.
Ganz Nissen                   70638    18    Vonhava          "    18.4.
Havas Georg                   68308    16    Mukacevo         "     7.6.
Friedmann Jakob               119719   36    Hanuslyce m/S    "    23.4.
```

Figure 19H: List of Czechoslovak Male Prisoners in Ebensee recorded by the Military Government of Germany.

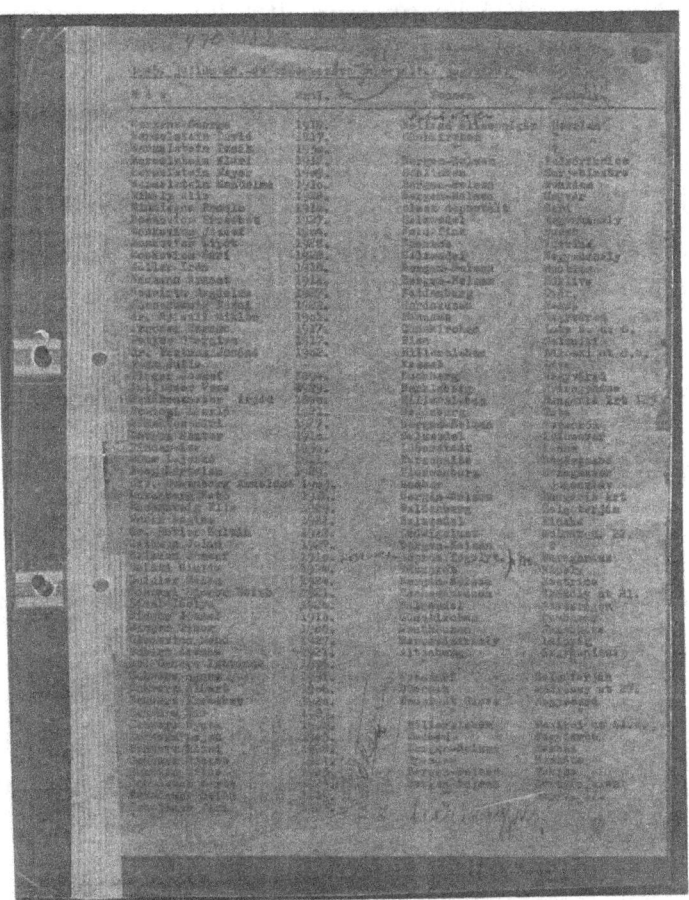

Figure 19I: List recording Leib on the 11th line from top. He is listed as Moscovics Lipot 1928 Ebensee (honnen/liberated), Kuzmina.

Figures 19A-Front, and 19A-Back, are copies of Mauthausen Liberation papers issued to Lipot Moscovitc. Information contained in this note includes name, birthdate, place of birth and prisoner number (68576). Note that the lower left frame is stamped 'Liberated of Ebensee'. Below the words 'Ebensee Mauthausen' is the hand written liberation date: June (VI) 17, 1945.

Fig 19B is the heading page of the list of those freed (Befreiungslisten) from Ebensee.

Figure 19C lists Lipot Moskovics 68.576 on the top line of the second column and is identified by his prisoner number 68.576.

Figure 19D lists Lipot by his number 68576 on the second column, third line from the bottom (Moskovi...).

Figure 19E lists on the seventh line from the bottom, Leib's name and identification which are written in script as Moskovic Lipold, 11 XI 1928, Kusminov.

Figures 19F-I are lists of Czechoslovak male prisoners in Ebensee Concentration camp. Refer to Figure 19F, 12th line from the bottom; Leib is listed as Moskowits Lipot 68576, age 17, Kuzmina. Refer to Fig 19I, 11th line from top; Leib is listed as Moscovics Lipot 1928 Ebensee (honnen/liberated), Kuzmina.

KUZMINO CHRONICLES

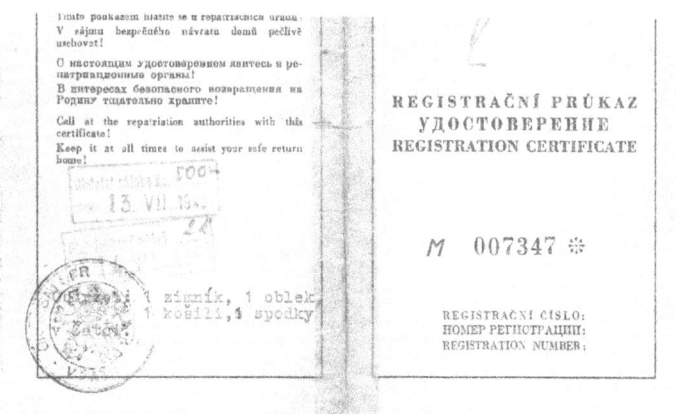

Figure 20A: Outside cover of Leib's Zatec registration certificate written in Czech and Russian.

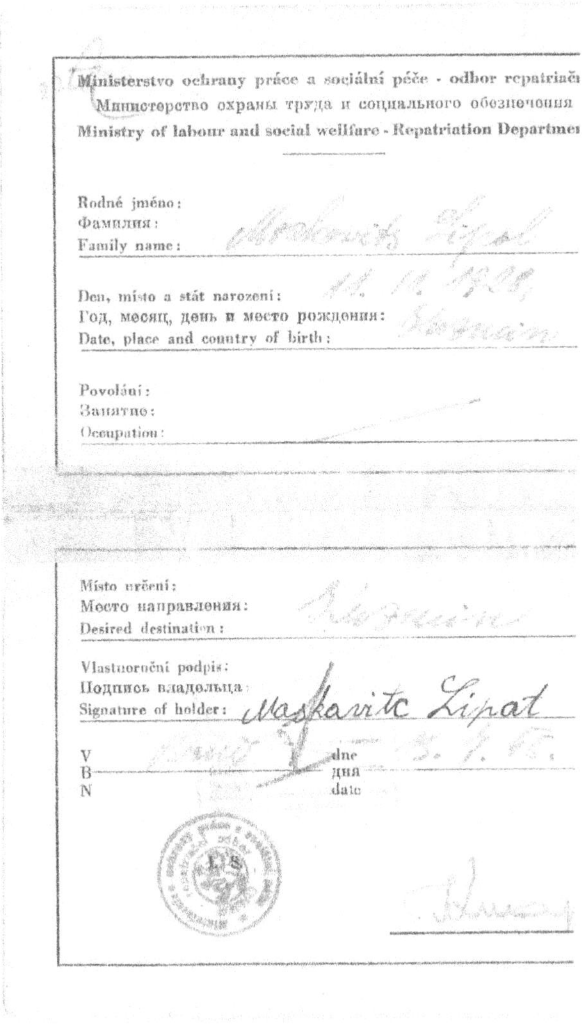

Ministerstvo ochrany práce a sociální péče - odbor repatriač
Министерство охраны труда и социального обезпечения
Ministry of labour and social weilfare - Repatriation Departme

Rodné jméno:
Фамилия:
Family name:

Den, místo a stát narození:
Год, месяц, день и место рождения:
Date, place and country of birth:

Povolání:
Занятие:
Occupation:

Místo určení:
Место направления:
Desired destination:

Vlastnoruční podpis:
Подпись владельца:
Signature of holder: Maskavitc Lipat

V ... dne
B ... дня
N ... date

L.S.

Figure 20B: Inside cover of Leib's Zatec registration certificate written in Czech and Russian.

Hand-written in Figure 20A on the left, in the middle of the page is '500' - for 500 Cronin. It is dated July (VII) 13 1945. It also documents on the lower portion of that page that he was given 1 zimnik (coat), 1 oblek (dress suit), 1 kosili (shirt), and 1 spodky (underpants).

Figure 20 B documents Leib's name, Lipot Moskovits, his date of birth and place of birth, Kusmain. The lower document on the last line in hand written letters is written Bruno, July 13, 1945.

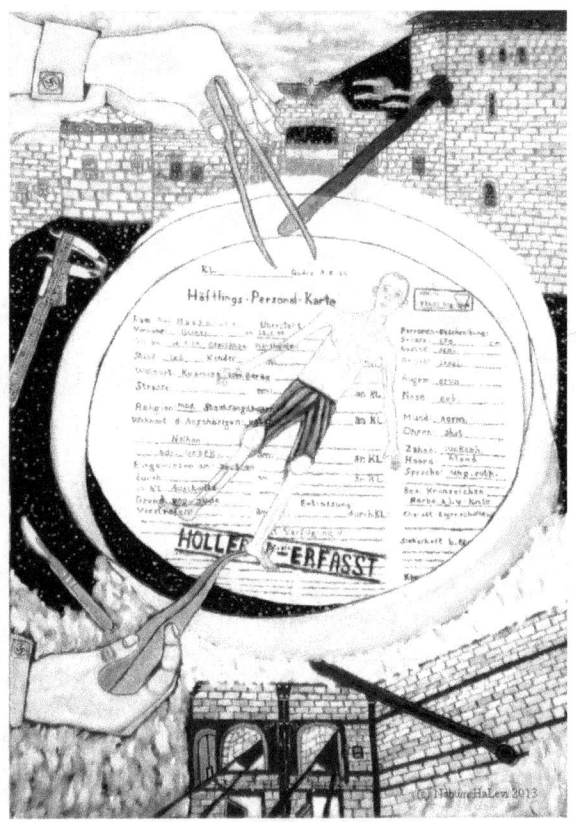

Photo3: *Painting of Herman by Nathan C. Moskowitz entitled "Shoah Forensics I: Reconstruction ex-nihilo" (oil on canvas, 2009, www.nahumhalevi.com). The original painting is in the permanent collection of the Yad Vashem Museum in Jerusalem.*

Photo 4: Painting of Herman by Nathan C. Moskowitz entitled "Shoah Forensics II: Recreation ex-nihilo" (oil on canvas, 2009, www.nahumhalevi.com).

8

Return to my house in Kuzmino after liberation

As I mentioned earlier, my father was called Munkotabor; he was in Hungarian slave labor camp. He was first enlisted in the army and was given a regular uniform to wear. Then later, they took away his uniform, but they allowed him to wear a military cap and civilian clothes. He also had to wear a yellow arm band. He was drafted and taken away at the end of 1938 or 1939. He used to write letters to us about once a month. When he was near Budapest. He once sent us a package of geese fat; two big bottles from Budapest sent by mail.

KUZMINO CHRONICLES

Sometime In 1940 he sent a letter to my mother asking her to please mail him a photograph of her and the two kids (The relevance of this recollection becomes apparent below).

We didn't have anything like cameras. To take a photograph we had to go to a special photographer. The closest one was in a nearby town of Seredna. We walked from Kuzmino to Seredna to get the photograph taken. First we crossed a little bridge over a river. Then we walked through a few towns until you got to Seredna. The photograph that my father requested was taken in a photography studio. We posed for it. My father used to mail us photographs of himself wearing a uniform. I don't have any of those pictures. I never found them.

After my liberation, when I arrived at Pressburg /Bratislava, I met two of my cousins, Dvora and Judie Salomon. They told me "Mamma leibt" ("Your mother is alive"). *She is either in Davidkov or Kuzmina. At the Bratislava Czech transit camp you could stay there for three days, then you had to move on. From Bratislava I took*

RETURN TO MY HOUSE IN KUZMINO AFTER LIBERATION

a train going to Budapest. I stayed three days in Budapest. Then I took a train to Munkatch during the hours somewhere between day and night. When I arrived at Munkatch, I went to a market which was open twice a week.

There they sold animals, vegetables, and other things. While I was there I recognized someone from my town who had a horse and wagon. I said to him "are you going home by any chance?"

He said "Why?"

"I need a ride to Kuzmino". So he gave me a ride and I came home. It was dark. The mayor, the shofet, lived three houses down. I said to myself 'I'm going to go to the mayor's house'.

I knock on his door, he recognized me. He said "Hello Leiba", and all of a sudden my mother comes out of the kitchen. The first thing she says is "Where's Chaym Hersch (my brother)?" I knew he's not here so I told her "He's not here". Of course she started to cry. So both of us cried. I told her he was very sick.

At day break I wanted to go see our house. I approach my house and see that there are no windows and no doors. One room had iron gates. They were still there, they weren't taken away. I walked in, and saw that there was nothing inside; not even a stick of furniture.

One room had wooden floors. We're walking around and I see what looks like a small piece of paper on the floor, the only thing that was left in the whole house. I bend down, and pick it up. It was the photograph of me, my brother and mother that we had taken in Seredna and mailed to my father. It was probably a duplicate that we kept. I have no idea. I pick it up and put it in my pocket. There was ground -in dirt still on the picture. I didn't rub it off; I was scared to ruin it. It was already partially ruined. I still have this picture, and the dirt is still on it (See Photos 5 and 6 and, the back cover and front cover of this book, respectively).

There was a Jewish family in town. They got married after the liberation and they tried to settle in the town. Her name was Abramovitz,

RETURN TO MY HOUSE IN KUZMINO AFTER LIBERATION

he was Avram Feldman. I figured I was going to make a life here too, and stay in my old house. I started asking people if they knew where a lot of our stuff was, and what happened to it.

I found out where our stove was. This stove we had to heat it with wood. It was in another town in somebody's house. I knocked on his door and I said "That's my stove and I want it back".

He said "Fine". We (my mother and I) took a kulya, a long piece of wood like a two by four, and carried that stove home.

I found a night table in another person's house. We took it back. There were bed covers, woolen bedspreads (dochanas), a very expensive dowry which was handed down for generations, they were red.

Our teacher from our town became the principal in Seredna. I was told they were in her house, so I went with my mother, and I said to her: "I understand you have our bedcovers, can we please have them back?"

She said: "Of course".

So we took that back. Then we thought we were going to settle down and look for more stuff. One night we are sleeping in the bedroom with the iron gates. Two guys come to the window. In Ukrainian- Russian one of them says: "You Jews, you're still alive?"

I says to mother: "Let's stay still and not answer".

There were no doors or windows. It got quiet, I got up, I looked around. I didn't see anything, it was dark. A half hour later I said to my mother "Let's go". We crossed the street and went into a neighbor's barn where the animals stay, and we stayed there overnight. It was then that we decided that we cannot stay in Kuzmino.

In the meantime my Uncle Shloymo (my mother's brother) is in Czechoslovakia the city of Zatec in the Sudtenlands and he said after hearing the story "Leave everything and come to Czechoslovakia".

RETURN TO MY HOUSE IN KUZMINO AFTER LIBERATION

I found somebody, a merchant who was settled in Kuzmino. His name was Hersch Leib. I said to him "I want to sell you my garden of fruit. Will you buy it?"

He said "I have no money. But I have slivovitz. I'll give you twelve bottles of slivovitz".

I took the deal. I packed up the Slivovitz to go to Czech. In the meantime I went to the town of Kalnik where you register when you were born. I asked for my birth certificate. They found the records, it was written in Russian and they gave it to me. I asked the guy who got married, Avrum Feldman "I have a night table you can use it, but if I return can you give it back to me?"

He said "Sure".

I left the dochenas with Surah. I asked her "If I come back will you give it back to me?"

She also said: "Sure".

I never came back to my house after that. When I arranged all that, I went back to the mayor and said I want you to give me a paper that you know me, who I am. He had a secretary who wrote everything out and put a stamp on it (see Figure 2B). I wanted to let everyone know who I am. When I came back to Kuzmina it was officially Russia and occupied by the Russian army.

I was going to meet up with my Uncle in Czechoslovakia in the Sudetenlands. That was sixty kilometers from Prague. It was safe there. The Russian army wasn't there; there was a Jewish community there. Uncle Shloymo had a brother-in-law who was captured by the Russians. They had formed a Czech army and came back fighting Germans. He survived as a Czech soldier. The Czech army threw out the Germans. I got there a week before Rosh Hashanah, in 1945.

RETURN TO MY HOUSE IN KUZMINO AFTER LIBERATION

Photo 5: Family photograph Herman Moskowitz (His face is not visible due to the damage done to the photo), Leah Moskowitz and Leib Moskowitz. The single photo found ground into the dirt floor of their home, upon return to their home after liberation.

Photo 6: Painting by Nathan C. Moskowitz (with assistance from Judy Horowitz) entitled "Shoah Forensics III: Family Photograph Re-illumination" (oil on canvas, 2014). Herman's face is forensically reconstructed from his Mauthausen card personal characteristics, and family facial resemblance. Leib Moskowitz maintains he cannot remember how he looked, and that he has completely forgotten.

9

Journeying from Kuzmino to Czechoslovakia

We left Kuzmino and we walked to Seredna, and then we took a little train to Ungvar. There we took a train to a city called Chop at the Czech border between Russia and Czechoslovakia. The borders were supposed to be open until December 1945. When we arrived the Russian army asked us for papers to enter Czech.

I said to der mama: "Sit on the whiskey and you sleep. I have a birth certificate. If they ask for papers I'll give them my birth certificate" (See Figures 1 and 2).

There were Russian words on the certificate and a Russian stamp. The soldiers looked at my certificate and they said: "Go; Charasha".

So I went, and from my mother they didn't say or ask anything. We crossed the border. We're waiting for a train to Prague. I boarded the train and I saw Moishe and Chana Weiss (my cousin) walking by the train, so I went out, and said hello.

They ask "Where you going?"

"I'm going to Uncle Shloymo".

They said: "We're also going there".

So I said "Let's go together".

We arrived to Prague. We then took another train and we arrived at Zatec (Sudentland). We arrived at uncle Shloymo. To get to him we took an electric street car from the train station to his house.

The Czechs, if they knew you were survivor they gave you double rations. At that time everything was rationed.

JOURNEYING FROM KUZMINO TO CZECHOSLOVAKIA

Shloymo's brother in-law was a Czech soldier. He lived in a twenty room mansion after throwing out the Germans who were living there. The Germans had to wear white armbands. Subsequently Russian soldiers confiscated the manor. They left Shloymo one room to sleep in. Then came in the Voliner soldiers and told Shloymo to get out. They took over, I had to leave with my mother and Ruchie (Shloymo's daughter, my first cousin).

Sura travelled to Davidkov to sell stuff that she bought in Zatec, but then they wouldn't let her out. She thought she could travel back and forth from Czechoslovakia and Davidkov (now Russian territory). But then the iron curtain came down and she got stuck in Davidkov.

Shloymo knew there was a Jewish committee in Zatec. He got a room there, and we went to the police and I said "I have nowhere to stay I'm a survivor from concentration camp, I need a place to stay".

"How many rooms you need?"

They took us to a place on the second floor. There was a big room and a kitchen and Germans are living there.

"Do you like this place?" they asked us.

"Yes".

They told the Germans: "Raus shwhinehund" ("get out swine").

They gave me the key and said: "This is yours".

I had a place. There was one bathroom for the whole floor. There was no running water. We had where to sleep. Lunchtime, the main meal was noon time. Feter (Uncle) Shloymo came every day for a meal with his daughter Ruchie. My mother used to cook.

[Figures 21 and 22 document Leah's registration certificate in Zatec. Figure 23 is correspondence sent from Leib with postmarks from New Jersey, Munkatch, and Zatec. The correspondence relates to sponsoring him and his mother to come to America. Figure

24 lists Leib and Lea as Jews of racial persecution in Bohemia and Moravia. There present address is listed as Zatec, Smejkalova 839. Photo 7 is a photograph of Leib Moskowitz in Zatec 1946]

There was a man here, Melvin Diamondstein (He later cut his name short to Diamond) *who was there by himself. He had a furnished room, and he didn't have where to eat. I said to him "My mother is going to cook; we'll share it three ways. You can come to us, and we can eat together".*

He said: "That would be nice".

My mother used to wash clothes. In 1946 in January Melvin's sister, and then Phyllis, another sister and other people including Gizela (Gittel), my future wife (I didn't know that at the time) show up. We welcomed them. My mother made room and cooked for everybody, and other people. We welcomed them. My mother made room and cooked for everybody and my mother gave up her bed. The sisters were making a big ruckus and were speaking loud. The neighbors complained to the Czech police.

The Czech police asked for their papers. They took them to the police station they said you have to disappear from here. Gizela (Gittel) went to Ash. They had to disperse.

Melvin came to eat with us. Phyllis Diamond and Melvin came to eat and they are eating and are getting one third of what we had, but they're contributing no money. Pesach was coming up. Phyllis was not doing anything. She didn't help cook or clean, and my mother is killing herself washing dishes and doing all the housework. So I said to Phyllis "Get the hell out of my house", a couple days before Pesach. "My mother can't clean for you anymore".

After Pesach 1946 word is out that the people who came out of former Czechoslovakia, the Russians are going to ship them all back. We were afraid to ride trains because if they're going to catch you they'll send you back there. So we

JOURNEYING FROM KUZMINO TO CZECHOSLOVAKIA

decided to go to Germany to the American zone.
[Figure 25 documents Leib's and Leah's presence in Prague Czechoslovakia dated March 12, 1946, and September 3, 1946.]

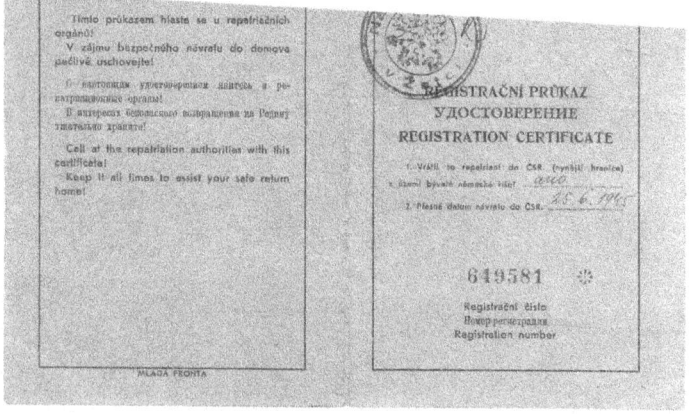

Figure 21A: Outside cover of Lea's Zatec registration (repatriation) certificate written in Czech and Russian.

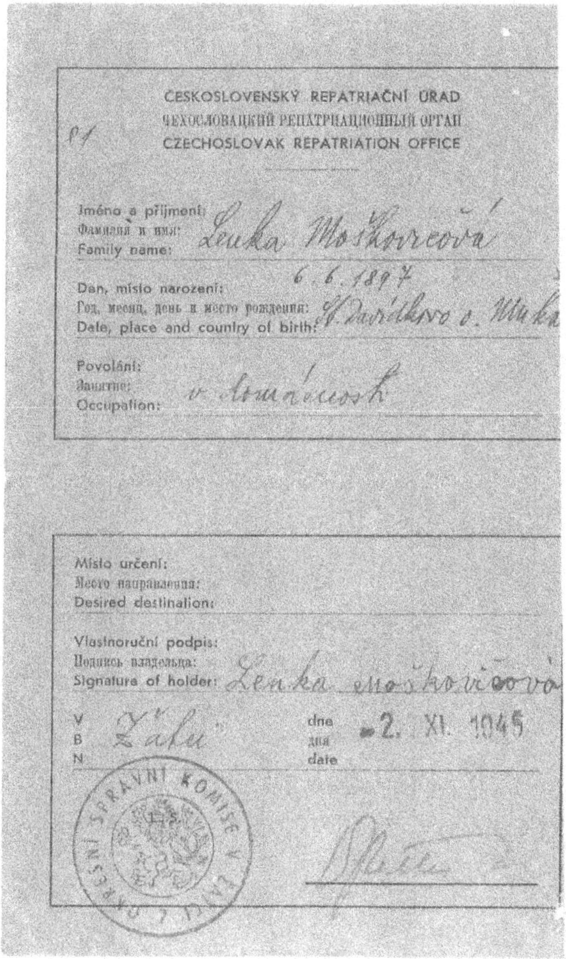

ČESKOSLOVENSKÝ REPATRIAČNÍ ÚRAD
ЧЕХОСЛОВАЦКИЙ РЕПАТРИАЦИОННЫЙ ОРГАН
CZECHOSLOVAK REPATRIATION OFFICE

Jméno a příjmení:
Фамилия и имя:
Family name:

Den, místo narození:
Год, месяц, день и место рождения:
Date, place and country of birth:

Povolání:
Занятие:
Occupation:

Místo určení:
Место направления:
Desired destination:

Vlastnoruční podpis:
Подпись владельца:
Signature of holder:

V
В
N

dne
дня
date
2. XI. 1945

Figure 21B: Inside cover of Lea's Zatec registration (repatriation) certificate written in Czech and Russian which states "Czechoslovak Repatriation Office" for Lenka Moskovicova who was born on 6/6/87 in St. Davidkovo, Mukacevo. The lower portion is dated November 2, 1945. Zatec is hand written on the bottom left, and the stamp says Zatec.

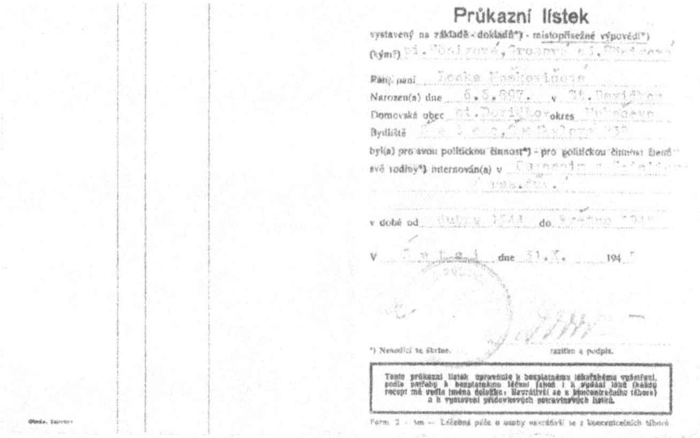

Průkazní lístek

vystavený na základě - dokladů*) - místopřísežné výpovědi*)

(kým?)

Ctěný pan - paní Lenka Moskovicova

Narozen(a) dne 6.5.897. v

Domovská obec okres

Bydliště

byl(a) pro svou politickou činnost*) - pro politickou činnost členů své rodiny*) internován(a) v

v době od do

V dne 31.X. 194

*) Nehodící se škrtne.

razítko a podpis.

Tento průkazní lístek opravňuje k bezplatnému lékařskému vyšetření, podle potřeby k bezplatnému léčení (zdarma i k vydání léků (každý recept má vedle jména doložku: Navrátivší se z koncentračního tábora) a k vystavení přídavkových potravinových lístků.

Form. 2 - 5m — Léčebná péče o osoby navrátivší se z koncentračních táborů

Figure 22A: Front of paperwork for Lea (Lenka) Moskowitz from Zatec which refers to Lenka Moskovicova, Zatec, Smejkalova 839 dated October 31, 1945, stamped Zatec.

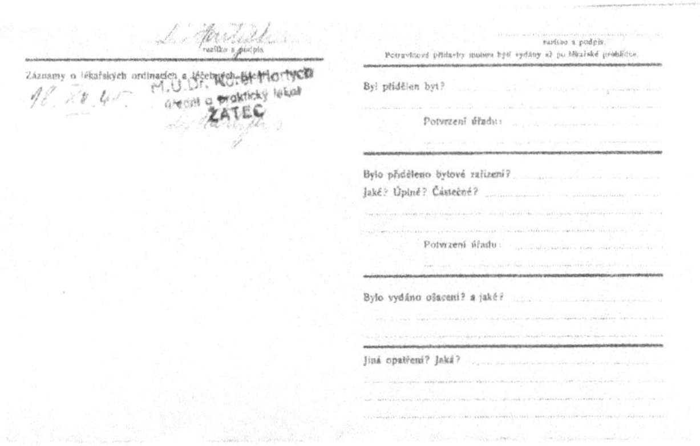
razítko a podpis

Záznamy o lékařských ordinacích a léčebných

úřední a praktický lékař
ŽATEC

razítko a podpis.
Potravinové přídavky mohou být vydány až po lékařské prohlídce.

Byl přidělen byt?

Potvrzení úřadu:

Bylo přiděleno bytové zařízení?
Jaké? Úplné? Částečné?

Potvrzení úřadu:

Bylo vydáno ošacení? a jaké?

Jiná opatření? Jaká?

Figure 22B: Back of paperwork for Lea (Lenka) Moskowitz from Zatec.

KUZMINO CHRONICLES

Figure 23: Copies of envelopes containing correspondence from Moskovics Louis in Mukachevo St. Davidkovo 116 to 590 Prospect Avenue Bronx, NY in English and Russian (top and bottom envelopes). The middle envelope is correspondence from New Jersey (1945) to Leopolt Moskovics living at 116 Smiykolova ulica isl 839 Zatec CSR. The postal stamp on the bottom envelope is that of Moukatchevo written in both Russian and Czech.

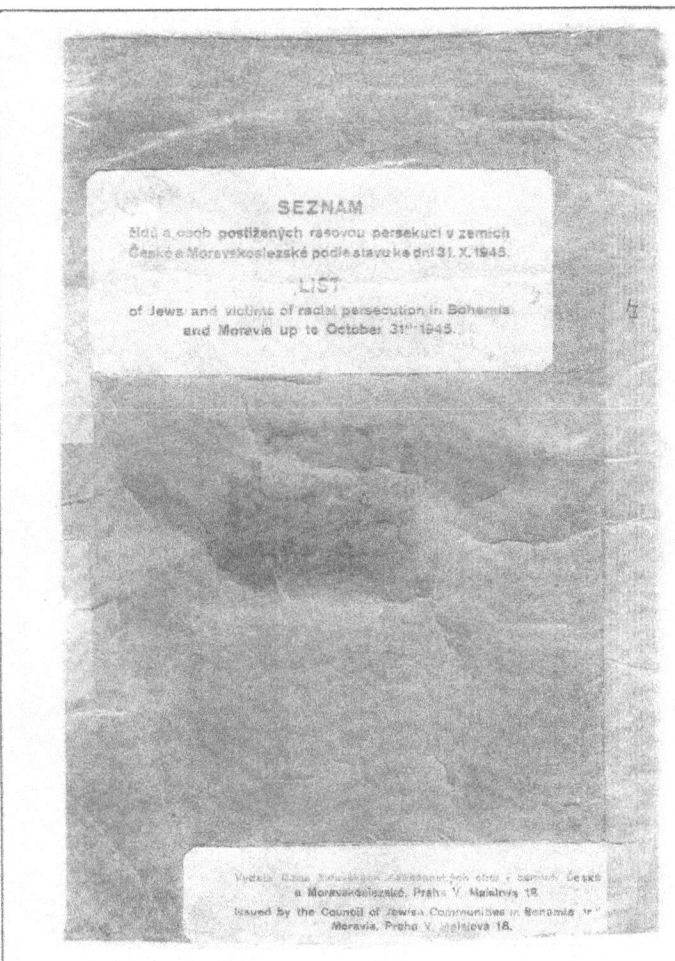

Figure 24A: Cover page for list of Jews and victims of racial persecution issued by Council of Jewish Communities in Bohemia and Moravia, Praha.

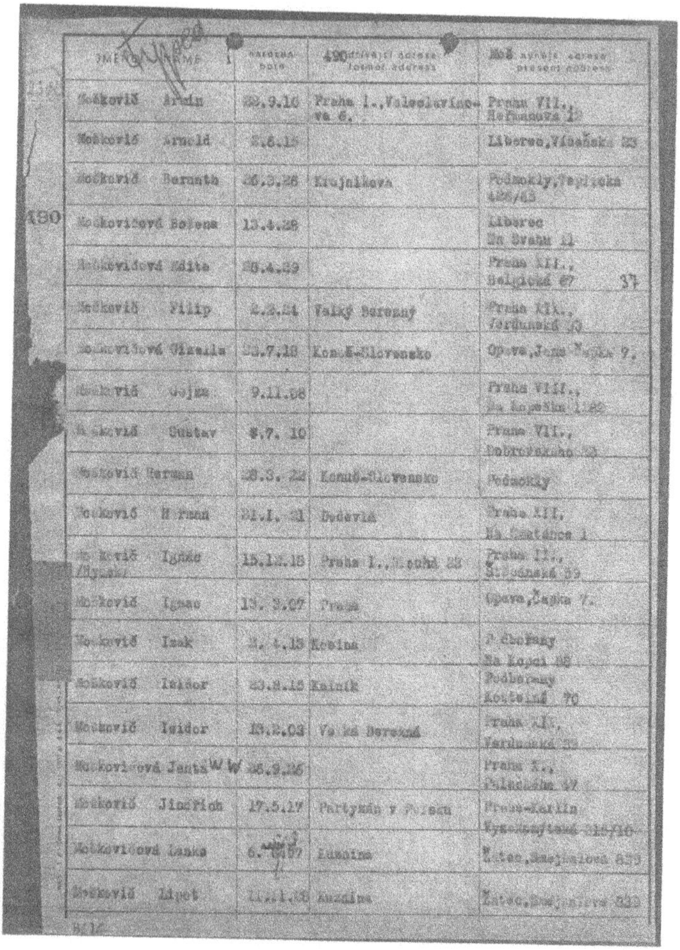

KUZMINO CHRONICLES

Figure 24B: List of Jews and victims of racial persecution issued by Council of Jewish Communities in Bohemia and Moravia, Praha. Refer specifically to the last two lines listing Moskovicova Lenke and Moskovic Lipot both from Kuzmin are residing in Zatec, Smejkalova 839.

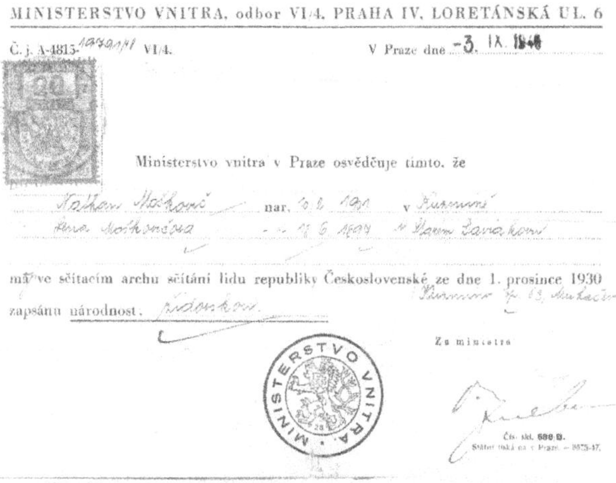

JOURNEYING FROM KUZMINO TO CZECHOSLOVAKIA

Figure 25: Papers from Praha with Leib's and Leah's birthdates and birth towns dated 3/12/1946 (bottom), and 9/3/1946 (top).

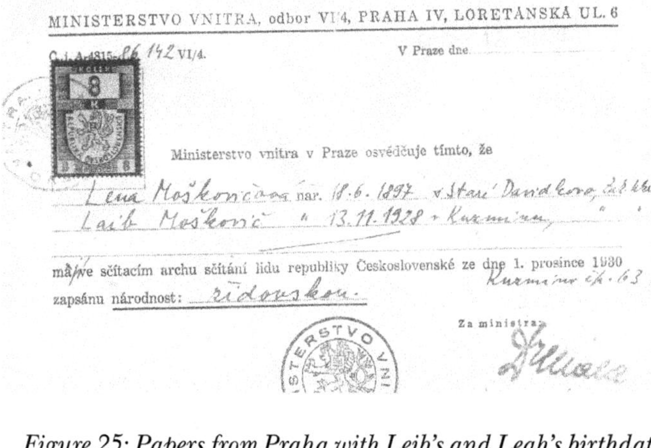

Photo 7: Photograph of Leib Moskowitz, Zatec, 1946.

10

Journeying from Czechoslovakia to Germany

Uncle Shloymo, Moshe Pasthkanover, and Ruchie decided to go to the city of Ash (a Czech city on the border with Germany), and from there the destination was to go to the American DP camp in Germany. We rented a truck for 10,000 Cronin to get to Ash. We come halfway, the truck driver says "Let's have the money". We give them money; we finally arrive at night to Ash.

In Ash there was a bunch of Israeli (Bricha) boys smuggling Jews over the border wherever they wanted to go. We come to a collection place and they said when they collect a total of 300 people we will smuggle them along with you through the border to Germany.

"Bricha ("escape" or "flight" in Hebrew) was the underground organized effort that helped Jewish Holocaust survivors escape post–World War II Europe to the British Mandate for Palestine in violation of the White Paper of 1939. It ended when Israel declared independence and annulled the White Paper...Almost immediately, the explicitly Zionist Bricha became the main conduit for Jews coming to Palestine, especially from the displaced person camps, and it initially had to turn people away due to too much demand...After the Kielce pogrom of 1946, the flight of Jews accelerated, with 100,000 Jews leaving Eastern Europe in three months. Operating in Poland, Romania, Hungary, Czechoslovakia, and Yugoslavia through 1948, Bricha transferred approximately 250,000 survivors into Austria,

Germany, and Italy through elaborate smuggling networks. Using ships supplied at great cost by the Mossad Le'aliyah Bet, then the immigration arm of the Yishuv, these refugees were then smuggled through the British cordon around Palestine. Bricha was part of the larger operation known as Aliyah Bet, and ended with the establishment of Israel, after which immigration to the Jewish state was legal, although emigration was still sometimes prohibited, as happened in both the Eastern Bloc and Arab countries" (From: http://en.wikipedia.org/wiki/Bricha).

They collected a group of people at night at twelve o'clock. I had a backpack and a suitcase with shmattas and we're going walking through the forest and the Czech police are with us. It starts to rain, my back gives out and I had to throw away my suitcase.

The Bricha come, it's raining. They tell me "You have a few more meters you must keep going or you'll be in trouble. They will catch you. In a few minutes we'll be there". On account of me we were left behind the rest of the people. We crossed the border into Germany, the other people left before us.

We're lagging behind but we're safe. Day break is coming out, and Uncle Shloymo sees a light in a window and says I'm going to walk over there and ask where we are, and where there's a train. The man in that house had a horse and wagon and took us to a train station. The next station was Hoff. We arrive there, and we go into an inn. We went in there, and within the hour the German police and the MP (Americans) come in.

We couldn't communicate with them. They took us in a jeep, outside the inn. One of the Brichas says: "Zug er zeit palishe yeedin (Say yours Polish Jews)". They didn't bother Polish Jews.

I had a Czech passport so I can't say that (they'll prove I'm a liar). So as we were riding

JOURNEYING FROM CZECHOSLOVAKIA TO GERMANY

in the open Jeep, I'm ripping up my passport (nobody could see), and as the Jeep is going, I'm slowly throwing out small torn pieces of my passport, bit by bit. They took us to American headquarters, and we're sitting there like four dummies. Nobody is asking us questions.

Comes in one of the Israelis and tells us in Yiddish "One at a time get out and don't look back or say anything". First the Uncle, then Ruchel, then mother, then I go.

Two to three guys shoved me in a car that was going, and the car is running to a train station. They gave us four train tickets and set us up on a train going to Munich.

11

ARRIVAL AT GERMANY: AMERICAN DP CAMP

In Munich there is a Jewish committee and they register you, and they took us to DP camp at Garbersee by Wasserburg. [See Figures 26-29 for Leib's and Leah's registration papers at Gabersee. See Figures 30-32 for lists of displaced persons in Gabersee which include Leib and Leah]

This was a DP camp. The houses were numbered from A-Z. A block was called a house. That housing was originally built for the German Nazi soldiers to be rehabilitated in. The UN and the Jewish Joint committee ran this place. They elected a president; we had our own

ARRIVAL AT GERMANY: AMERICAN DP CAMP

post office and kosher facilities. There were quite a few thousand people there.

There was running water, and toilets with flush. They gave you three meals a day, no questions. Just stay on line, they give you a siddur and tzitzis (fringed ritual garment) *if you want.*

I started working at the Post office for a while. I had a bicycle. I had to pick up the mail from the German post office and bring it to the camp. After 12 O'clock I went from block to block and delivered mail. In the afternoon they had to drop off mail at the post office, at night I picked it up and delivered to the German post office. For that I got a carton of cigarettes, three pounds of Crisco, and 5 pounds of flour per month.

I sold the cigarettes on the black market. If I wanted to smoke, I picked up the butts of cigarettes that American soldiers smoked and dropped. I tried to sell the flour. I bought two chickens. I fed the chickens; they laid eggs, so we had fresh eggs.

In 1946 Ruchela went to kindercamp -they were treated better and were going to be the first to leave Germany to go to England or the US. It was for people who were orphans and didn't have any parents. Her father Shloymo was alive so she didn't qualify, so she lied, and said both her parents were dead, and so she went to kindercamp.

After she left, we had one room for the three of us. We had folding cots and blankets. It wasn't bad. Food we had. Once in a while they gave you a shirt or pants from the US through the Joint (United Nations Relief and Rehabilitation Administration).

While we were there, my uncle was on the committee. They had a real little Medina (mini-country), *he was a judge. My mother was working in the kitchen koshering the meat; she got the same pay I got. Food we had enough.*

I had no problems selling cigarettes. I also helped selling ice cream on the street. Later on, towards the end of my stay, I joined a Tailor group. I put aside the money. I bought a watch

ARRIVAL AT GERMANY: AMERICAN DP CAMP

for 27 dollars. I still have it. My mother was going to kill me for buying that watch.

They had a Rabbi there from Budapest, Rabbi Shyavitz who survived with seven children.

There was a bus going to Munich every day to Berza. I seen that the Rabbi was walking with a cane, and he had a long red beard. He was dressed up as a Hungarian soldier during the war and that's how he survived. His cane was hollow and was filled up with golden coins. In 1946 Rosh Hashana in camp he was hired to be the shleich tzibur (Cantor). The committee paid him 300 dollars. That was a lot of money those days.

On Yom Kippur when he davened 'hineni' (a solemn hymn) he let out a voice... it was something not to be believed...Very moving. I never heard anything like that again.

[While there, Leib and Leah signed multiple legal certificates in front of lawyers and witnesses testifying to who they were where they were born, and that Nathan Moskowitz had indeed perished (See Figures 33-35).

They were also provided with DP immunization cards under UNRRA (See Figures 36A (Front and Back), and 36B (Front and Back)].

In the DP camp I had to register, so I registered both myself and my mother with Aguda (See Figures 37A, 37B1, 37B2, 37C, and 37D).

We're still waiting for papers to come to the US. My father had three sisters in the US; Feiga, Golda and Shifra (they left Kuzmino after WW I). That was three fewer mouths to feed.

Melvin Diamantstein (Diamond) *had a sister who left in 1938 on the last boat. Her name was Shirley Diamond. She left when she was 18 yrs. old and no one heard from her. Her mother used to cry: "I buried a daughter, I sent her to drown".*

That sister was engaged to a guy named Weinberg whose father had a grocery store in Kalnik. He was an American soldier and visited.

I said to Melvin in Zatec: "Do me a favor. My mother says she has relatives in America,

ARRIVAL AT GERMANY: AMERICAN DP CAMP

sister in laws; one Family name she remembers is Einczig. The first name is William".

Shirley got in touch with them. Before we got a letter from my aunt Feiga (Eleanor's mother). I had a suit, my mother has a dress and pocketbook and shoes from America.

We got a letter and she knew who survived. We got a letter from Feiga requesting our exact names and birthdates and she said to write to her immediately and tell her what's what.

We started corresponding and learned that Einczig had a grocery store. We had once gotten an affidavit from America to Czech to apply for a visa. In Germany this affidavit was null and void. We wrote again and they sent us new papers and we had to wait.

[Refer to Figures 38, 39 and 40 for Immigration papers filled out by William Einczig for Lipot Moskovits (38) and Leah Moskovitz (39), and his own personal financial and tax testimony (40). Refer to Photos

8-10 portraying Leib during his stay at Gabersee/Wasserburg.]

Uncle Einczig wrote nice letters… "I'll find you work don't worry about'. Just get here."

We didn't hear from my two other aunts, Shifra or Golda at all. We got papers and we had to wait. They sent me pictures. In 1949 everything went through and we were ready to leave.

We were in the DP camp waiting for four years to go to America. A year before we left American CIA men questioned us, and wanted to confirm our stories. They wanted to make sure you were really there. They asked me what does it look like? Where exactly were you? They tried to trick me with their questions, but I couldn't be tricked. I told them the exact block numbers … They tried to put obstacles in the way to keep you out of America. My guess is that the Latvians and Ukrainians who were also in DP camps, and who were Nazis, and came to America were probably not asked these questions, and were just let in.

ARRIVAL AT GERMANY: AMERICAN DP CAMP

Displaced Persons Camps : "In 1946 and 1947, the number of DPs in the camps rose substantially, as additional Jewish refugees continued to arrive from Eastern Europe, many through the Beriha' movement (The Beriha was a Zionist organization, which tried to aid survivors in leaving Europe for the Jewish Homeland). The increase of the DPs population affected the international public opinion, a fact that exerted increasing pressure on the British and American governments in order to find a solution to their situation. This kind of activity was especially evident in Zionist political groups, where attempts at clandestine emigration to Palestine increased. The opening of Israel's borders after its independence, as well as the adoption of more lenient regulations in western countries regarding the immigration of survivors, led to the closure of most of the DP camps by 1950".

(From http://www.yadvashem.org/yv/en/holocaust/resource_center/item.asp?gate=2-62)

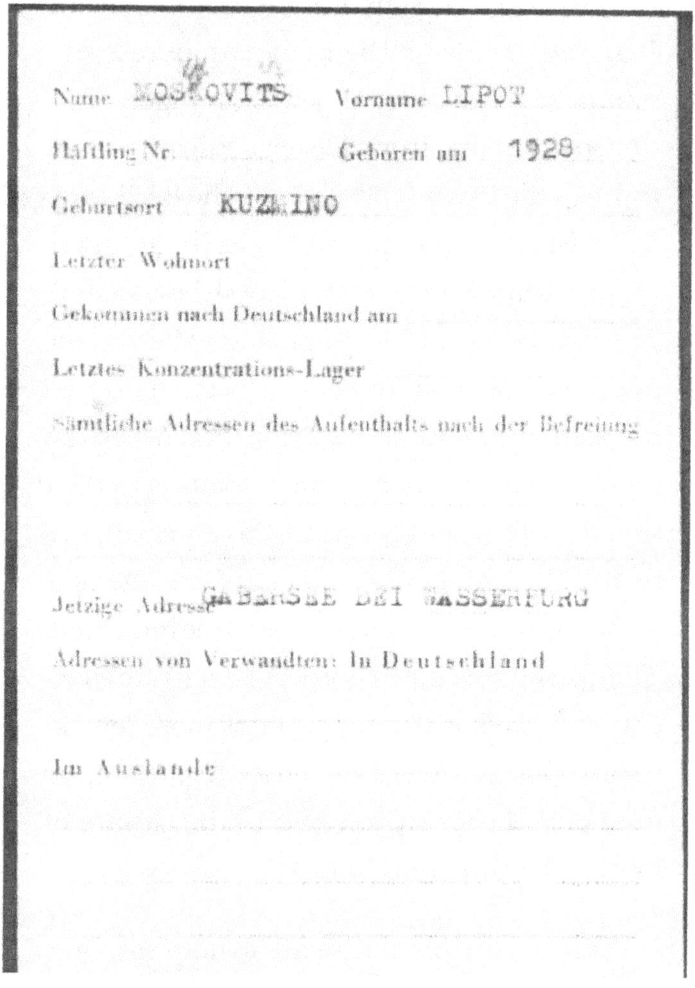

```
Name  MOSKOVITS     Vorname  LIPOT
Häftling Nr.              Geboren am    1928
Geburtsort    KUZMINO
Letzter Wohnort
Gekommen nach Deutschland am
Letztes Konzentrations-Lager
Sämtliche Adressen des Aufenthalts nach der Befreiung



Jetzige Adresse GABERSEE BEI WASSERBURG
Adressen von Verwandten: In Deutschland


Im Auslande
```

Figure 26A: Registration paper for Leib (Lipot Moskovits) which lists his current address as Gabersee Bei Wasserburg.

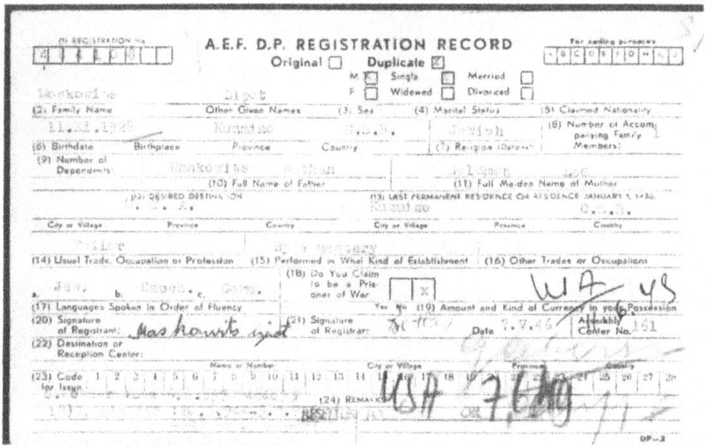
A.E.F. D.P. REGISTRATION RECORD

Original ☐ Duplicate ☒

(1) Registration No.

For coding purposes

M ☒ F ☐ Single ☒ Married ☐ Widowed ☐ Divorced ☐

(2) Family Name | Other Given Names | (3) Sex | (4) Marital Status | (5) Claimed Nationality

(6) Birthdate | Birthplace | Province | Country | (7) Religion (Optional) | (8) Number of Accompanying Family Members:

(9) Number of Dependents:

(10) Full Name of Father | (11) Full Maiden Name of Mother

(12) Desired Destination | (13) Last Permanent Residence or Residence January 1, 1938

City or Village | Province | Country | City or Village | Province | Country

(14) Usual Trade, Occupation or Profession | (15) Performed in What Kind of Establishment | (16) Other Trades or Occupations

(17) Languages Spoken in Order of Fluency a. b. c.

(18) Do You Claim to be a Prisoner of War Yes No

(19) Amount and Kind of Currency in your Possession

(20) Signature of Registrant: Moskowits Lipot

(21) Signature of Registrar:

Date 7.V.46

Assembly Center No. 161

(22) Destination or Reception Center:

Name or Number | City or Village | Province | Country

(23) Code for Issue 1 2 3 4 5 6 7 8 9 10 11 12 13 14 15 16 17 18 19 20 21 22 23 24 25 26 27 28

(24) Remarks

USA

DP-2

Figure 26B: AEF DP (American Expeditionary Forces Displaced Persons) Registration record dated V (May) 7, 1946 for Lipot Moskowits (Version 1).

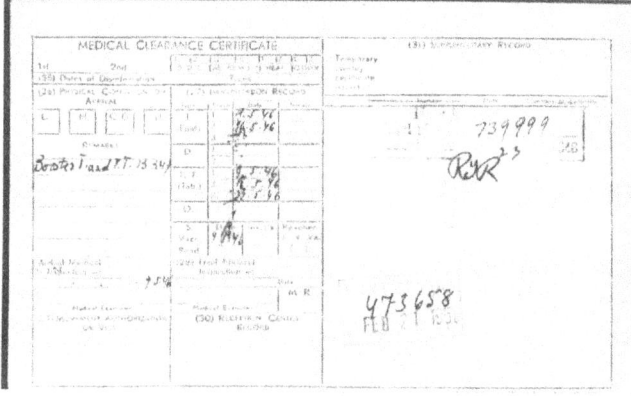

Figure 26C: Medical clearance certificate documenting Leib's immunization record.

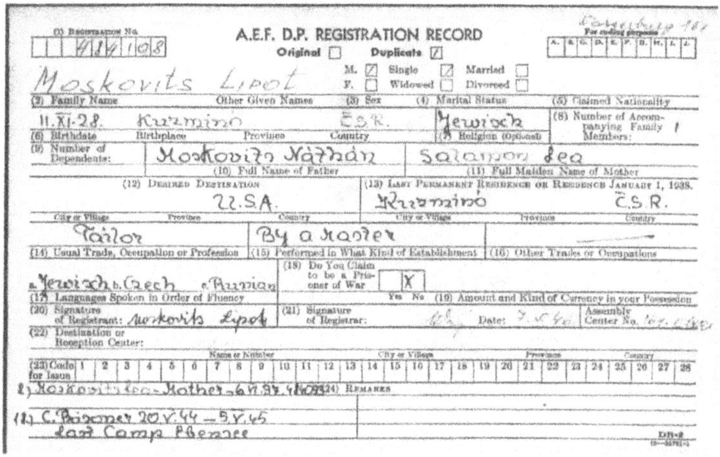

ARRIVAL AT GERMANY: AMERICAN DP CAMP

Figure 26D: AEF DP Registration record (Version 2) similar to Figure 26B although it differs by recording different language fluencies in Jewish, Czech and Russian. It records similarly that his mother is Lea that he was a prisoner from 5/20/44 – 5/5/45, and that he was liberated from camp Ebensee.

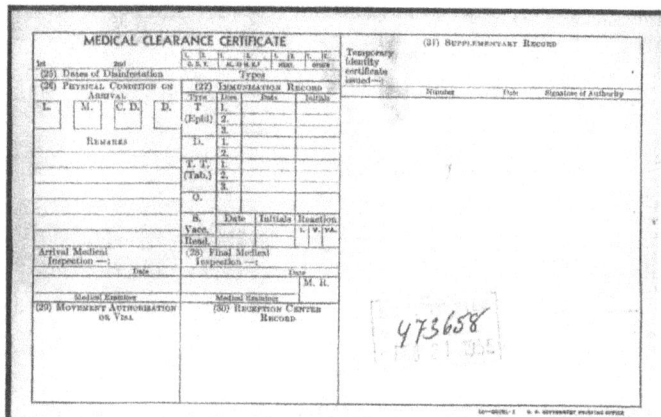

Figure 26E: An uncharted medical clearance certificate in Leib's file.

ARRIVAL AT GERMANY: AMERICAN DP CAMP

Figure 26A is a registration paper for Leib (Lipot Moskovits) which lists his current address as Gabersee Bei Wasserburg.

Figure 26 B is an AEF DP (American Expeditionary Forces Displaced Persons') Registration record (one version dated V (May) 7, 1946 for Lipot Moskowits who is Jewish from Kuzmino. His desired destination is USA. His trade is Tailor Performed by a mastery. His languages spoken in order of fluency are Jewish, Czech and German.

Figure 26C is a Medical clearance certificate documenting his immunization record. He arrived for medical inspection on May 4, 1946.

Fig 26D is similar to Figure 26B although it differs by recording different language fluencies in Jewish, Czech and Russian. It records similarly that his mother is Lea that he was a prisoner from 5/20/44 – 5/5/45, and that he was liberated from camp Ebensee.

Figure 26E is an uncharted medical clearance certificate.

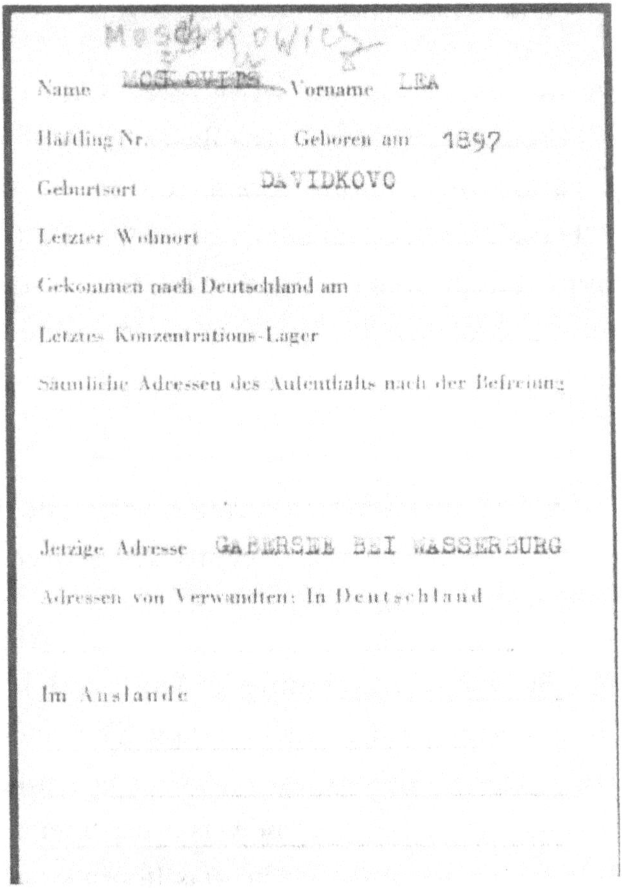

```
Name  M̶O̶S̶K̶O̶W̶I̶C̶S̶  Moskowicz  Vorname  LEA

Häftling Nr.              Geboren am   1897

Geburtsort        DAVIDKOVO

Letzter Wohnort

Gekommen nach Deutschland am

Letztes Konzentrations-Lager

Sämtliche Adressen des Aufenthalts nach der Befreiung




Jetzige Adresse   GABERSEE BEI WASSERBURG

Adressen von Verwandten: In Deutschland



Im Auslande
```

Figure 27: Registration paper for Lea Moskowicz listing her current address as Gabersee Bei Wasserburg.

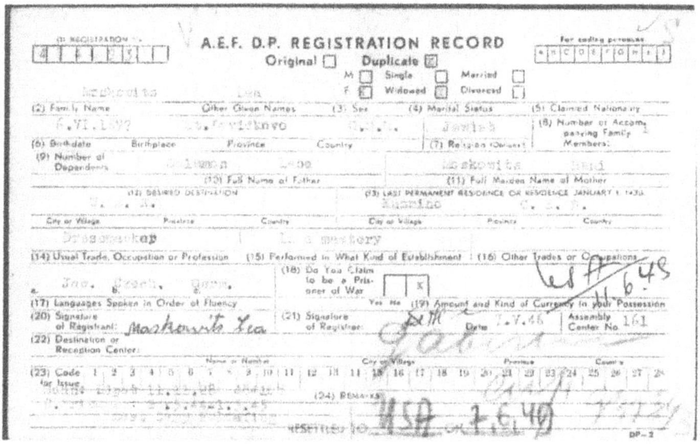

ARRIVAL AT GERMANY: AMERICAN DP CAMP

Figure 28A: AEF DP Registration record dated V (May) 7 1946 for Lea Moskowits who is Jewish from St Davidkovo CSR (Version 1). Her desired destination is USA. Her trade is Dressmaker Performed by a mastery. Her languages spoken in order of fluency are Jewish, Czech and German. She has a son Lipot. Her last Camp was Feldafing.

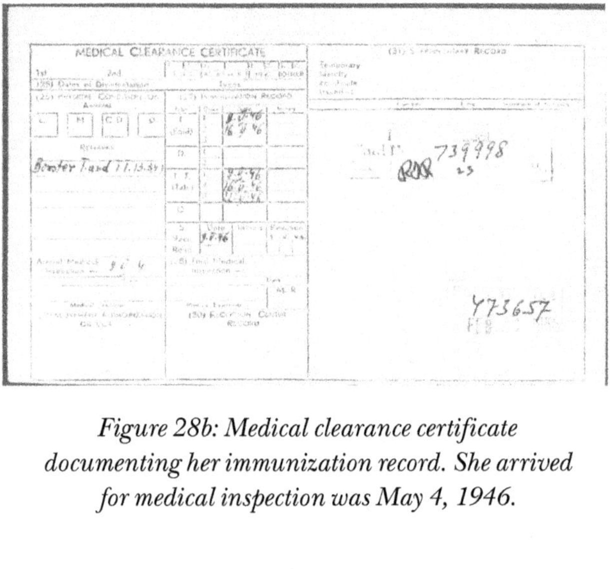

Figure 28b: Medical clearance certificate documenting her immunization record. She arrived for medical inspection was May 4, 1946.

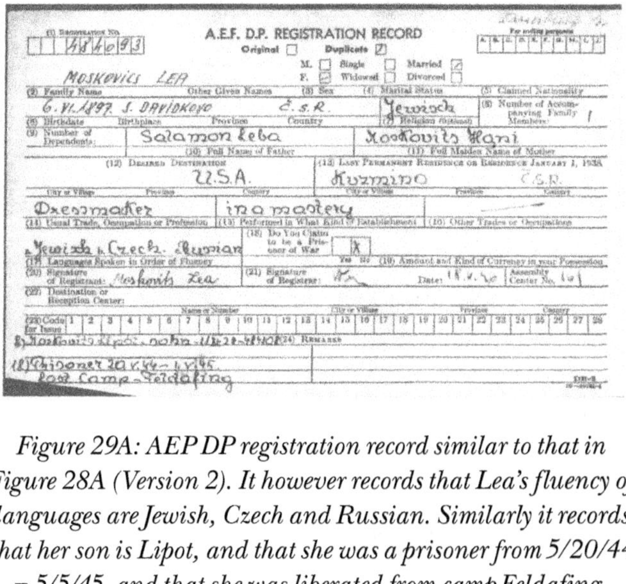

ARRIVAL AT GERMANY: AMERICAN DP CAMP

Figure 29A: AEP DP registration record similar to that in Figure 28A (Version 2). It however records that Lea's fluency of languages are Jewish, Czech and Russian. Similarly it records that her son is Lipot, and that she was a prisoner from 5/20/44 – 5/5/45, and that she was liberated from camp Feldafing.

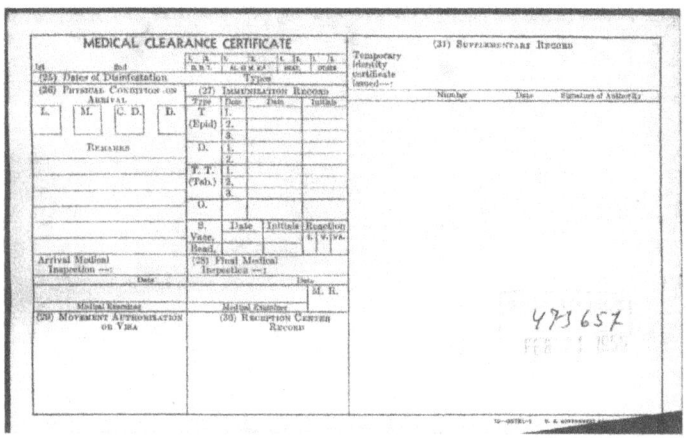

Figure 29b: An uncharted Medical clearance certificate.

ARRIVAL AT GERMANY: AMERICAN DP CAMP

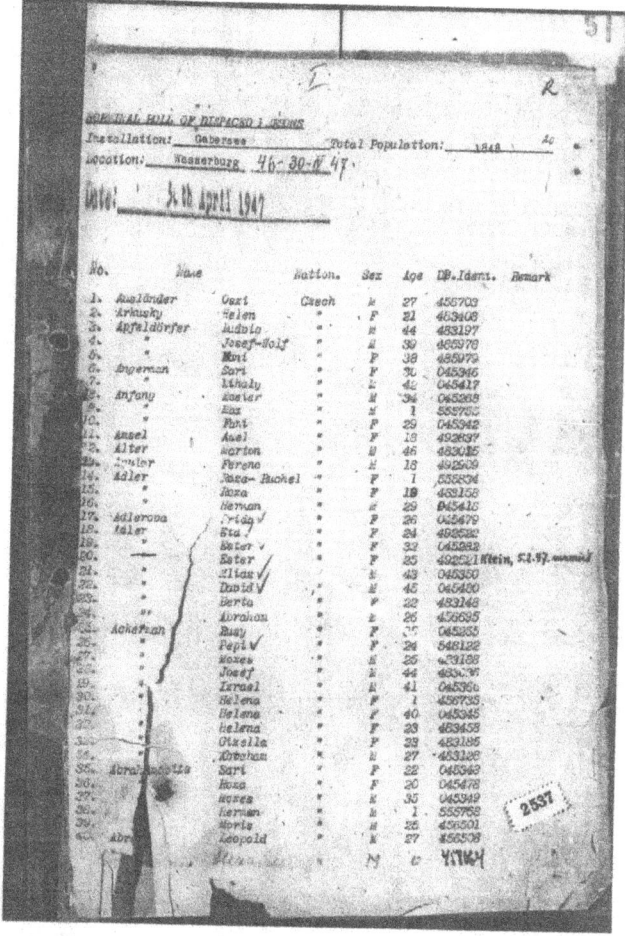

Figure 30A: Alphabetical Roll of displaced persons in installation Gaberseee at location Wasserburg with a total population of 1848 persons, dated April 30th 1947.

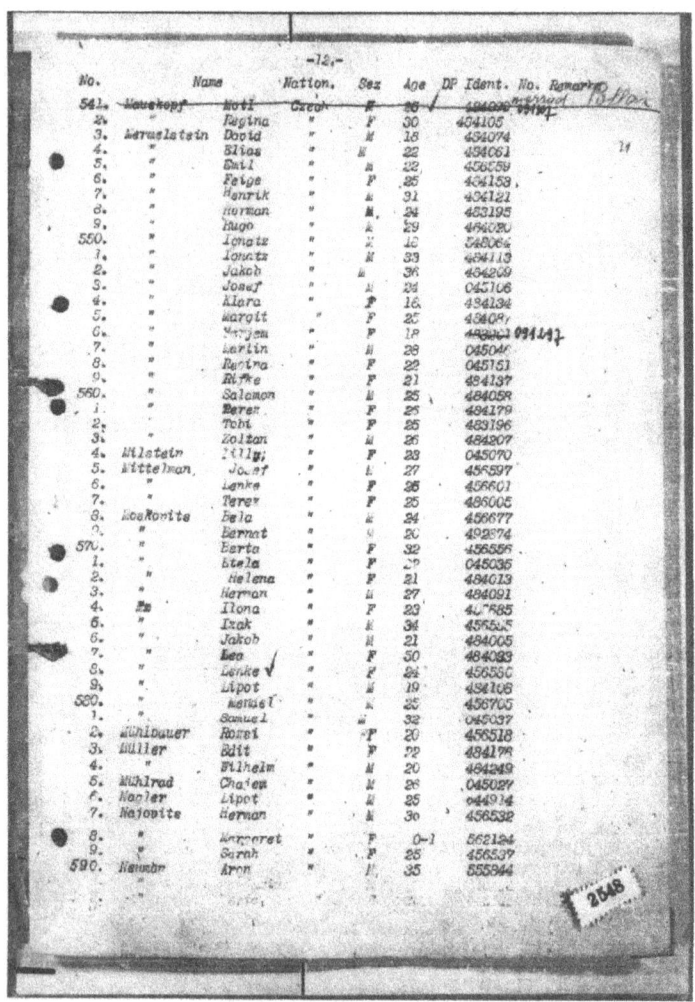

Figure 30B: Roll of displaced persons. Refer to line 577 which lists Lea, a Czech, female, age 50. Line 579 lists Lipot Moskovits, a Czech, male, age 19.

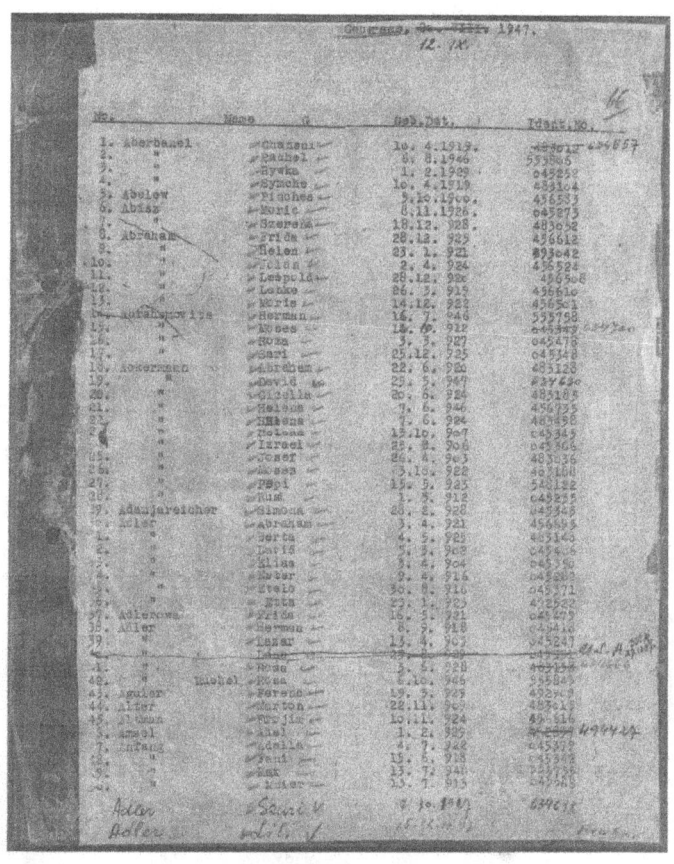

Figure 30C: List of Displaced persons from Gabersee dated September 12, 1947.

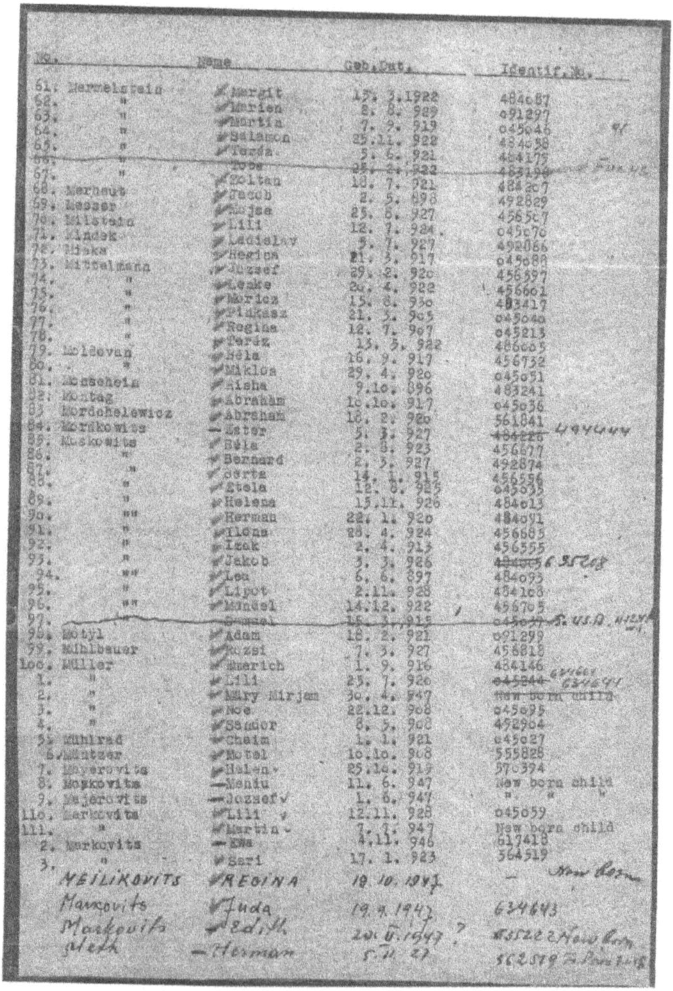

No.		Name	Geb. Dat.	Identif. No.	
61.	Mermelstein	Margit	15. 3.1922	484087	
62.	"	Marien	8. 8. 929	091297	
63.	"	Martin	7. 9. 919	045046	
64.	"	Salamon	25.11. 922	484058	
65.	"	Tersa	5. 6. 921	484175	
~~66.~~	~~"~~	~~Tobe~~	~~25. 2. 922~~	~~483194~~	[illegible]
67.	"	Zoltan	18. 7. 921	484207	
68.	Merhaut	Jacob	2. 5. 898	492829	
69.	Messer	Mojse	25. 8. 927	456567	
70.	Milstein	Lili	12. 7. 924	045070	
71.	Mindek	Ladislav	5. 7. 927	492066	
72.	Miska	Regina	21. 3. 917	045088	
73.	Mittelmann	Jozsef	29. 2. 920	456597	
74.	"	Lenke	20. 4. 922	456601	
75.	"	Moricz	15. 8. 930	483417	
76.	"	Pinkasz	21. 3. 905	045040	
77.	"	Regina	12. 7. 907	045213	
78.	"	Teréz	13. 5. 922	486005	
79.	Moldovan	Béla	16. 9. 917	456732	
80.	"	Miklos	29. 4. 920	045051	
81.	Monschein	Aisha	9.10. 896	483241	
82.	Montag	Abraham	10.10. 917	045036	
83.	Mordchelewicz	Abraham	18. 2. 920	561841	
84.	Morákowits	Ester	5. 3. 927	~~484226~~	494444
85.	Moskowits	Béla	2. 8. 923	456677	
86.	"	Bernard	2. 5. 927	492874	
87.	"	Berta	14. 1. 915	456556	
88.	"	Etela	12. 8. 925	045035	
89.	"	Helena	15.11. 926	484013	
90.	"	Herman	22. 1. 920	484091	
91.	"	Ilona	28. 4. 924	456683	
92.	"	Izak	2. 4. 913	456555	
93.	"	Jakob	3. 3. 926	~~[illegible]~~	635208
94.	"	Lea	6. 6. 897	484093	
95.	"	Lipot	2.11. 928	484108	
96.	"	Mindel	14.12. 922	456705	
~~97.~~	~~"~~	~~Samuel~~	~~15. 3. 915~~	~~045037~~	to U.S.A. [illegible]
98.	Motyl	Adam	18. 2. 921	091299	
99.	Mühlbauer	Rozsi	7. 3. 927	458818	
100.	Müller	Emerich	1. 9. 916	484146	
1.	"	Lili	25. 7. 920	~~045244~~	634644
2.	"	Mary Mirjam	30. 4. 947	~~New born child~~	
3.	"	Noe	22.12. 908	045095	
4.	"	Sandor	8. 5. 908	492904	
5.	Mühlrad	Chaim	1. 1. 921	045027	
6.	Müntzer	Motel	10.10. 908	555828	
7.	Mayerovits	Helen	25.10. 919	570394	
8.	Moskovits	Meniu	11. 6. 947	New born child	
9.	Majerovits	Jozsef	1. 8. 947	" " "	
110.	Markovits	Lili	12.11. 928	045059	
111.	"	Martin	7. 9. 947	New born child	
2.	Markovits	Ella	4.11. 946	617418	
3.	"	Sari	17. 1. 923	564519	
	MEILIKOVITS	REGINA	18. 10. 1947	—	New born
	Markovits	Juda	19. 9. 1947	634643	
	Markovits	Edith	20. [illegible]. 1947 ?	[illegible]	New born
	[illegible]	Herman	5. [illegible] 27	562579	[illegible]

Figure 30D: Line 94 lists Moskowits Lea, birth date 6/6/1897.
Line 95 lists Moskowits Lipot, birth date 2/11/1928.

ARRIVAL AT GERMANY: AMERICAN DP CAMP

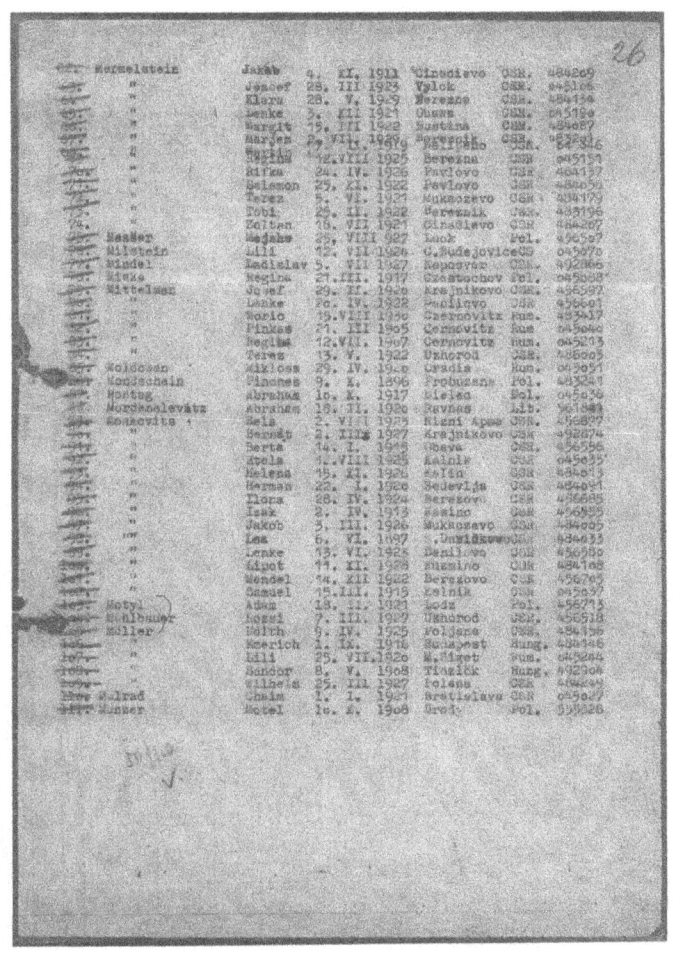

Figure 30E: Line 98 lists Moskovits Lea, birth date 6/6/1897, born in S Davidkovo CSR. Line 100 lists Moskovits Lipot, birth date 11/11/1928, born in Kuzmino CSR.

```
Kammer VII                    US-Zone
Der Vorsitzende:         (14a) Stgt.-Feuerbach, den   2.12.1947
                             Wiener Straße 60   Telefon 81073

                         v.K/Jo


               B e s c h e i n i g u n g :

In dem Spruchkammerverfahren

              Gertrud Rosa  M ü l l e r

vor der Spruchkammer 7 Stgt.-Feuerbach wurde fest-
gestellt, dass

              Frau Lea  M o s k o w i t z

vom Aug. 1944 bis März 1945 im Konzentrationslager
Geislingen/Steige inhaftiert war. Von dort wurde
sie nach Alach bei München transportiert und in
Staltach befreit.

Vor der Zeit in Geislingen befand sich die Genannte
in Auschwitz.


                              Der Vorsitzende:
                         Spruchkammer 7 Stgt.-Feuerbach

                                  (v.Kirn)
```

Figure 31: Official document titled Bescheinigung (the presiding) in the US zone by Sgt. Feurbach certified on Dec 2, 1947 that Frau Lea Moskowitz was in the concentration camp Geislingen/Steige from August 1944 to March 1945. From there she was transported to Alach near Munich and from there she was liberated.

ARRIVAL AT GERMANY: AMERICAN DP CAMP

```
                    TRACING SECTION,
                    LUDWIGSBURG (14a),
                    Hohenzollernstrasse 46.
                    c/o Area Team 1002 .
                    APO          154 .

No. 109                              Date :  5.2.1948
TO      : Miss. Lea MOSKOVITS, D.P. Camp Gabersee near Wasserburg/Inn.
SUBJECT : MOSKOVITS      Christ. Name: Lenke        Nat.: Czech/Jew
          Birth Date:  9.7.1897    Birth Place: Stara Davydovo

  1. Your letter dated  ------  on above subject has been re-
     ceived by this Bureau.
  2. Upon investigation of this case we have to advise you that
     the following information is available in the records, held
     by this Bureau.

     MOSKOVITS      Lenke       11..1904-  ------  Ungar/Jew
     (Name)       (Christ. Name) (Birth Date - Place) (Nation.)

     Last known address:  --------

     has entered the Concentration Camp of:  Dachau
     coming from : Natzweiler   on: 11.4.1945  and has
     been registered under the Number(s) 154067 . The reason
     for imprisonment, according to the records was: Political
     Prisoner (Jewish-Ungar) . Transferred on : ------
     to:  Allach      / Died in : ------
     on:   ----       . Cause of Death: ------
     Location of grave : ------
     Liberated from:  Dachau       on:  by US army
     Present address:     as above
     Further information available:  ------

                                       F. Przyluski
                                       F. PRZYLUSKI,
                                       Chief, Tracing Section.
     vs
     Note: If information in the above report is not complete we
           are automatically continuing our search and any further
           information secured will be forwarded to you.

     Form : T - 12.
```

Figure 32: Record documented by the Tracing Section (Area Team 1002) of Miss Lenke (Lea) Moskovitz a Hungarian Jew who is in DP camp Gabersee near Wasserburg on Feb 5, 1948 dame to Dachau from Natzweilar on 4/11/45, and was registered under the number 154067. She was imprisoned for the political reason of being a Hungarian Jew. She was transferred to Allach. She was liberated from Dachau by the US army. This document was signed by F. Przyluski Chief of the Tracing Section.

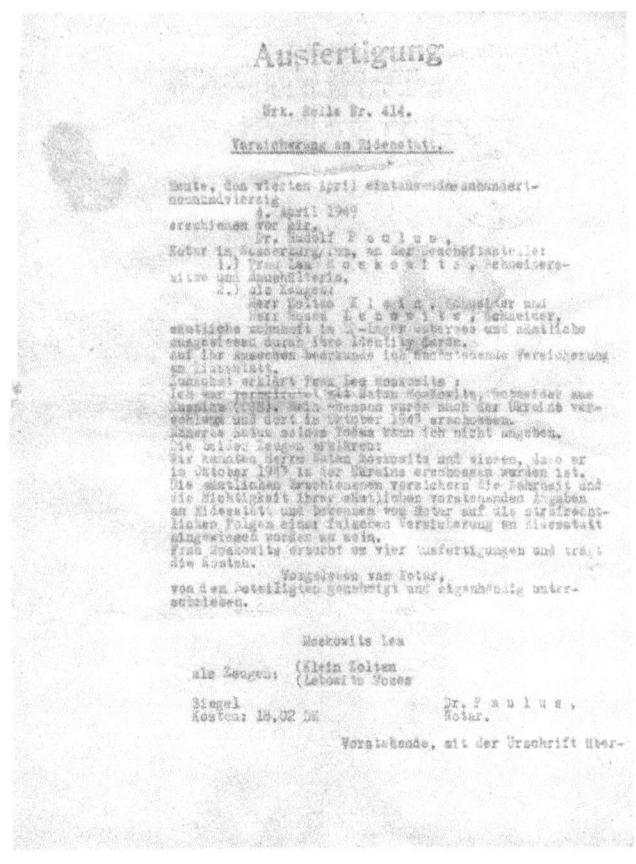

Figure 33A: Statuary Declaration (Versicherung an Eidesstatt) dated April 4, 1949. Lea testifies before two witnesses, Zoltan Klein and Moses Lebowitz that she was married to Natan Moskowits a tailor from Kussina (CSR). He was sent to the Ukraine and in October 1943 was shot. The witnesses declared that they knew Natan Moskowits and know that he was shot in Ukraine in October 1943. This document was notarized by Dr. Paulus.

ARRIVAL AT GERMANY: AMERICAN DP CAMP

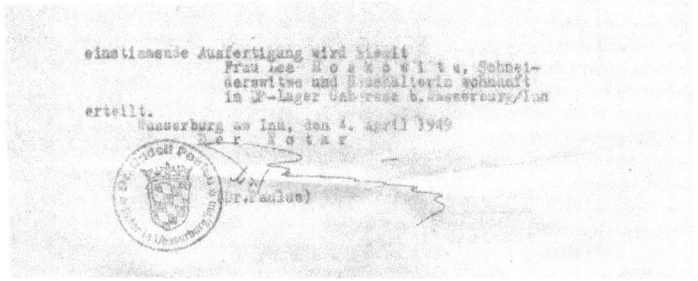

Figure 33B: Statuary Declaration (Versicherung an Eidesstatt) dated April 4, 1949. This document was notarized by Dr. Paulus.

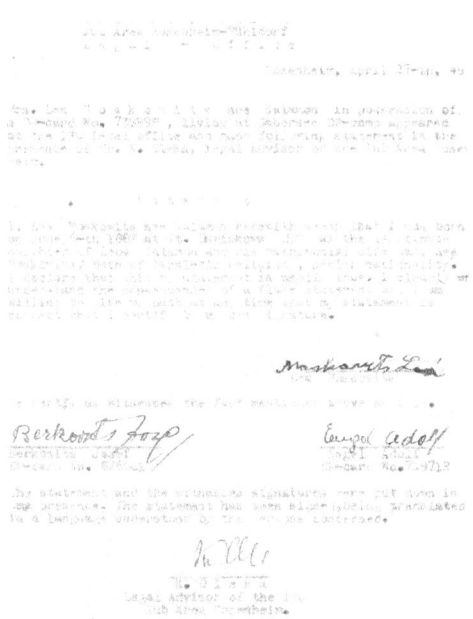

Figure 34: Witnessed certified statement made by Lea Moskowitz at the IRO legal office. She swears she was born on June 6, 1897, is the legitimate daughter of her parents and is of the Jewish Nationality. Two other witnesses in possession of DP cards, Josef Berkowitz and Adolf Engel, testify that what she said was true. This was witnessed and signed by K. Oleka, Legal advisor of the IRO in Sub Area Rosenheim on April 27, 1949.

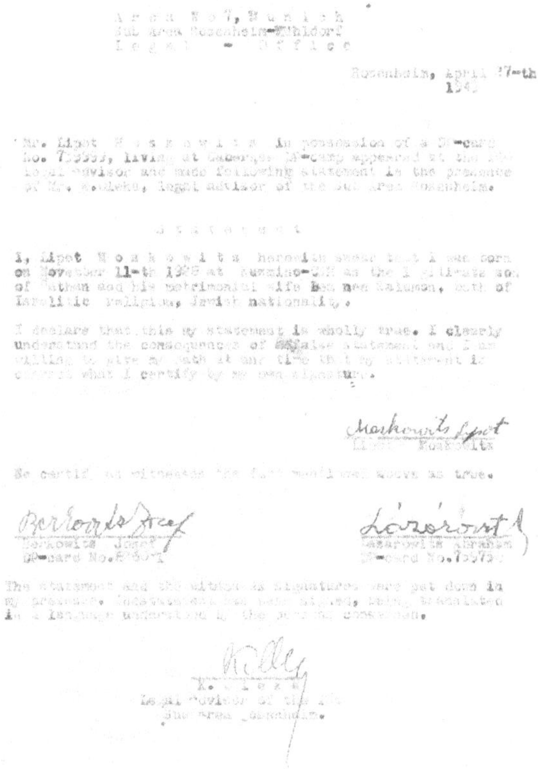

ARRIVAL AT GERMANY: AMERICAN DP CAMP

Figure 35: Witnessed certified statement made by Lipot Moskowitz at the IRO legal office. He swears he was born on November 11, 1928, that he is the legitimate child of his parents, and he is of the Jewish nationality. Two witnesses in possession of DP cards, Josef Berkowitz and Abraham Lazarowitz testify that what he said was true. This was witnessed and signed by K. Oleka, Legal advisor of the IRO in Sub Area Rosenheim on April 27, 1949.

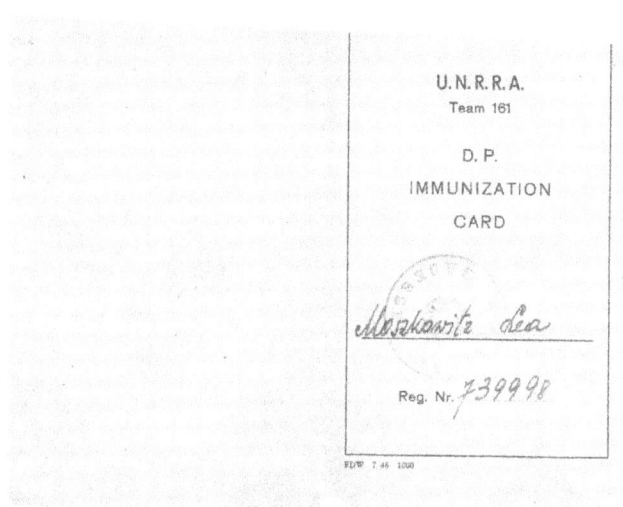

Figure 36A-Front: Front of DP immunization card under UNRRA (United Nations Relief and Rehabilitation Administration) for Lea.

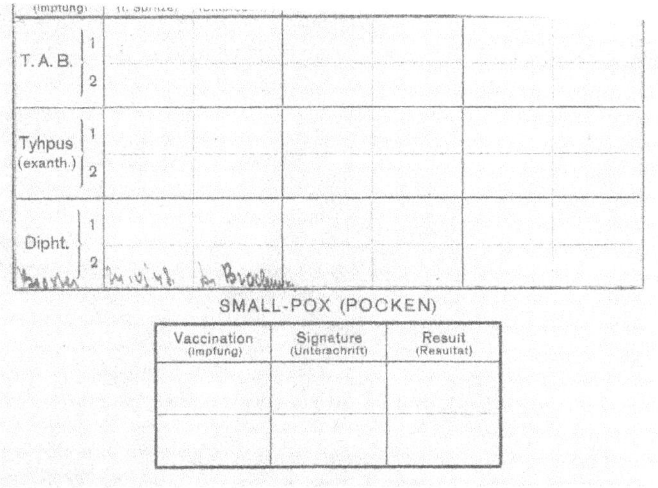

ARRIVAL AT GERMANY: AMERICAN DP CAMP

Figure 36A-Back: Back of DP immunization card under UNRRA (United Nations Relief and Rehabilitation Administration) for Lea.

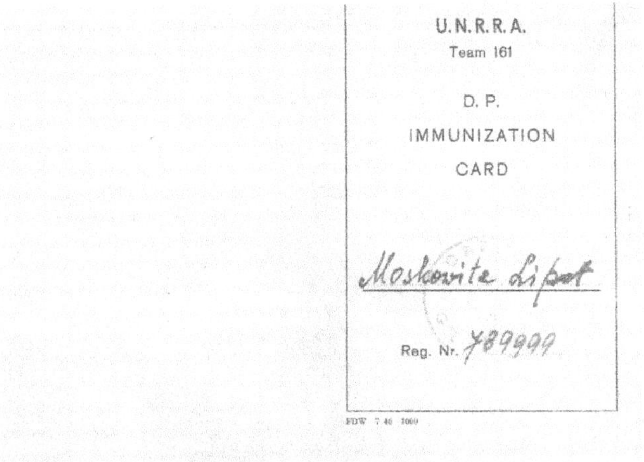

U.N.R.R.A.
Team 161

D. P.
IMMUNIZATION
CARD

Moskovitz Lipot

Reg. Nr. 789999

Figure 36B-Front: Front of DP immunization card under UNRRA(United Nations Relief and Rehabilitation Administration) for Leib (Lipot).

ARRIVAL AT GERMANY: AMERICAN DP CAMP

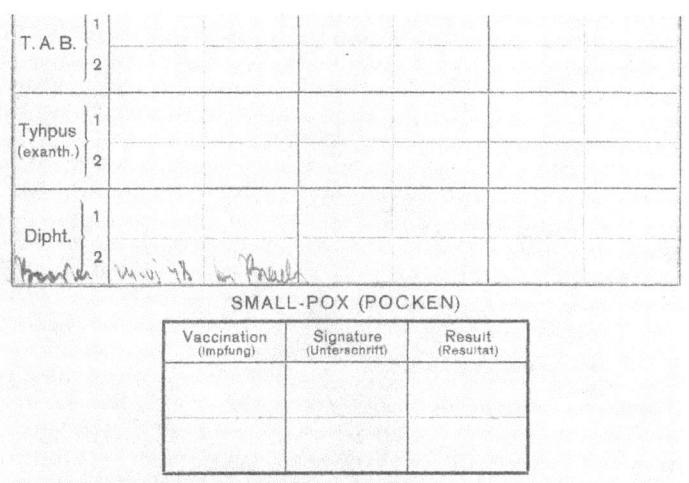

Figure 36B-Back: Back of DP immunization card under UNRRA (United Nations Relief and Rehabilitation Administration) for Leib (Lipot).

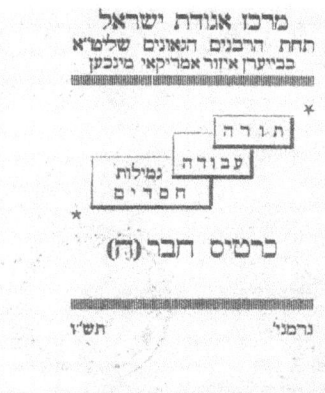

Figure 37A-Front: Front of a registration card for Agudath Israel in Gabersee bei Wasserberg written in Hebrew.

ARRIVAL AT GERMANY: AMERICAN DP CAMP

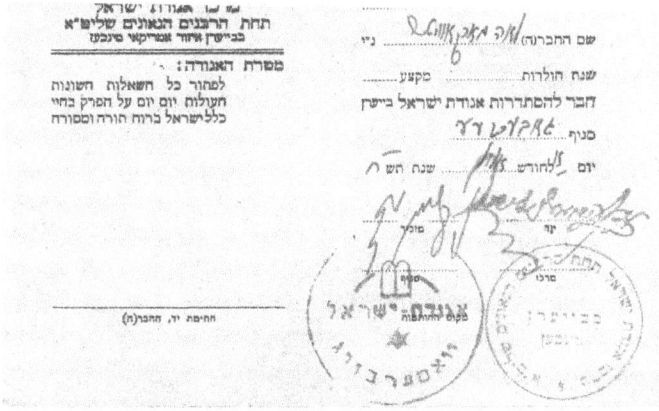

Figure 37A-Back: Lea's registration card for Agudath Israel in Gabersee bei Wasserberg written in Hebrew.

Belonges to the Organisation of the
„AGUDATH ISRAEL"
in Gabersee bei Wasserburg.

photograph

Name MOSKOVITS
Surname LEA
Birth 6. VI 1897
Adress of Residence Gabersee bei Wasserburg./Inn.
Height 170 cm.
Colour of Eyes blue
Colour of Hair Blond.

Signature of holder
Gabersee 6. VI. 1949
Place and Date
Direktor
Secretary

Belonges to the Organisation of the
„AGUDATH ISRAEL"
in Gabersee bei Wasserburg

photograph

Name MOSKOVITS
Surname LIPOT
Birth 11. XI. 1928.
Adress of Residence Gabersee-Germany - U.S. Zone.
Height 178 cm.
Colour of Eyes Grey.
Colour of Hair Brown

Signature of holder
Gabersee 6. VI. 49 Germany
Place and Date
Direktor
Secretary

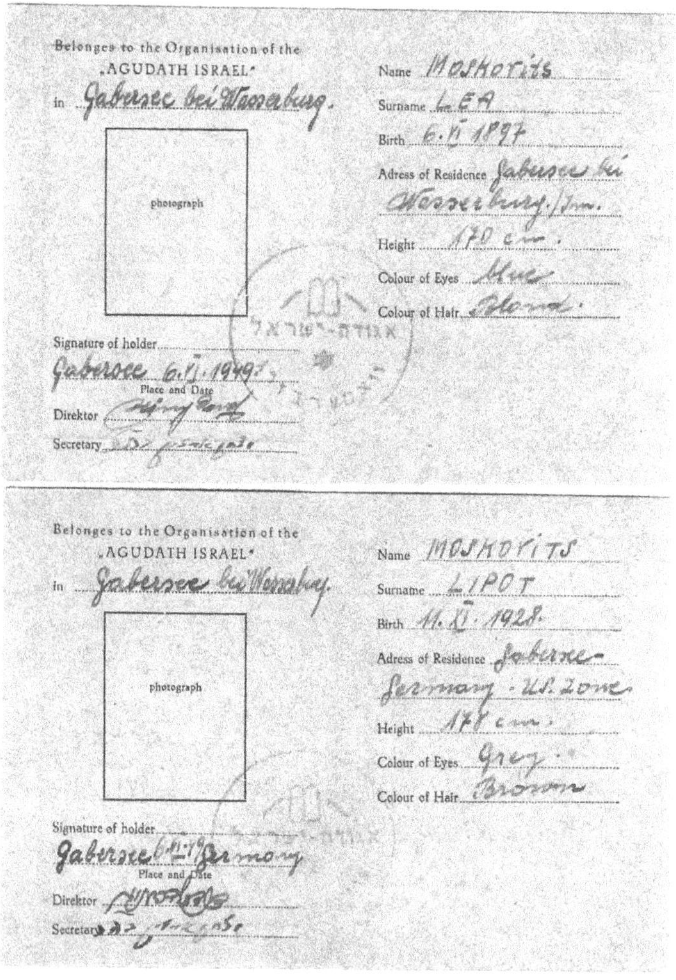

Figure 37B1: Leib and Lea's registration cards (inside) for Agudath Israel in Gabersee bei Wasserberg written in English.

ARRIVAL AT GERMANY: AMERICAN DP CAMP

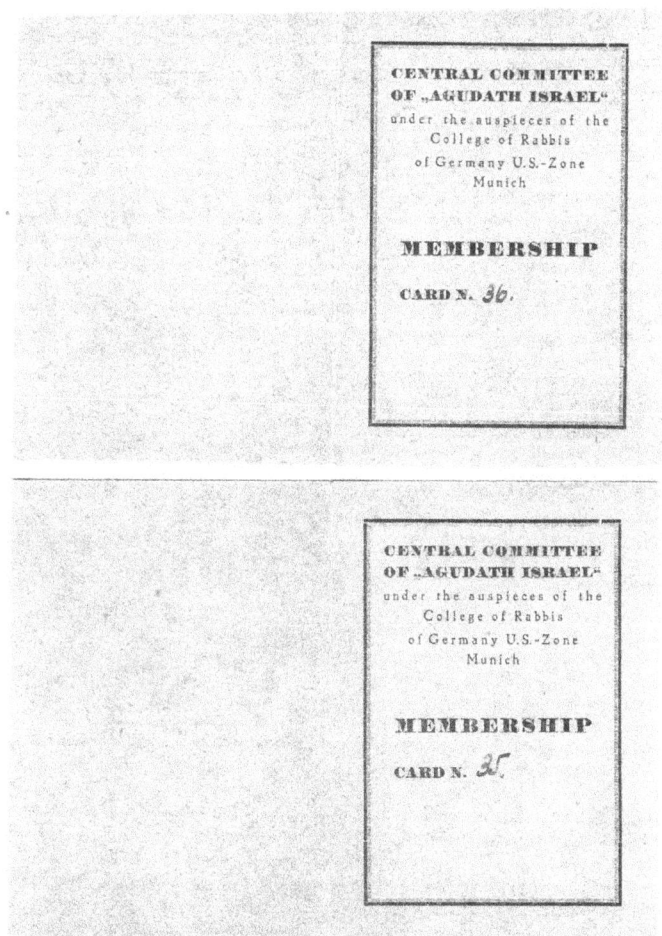

Figure 37B2: Leib and Lea's registration cards (outside) for Agudath Israel in Gabersee bei Wasserberg written in English.

Figure 37C: Receipts for Agudath Israel in Gabersee bei Wasserberg for Lea at Wasserburg written in Hebrew.

ARRIVAL AT GERMANY: AMERICAN DP CAMP

Figure 37D: Receipts for Agudath Israel in Gabersee bei Wasserberg for Leib (Lipot) and Lea at Wasserburg, and baggage check stub for passenger 789 (Lipot) on the USA Muir from Bremerhaven to Boston US.

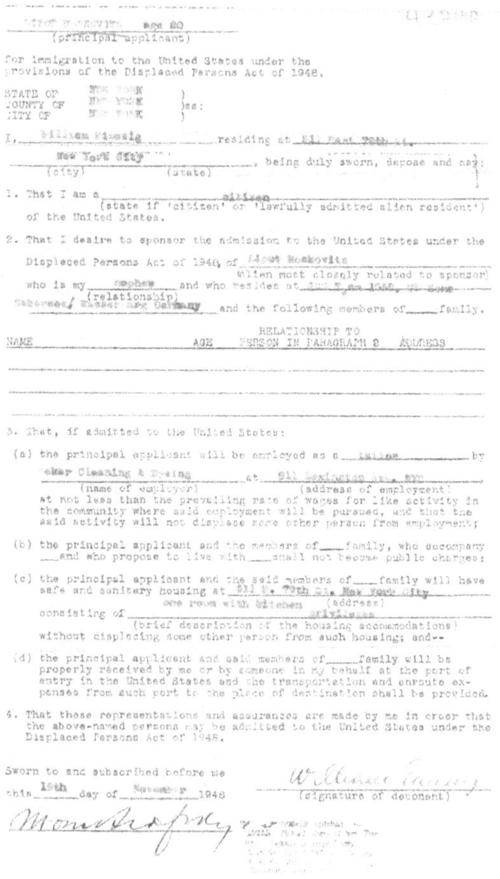

Figure 38: Application for immigration of Lipot Moskovits age 20 to come to the US sponsored by his Uncle William Einczig. William documents that he is a citizen of the US, that his nephew who resides at IRO T am 1059, US zone in Gabersee/ Wasserburg Germany. If admitted he will be employed as a tailor, and will live in NYC. This was notarized on November 16, 1948.

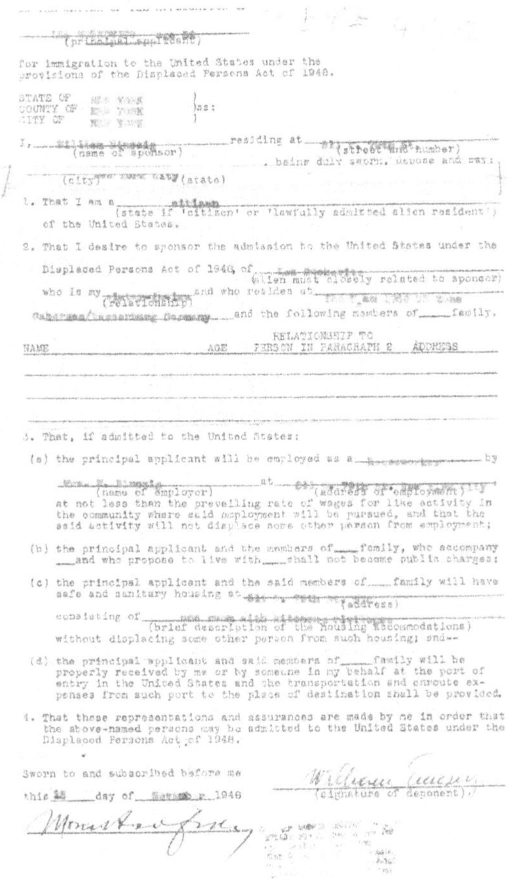

ARRIVAL AT GERMANY: AMERICAN DP CAMP

Figure 39: Application for immigration of Lea Moskovits age 52 to come to the US sponsored by her brother-in-law William Einczig. William documents that Lea is his sister-in-law who resides in Gabersee/ Wasserburg Germany. If admitted she will be employed as a house worker for his wife, and will live in NYC. This was notarized on November 16, 1948.

KUZMINO CHRONICLES

State of New York
City of New York } ss.:
County of New York

I William Einzig

age 58 yrs being duly sworn, depose and say:

I reside at 511 East 79th Street
New York City, N.Y.

I am a Native American or Naturalized Citizen of the United States as evidenced by (indicate which) my My Naturalization Certificate No. 815250 issued on June 13, 1918 by U.S. Southern District Court at New York

I am Married and dependent on me for support are My wife (married or single)

I am in the Retail Grocery Business and in the (State fully business or occupation, location, earnings) Real Estate Business at 342 East 94th Street, New York City; and my Income for the Year 1947 amounted to $4319.08 as evidenced by the attached Tax Report.

In addition, I have assets consisting of As follows: (State investments, savings, life insurance, real property, etc.)

Interest in Real Estate $13590.95
Interest in Grocery Business 4759.00
Mfrs. Trust Co. 2345.63
Cash Value – Life Insurance 2851.00 Total $ 23,554.58

I am the Cousin of Leo Moskovits 50 Years of Age (state relationship) (give names and ages of persons abroad)

now residing at P.G. Ira Team 1069
Gabersee / Vasserburg Wasserburg Obayern Germany

who desire s to come to the United States to join me and others of the family, and whom I am most anxious to bring over.

I do hereby promise and guarantee that I will receive and take care of my Cousin who is applying for an immigration visa, and will at no time allow Her to become public charges to any community or municipality. I do further promise and agree that those of my relatives covered by this affidavit within school age will attend public school, and will not be permitted to work until they are of age.

I make this affidavit for the purpose of inducing the United States Consular authorities to grant the visa to my said relative, and herewith submit corroborative proof as to my personal standing.

Sworn to before me this ____ day
of _____ 1948.

Notary Public

Figure 40: Testimony by William Einczig regarding his US citizenship, his net worth, his income and taxes, all documenting his ability to lend support. This was notarized on June 1948.

ARRIVAL AT GERMANY: AMERICAN DP CAMP

Photo 8: Leib selling ice cream on a street in Gabersee/Wasserburg, Germany, 1947.

Photo 9: Leib marching in a parade carrying a Jewish flag with a Magen David (not seen), Gabersee/Wasserburg, Germany, 1947.

ARRIVAL AT GERMANY: AMERICAN DP CAMP

Photo 10: Group photo of the Arbeiter (Workers) collective, specifically the Tailors of Gabersee. Leib is in the fourth row from the top in the center, sixth from left, above the woman below him, Gabersee/Wasserburg, Germany, 1948.

12

EN ROUTE TO AMERICA

We first went to Munich. They put us on trains and we were going to Bremerhaven (See Figures 41A and B, and Photo 11). *We got to stay there for three days before you board a ship* (General Muir), *an army troop ship (See* Figures 42A and B). *They said "Whoever wants to volunteer to work on ship, you can work and you get to pick a cabin". I went on the boat, I had to see where everybody was supposed to be, whatever. I got an arm band that said MP. When we boarded I had a cabin for my mother. Finally when they are untying the ropes I'm saying to myself impatiently "nu let us move already". I couldn't believe we were finally leaving.*

EN ROUTE TO AMERICA

The boat starts to move and everybody was puking like crazy. I was hungry. Aunt Feiga in the meantime died while we were in DP camp. She died of a bad heart valve (at the age of 55). When she died, Uncle Willy took over and took over the writing. He said: "I see refugees where are you?" They had to work out the quota. "I'm going to wait for you".

After travelling on the water for nine days (See Photo 12) we arrive at Boston on Friday at 10 am. I see the border police dressed like Nazis, I got scared. I had a hundred bucks on me from selling cigarettes. I had a three armed candlestick; I bought a camera at Bremerhaven, and coats for both of us.

We came off the boat. The boat carried Jews, Ukrainians, and former SS Latvians. The Ukranian bastards were in displaced camps, like Jews. Most were ex- Nazis. When we disembarked everyone had someone to pick them up.

I'm holding a picture of Uncle Willy, and I didn't see him. It's 12:30PM and everyone is leaving. I figure he got cold feet. All of a sudden a few Jews from the city of Boston show up. They say:

"If you don't want to mechallel Shabbos (violate the Sabbath) stay here for Shabbas, and on Sunday we'll take you to a train".

My mother says "There are Yeeden in America, ich vill nisht furen in shabbas (I will not travel on the Sabbath)".

So a few families took us into the city to an empty house. There was nothing in there. They're bringing in mattresses, and they start cooking. I go on the street, and then I go into a store. I say to the guy in the store: "Rets Yiddish?" ("You talk Yiddish?")

"Voos vilste boychik?" ("What do you want sonny?")

I say: "My uncle is supposed to meet us here at the boat; the address is 511 east 79th street in New York. Can you send a telegram, and can I get in touch with William Einczig?"

EN ROUTE TO AMERICA

A woman asked us "You have two dollaren?"

"Ya". I had ten dollars, the rest I sewed into my jacket.

So she goes and makes a telephone call. Who answers? Shifra answers.

She says: "Rets Yiddish, ver is de?"

I said to her: "Rets Yiddish and Ich been dein brieder's a zein" ("I speak Yiddish and I am you brother's son").

Her answer was: "Zu mir sols nisht kumen ich, hob kein platz far dier. Ich vill kumin dech zehn, cum HIAS" ("To me you shouldn't come, I don't have any place for you. I will come and see you. Go to HIAS").

She told me: "Uncle Willie hat geshtorbin mit drei voch zurich" ("Uncle Willie died three weeks ago.")

Three to four days later she came to the HIAS She took us to her home on 511 east 79th street and she gave us five dollars so I shouldn't die from thirst.

She married Willie, her brother-in-law after her sister died.

After she told me Willie died, the phone slipped out of my hand, and I said to my mother

"Uncle Villie is geshtorben, let's go back on the boat and go back to Germany. I don't know anyone here".

The women who were making Shabbas, overheard me and start saying "You are going to leave the Goldena Medina? Bist de meshugga?" ("You're going to leave the Golden Nation, are you nuts?")

They made a beautiful Shabbas meal. They pick us up and made us a dessert of cantaloupe.

On Shabbas we went to shul. They gave me an aliya and I benched goimel (a blessing for surviving an ordeal). *Sunday they took us to a park. They were very hospitable. Sunday*

EN ROUTE TO AMERICA

afternoon they took us to the train station, and they gave us tickets to New York.

We arrived to 34th street Penn station. The people from HIAS recognized us. We were wearing cards on our necks.

"Greena kim" ("Greenhorn come"), we are instructed by the people. They take us to 8th street and Lafayette in New York, the HIAS (Hebrew Immigrant Aid Society) for refugees. We come there and there are two big rooms where the refugees are, but there is no room for us. But there is a hotel 3-4 blocks away. "We'll put you up there, but you can come here to eat". They took us to the hotel. We eat three square meals a day; plenty of food. The food was delicious.

Ruchela came to visit. The food is real nice, and I eat like a chazar (pig). You could have whatever you wanted. Friday afternoon, Eleanor's husband comes to look for the Moskowitz's, the greeners (greenhorns) from Kuzmino. He starts talking in Yiddish. His name was Irwin Werber.

He says "I'm a cousin from Eleanor. Eleanor wants you to come for Shabbas". We went there for Shabbas. I didn't tell HIAS that I'm leaving. Eleanor made a Friday and Shabbas meal with brisket and cabbage. We didn't have a meal like this since before World War II.

They lived On 77th Street between Second and Third Avenue. They lived on the third floor and owned a grocery store on the bottom. He worked on Shabbas. They had two small kids, Pauline and Seymour.

In the afternoon the telephone rings and someone asks Eleanor, "The grena dorten (Are the Greenhorns there?) I'm coming later".

That was Golda Neiderman. She comes with her son Jack. She sees me and says: "Oy yo, mein breeder's zein ..." ("Oh my, my brother's son...").

My cousin Jack asks "You smoke?"

He buys me two packs of cigarettes, and then he says "We'll show you where you live".

EN ROUTE TO AMERICA

It's Shabbas and my mother says in Yiddish "I'm not traveling on Shabbas".

So they waited until Shabbas ended. They took us to New Brunswick Saturday night.

That following Monday was July 4th.

We drove in a big Buick. They lived in a very nice house. Aunt Golda takes me to the bathroom and demonstrates saying "When you go to the toilet you have to pull this".

I said "I come from Kuzmino, but I've seen the world. Ich vise (I know)".

We slept there. I met an uncle there, I knew his father Neiderman an old man, with a beard.

Neiderman (Golda's husband) says "And what do you do for a leben (living)?"

"What are you talking about? Ich ken a bissele a schneider" ("I know a little about tailoring").

I'm sleeping in bed on Tuesday morning, and somebody is shaking me. My uncle is shaking me. "Come on let's look for work". I got up. We're in New Brunswick. It's a small shteitel. He walks into a cleaning store. He inquires about a job...no work. He goes from store to store, and nobody is hiring.

Finally he goes into a factory where they make flannel shirts. He says they need help.

"Stay here" my Uncle says "I'll come and get you".

I don't speak one word of English. They ask me my name, and they're applying for social security. Someone was talking Hungarian, and I understood a few words.

"How much do they pay?" I ask.

"Seventy five cents an hour. When the truck comes with a material, we stretch it out on the table, and somebody cuts it".

I stayed and always worked overtime. I bought a coke and a salami sandwich for lunch from a pushcart.

EN ROUTE TO AMERICA

Then my Uncle says "We have to look for an apartment".

I said "I have no money".

"I will lend you some money".

They took us to Spruce Street; the rent was 38 dollars a month. They dropped us off in an empty place. There wasn't a bolt in the ceiling, the same way I found my house in Kuzmino except it had windows and doors.

My Uncle said to us "You live here".

My mother said to my Aunt "Buy me a loaf of bread, you have to have bread and salt when you move into to a new place".

The Tanta (Aunt) came back and said "Bread is sold out". Across there's street a shvitzbath (sweat bath). A man Mr. Klein comes over, He was from Ungvar and he says: "Who are you?"

I speak Yiddish.

"Who is that big guy?" he asks.

"My Uncle Neiderman".

"So what are you going to do here?"

"I live here".

He said; "How?"

"You have to have a bed, a chair, and a table". He took his workers.

A couple people started bringing in beds, chairs and tables. His name was Klein. Within hours we had everything we needed. Mrs. Klein said "Whenever you want anything say yoohoo and I'll come over".

Mr. and Mrs. Klein were wonderful people. Mr. Klein took my mother to an appliance store and bought a refrigerator for $210.00. I believe he signed his name. When we left New Brunswick he put the refrigerator in his house. I told him if you can sell it ok, if not do with it what you want. He sold it I believe for $125. He sent me a check to New York when we settled in New York. We went to visit the Klein's pretty often. Mrs. Klein said to me 'go *visit your aunt'. I said to her 'you are my aunt talk to me'. I thanked them on Rosh Hashanah and Yom Kippur. Mr. Klein barely eked out a living. He had a Turkish shvitzbood* (sweat bath). *He also had a gambling problem.*

The first paycheck I get I go to Uncle Moishe and ask "Did you pay the rent?"

"How much?"

He said: "$38, sign here".

*He turned over the check to pay the rent (*See Figures 43-Front and 43-Back for electric and gas bill*).*

As I'm walking in the street I thought I recognized a refugee. We refugees had a password 'Amchu' ('Our Nation').

"Amchu" I say. "Amchu" he answers.

"Where do you work?" I ask him.

"At a factory".

"How much they pay you?"

"A dollar an hour".

"Do they need more help?"

"Yeah".

"Can you take me there?"

When I came to the factory the boss spoke Yiddish and said: "What can you do?"

"I can sew".

"Ok sit down".

So I'm making a dollar an hour. After 2 days I says to him "You need someone else?"

He said "Yes", so I brought my mother, and between the two of us we were making eighty dollars/week.

In the meantime Mr. Klein said come to my house. I ask my Uncle Neiderman if I could buy a refrigerator from him, he had an appliance store.

I said: "Uncle Moishe can you sell me a used refrigerator?"

"I'll give you an icebox".

"No I want a refrigerator. I have a job I'll pay for it".

I hung up. Mr. Klein heard the story, and he took my mother and bought her a refrigerator. He put down 10 dollars, and the rest was to be paid on credit. They delivered it right away.

Neiderman found out, and Tanta Golda said to my mother "Tell them they must take back the refrigerator, and we'll sell you a refrigerator. You must do this, if you don't do that they will ship you out of the country!" Mr. Klein, who was a friend acted like a real uncle to me, and he takes me to shul.

One day we're working. One day the boss asks "Who wants to go to New York, and get paid time and a half? That means you work an hour and you get paid for an hour and another half hour".

They needed four people. I volunteer. The overtime had to be on Shabbas. My mother went crazy. "*How can you work on Shabbas, if your father were alive...?*"

We went to a factory in New York. They make 70-80 dollars/week.

I'm working someplace on 30th street. HIAS is on 8th street. I slept over one night at the HIAS I call Klein to tell my mother not to worry, that I'm going to HIAS for the weekend. I come to 34th street. I can't talk English. I motion to a cop, saying "Uh... uh...", and the cop points me to where I have to go.

I come to HIAS Saturday night. I eat a good dinner. I seek out an empty bed and I lay down and figure I'll stay here until Monday. Somebody shakes me and says "What are you doing in my bed?" So I get up and find another bed.

Monday at 8:00 AM the HIAS office opens up, and I says "My name is so and so".

"*You checked out?*"

"*No I didn't. I got sick. I didn't leave*".

"*We have no room for you*".

"Ok I'm going to sit here. I have nowhere to go".

"Einczig sent papers for you".

"No, he's dead".

They wouldn't listen to me. Eventually they relented, and they gave me a room to sleep.

I take a train, I go to New Brunswick, I said to my mother "Come were going to New York".

I went to my boss and said "Thank you, please pay me".

My mother said "Lets say goodbye to Tanta Golda".

I said "No thanks".

Golda told my mother after she said goodbye "If you leave New Brunswick they will never let you in here again".

I approached Mr. Klein and I ask him a favor. "Please take the refrigerator. See if you can sell it. I'm going to NY".

"Good for you! This is not a young man's place".

I found a job in Brooklyn for one dollar an hour making clothes for the air force. We were staying in HIAS. A woman comes to look for someone to rent rooms in the Bronx. She was renting for 35$/month an apartment with a kitchen a bedroom, I left HIAS and went to 590 Prospect Avenue. I got a job in Williamsburg for 40$/week. HIAS and the Joint told me we'll help you until you can make enough money to support yourself.

At my work, the Union came in and put every section on piece work (no salary). I was given a choice: Either make a dollar an hour or get paid by the piece (do piece work). I wanted to see how much I can produce by piece work. The first week I earned 60 dollars.

I made twenty dollars more doing piece work so I told the boss next week I want to do piece work.

"Do you think you can make more than a dollar an hour?"

EN ROUTE TO AMERICA

"I'll try" I said. I started piece work. I was making $120-130/week. I took no lunch breaks. I cashed my checks and gave the money to my mother. She made supper and had clean shirts and prepared lunch every day.

I worked like this for nine months. OK the boss announced "The contract is finished everyone go home".

At the time I knew a guy, David Gelber. I got a job working on 38th street. The union is paying me out 12 dollars a day. After what I was making, that was a very bitter fall.

After a couple of months the previous job called me back. They had a contract for Navy uniforms. These uniforms were very thick. If I killed myself I couldn't make more than 60$ a week.

Dave Gelber then talked to me and said "Why do that? I work by the piece. We make lady suits. You can do that. Come we'll be partners we'll share 50-50".

I did the Navy uniforms, and after 6 weeks I made $100/ week. The Boss then says "No work, I'll call you if I need you".

I registered for unemployment. I was getting engaged. We started seeing each other. I want to get married. She has a cousin going out with Spitz, a grocery store owner. I was ashamed to go out from my apartment on 395 Fort Washington Avenue because I wasn't working when we got engaged.

My mother gave me $1500 which she had saved. She used to clean houses for $ 2-3/day. She saved that and from my salary.

Friday night I'm not coming home. I went to walk the beaches of Coney Island.

You (NCM)) were born in Bronx Lebanon Hospital. My mother was overjoyed when we named you Nathan Chaim. She said finally my husband (Nathan) has a name. Chaim came from my brother Chaym Hersch, so both my father's and my brother's names were carried on.

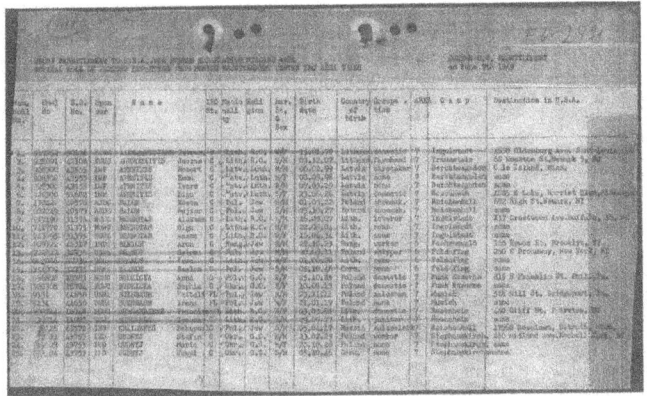

Figure 41A: The names of the first 25 people on the list departing from Munich resettlement center IRO area 7 AZG on June 7, 1949 to proceed to Bremerhaven (See text).

KUZMINO CHRONICLES

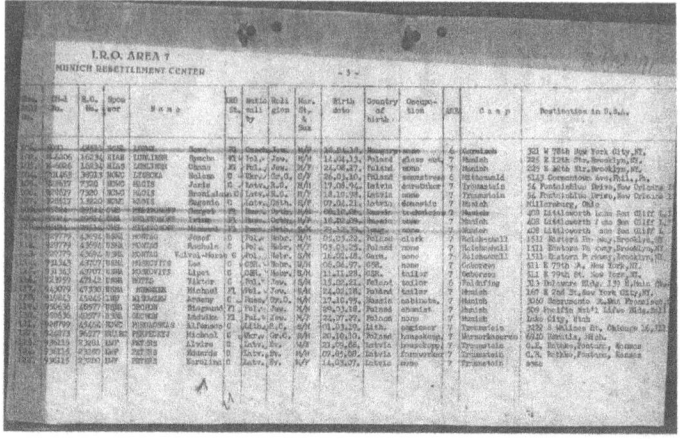

Figure 41B: List of the 101st to 125th people departing from Munich. Lea and Lipot are listed on lines 115 and 116, respectively departing from Munich resettlement center IRO area 7 AZG on June 7, 1949 to proceed to Bremerhaven (See text).

Figure 41A lists the first 25 people on the list.

Figure 41B lists the 101st to 125th people on the list Lea and Lipot are listed on lines 115 and 116, respectively. Information included are names, nationalities country of birth, occupation, camp and destination.

EN ROUTE TO AMERICA

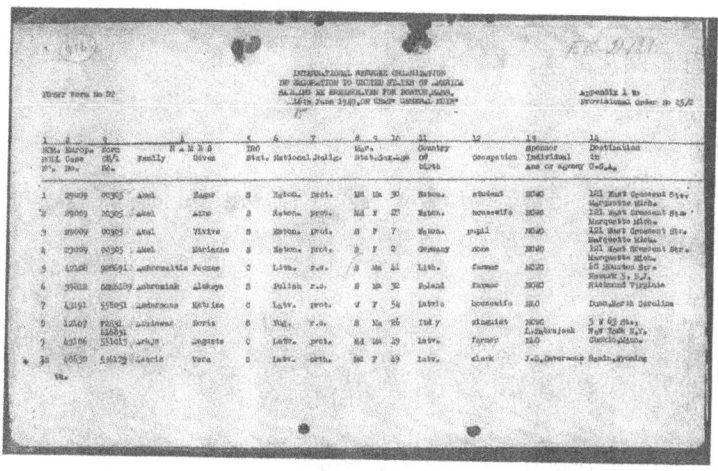

Figure 42A: List of passengers 1-10 immigrating to USA, sailing on the USAT Muir on June 15, 1949 (See text).

KUZMINO CHRONICLES

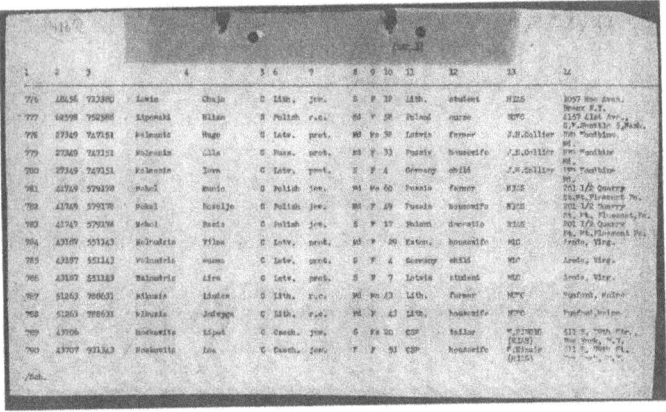

Figure 42B: Lists of passengers 776-790 immigrating to USA, sailing on the USAT Muir on June 15, 1949. Lipot and Lea appear on lines 789 and 790, respectively. (See text).

Figure 42A lists passengers 1-10.

Figure 42B lists passengers 776-790. Lipot and Lea appear on lines 789 and 790, respectively. The list includes names, nationalities, marital status, country of birth, occupation, sponsor and destination.

EN ROUTE TO AMERICA

Figure 43-Front: Electric and gas bills for Aug 2, 1949- Aug 31 1949 in New Brunswick addressed to Lela Moskovets.

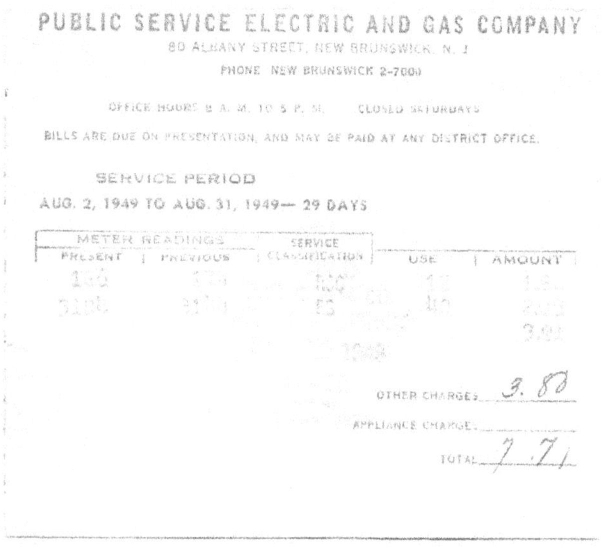

Figure 43-Back: Electric and gas bills for Aug 2, 1949- Aug 31 1949 in New Brunswick addressed to Lela Moskovets.

*Photo 11: Leib and Lea in Bremerhaven.
Leib is greeting a friend, 1949.*

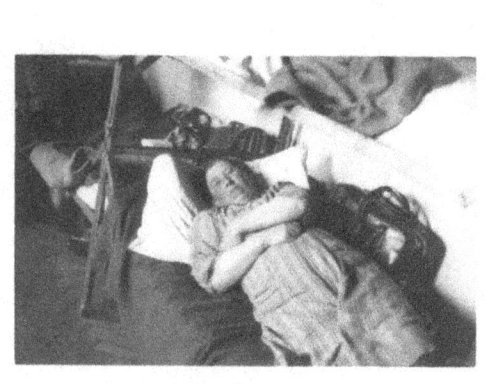

Photo 12: Leah sleeping in The US Muir on the way to the USA, 1949.

BOOK II

KUZMINO CHRONICLES OF GITTEL MOSKOWITZ

1

CHILDHOOD IN KUZMINO

I was born in Kuzmino on March 12, 1929. My name then was Gizella, Gittel in Yiddish. We were a family of eight kids. I was the second oldest child. My Grandmother was living with us. My older sister was older by one or two years. Her name was Leah. The third child, born after me, was my sister Shoshanna.

The fourth child was my sister Raizel. She died at the age of eight. One day she got up and was supposed to go to school. She had a headache, she then started getting sick. She lay in bed she didn't get up. They called a doctor. She couldn't get up. He came to the house. The doctor said: "She has meningitis. Even if she survives she would be either blind or deaf".

He gave her some useless medicine. She lay in bed and was kind of in coma with her eyes closed. The Doctor said: "It doesn't look good, I can come again but it wouldn't help you".

We gave her a bar of chocolate she threw it up. She started groping, and said "I can't see". She died within two weeks. My Mother was heartbroken. They made a funeral in the house. My parents didn't want the kids to see it, so they sent us away to a neighbor. She was buried in the cemetery, walking distance from our house.

The next and fifth child was my sister Pearela (Pearl). The sixth child was a boy, Wolf. My father's father was called Moshe Wolf. Because he was alive they couldn't give him that same name; we don't name children after people who are alive. Because my mother's father was Schmiel Moishe, and he too was alive, they couldn't give him that name either. So he was just called Wolf. The seventh child was Herschie.

CHILDHOOD IN KUZMINO

The eighth child was Yankel, the youngest. He was three years old when we left home.

My mother's name was Chana. Her maiden name was Itzcovitz. My father's name was Yisrael Bear (Berko). My father's mother lived with us and her name was Liba. My mother's mother name was Sara, and my mother's father's name was Schmiel Moishe. They were both alive when we were taken away. My mother had seven siblings who were all alive when we were taken away. None survived (more details below).

My father had two brothers, also alive. One was in the United States, his name was Abie Moskowitz. The other was Michal; he lived near Seredna (more details later). *My father also had a sister in the United States her name was Rivka. She died in the United States and had two daughters whose names were Chazie Gillete and Florence Kagan. They got together and sent me the papers and tickets to come on The Queen Mary from England to the US.*

KUZMINO CHRONICLES

Three out of my four grandparents were alive when I was growing up. We used to visit them. My mother's parents lived in Orliva (an hour's walk from us). They had a big house. They were horse breeders, and he had a lot of real estate; fields which produced corn, wheat, potatoes. My grandfather had a long white beard. He was very religious.

My grandmother, she was very good looking. She was bent over because she had a broken back. She had twelve children, with two sets of twins. Four didn't make it.

The other grandparents on my father's side lived in Kuzmino. My grandfather died at the age of sixty five before I was born. They told him you need surgery. He said "No thanks I lived long enough".

My grandmother (paternal) had problems with her stomach all her life. She couldn't eat heavy stuff. If she ate kugel she used to faint. She lived to eighty two. She looked like a hundred. She was short. She died a month before Purim before we were taken away.

CHILDHOOD IN KUZMINO

We lived in an average house. We had two big gardens. We first had one garden, and then my father bought another garden at the other end for an investment. We had all kinds of fruit, cherry trees, nut trees, apples, pears, plums.

We had a stable with four to five cows. We had a lot of milk. We didn't need so much, so you sold milk whatever we didn't need. We had chickens and geese. The chicken laid eggs. We had more than enough. We had a vineyard, and we made wine, not much. It was a nice life, no one complained.

We woke up at eight in the morning and you walked to school. Leib, my future husband (I didn't know that at the time) lived across the street from the school. That was a public school. There was a shortcut we could go, but not during winter because it was icy. I didn't go to Jewish school. My father hired a tutor to come once a week to teach us the Aleph Beit (Hebrew alphabet: ABC's)*, to read the brauches* (blessings)*, the Shema* (prayers)*. They would teach us to remember it all by heart.*

Public school, I liked to go to school. I was the teacher's pet. My teacher had a boyfriend. I was the courier. I walked over to give him notes, and he gave me notes to give to her. The boyfriend was another teacher, a Ukrainian who was a big anti-Semite. He married her at the end. He was the one who taught my husband. The principal and wife were also teaching. They taught up to fourth/fifth grade. School went up to eighth grade. I was a good student. A lot of children came to my house for me to help them with the homework.

I remember kids came to my house and asked "Do you want to play?" I couldn't go because I had chores and had to help take care of the younger kids.

My parents weren't poor. They sold nuts and grapes and plums. We used to get along. My older sister Leah whenever she was told to do something she did everything in the house. When Shoshanna was asked to do anything she said someone else should do it. She was very good looking. She was rebellious.

CHILDHOOD IN KUZMINO

After five girls we had a boy. They were very protective of the boys. If they had a cold they put shawls around their neck. My mother's father had a lot of seforim (holy books). *He sat and learned a lot. He didn't have to work physically.*

My father in winter did tailoring, like a hobby, but he was paid. He was a businessman; He sold and bought fields. Some of the fields he liked he kept. He sold fruits from the garden. If they weren't productive he sold him. He once bought a big field to have grass to feed animals. During summer grass was cut for hay and feeding animals. He held onto that field. He hired a non-Jew to cut the grass when it was tall, it had to be dried. He gave him a percentage to take care of it. He hired more people as he went along (as the need arose). *Wheat and corn had to be picked. When you needed it, you hired. Also we had potatoes in the field. People came to buy stuff from the fields.*

My father's father bought three townhouses. He had four sons. One was in the United States, Abie Moskowitz. Abie had two sons. They both changed their last names; each chose a different name. One changed his name to Moore, and the other to Merrill. He named himself after a famous opera singer (Robert Merrill). *My grandfather's three other sons; one lived in Seredna, his name was Yankel. His son Bumie survived* (more details later). *Another son lived in Kamarovitz near Seredna, his name was Michal. Michal and his wife perished. Michal had two daughters who survived, Anna and Lilly. Anna lived in Arizona, and Lilly lived in New Jersey. My father was the youngest son. My grandmother lived with us.*

My grandfather's three townhouses were in Seredna. One he gave to Yankel, he lived in it. The other he gave to Michal, he rented it out, and the third one was also rented, and both Michal and Yankel shared that rent. My grandfather dealt in real estate. He also had properties in Kuzmino. He bought the townhouse in Seredna for his other sons who didn't live in Kuzmino because he didn't want them to have a claim on anything in Kuzmino. What was theirs was in Seredna. In Kuzmino whatever real estate there was went to my father which included the house we lived in, three gardens with vegetables and fruit, and fields. There were between five to ten fields. My father bought even more fields, gardens and properties after my grandfather died; he added on. My grandfather left most things with my father, because he and my grandmother lived with us. The other children didn't live in Kuzmino.

During winter everything closed. We had to feed the cows. My father did tailoring during the winter. He made a minor living from that.

In winter the nights were long, so my father liked to play cards once a week with his buddies from shul. They all played. He also played with Leib's father. There were all of twenty Jewish families in Kuzmino. We all knew each other. Usually Saturday or Sunday night the men got together and played cards for money.

My mother didn't like my father to go and play cards; she thought it was gambling. One night he came home late from playing cards. He didn't have a key to the house, so he keeps knocking and knocking on the door, and my mother didn't open the door. She didn't want to let him in, she wanted to punish him. So he had to sleep in the stable with the animals that night.

My mother was a good swimmer. She took us to the river. We were scared to swim. All the little kids where my mother was born were living near a river; they were great swimmers. She also was a professional horse rider. When she grew up she had horses. They were horse breeders. My grandfather had steady workers. They used to shine the horses, clean them and feed them.

Someone in the United States told me what a good horse rider my mother was. I never saw her ride a horse. This person told me she was riding horses like a big shot. My mother was one of identical twins. Her twin's name was Ruchel. They looked like one. I couldn't tell a difference. Ruchel's husband survived. He lived to a hundred years old in Israel in Sanhedria. His name was Yehuda Leib Haberman. He remarried, he had two girls. One son survived from Ruchel, and seven other children perished. The name of the son who survived is Menachem Haberman. He lives in Israel. He is now in his eighties. He has three children. We met him in Israel, and he calls me once in a while. He lost his wife and moved. He has an apartment in assisted living. It cost him a million shekels.

My mother's siblings, not one of them survived. Her brothers were Shmuel Itzcovitz, Shea Itzcovitz, Yankel Itzcovitz, and Aaron Itzcovitz. Yankel was married to Tovy. They had many children. I don't know how many, what their names were, or how many were girls or boys. They all perished. Aaron was married. His wife and daughter also perished. In addition to my mother's identical twin sister Ruchel, she had two other sisters, Feiga and Dvora. Feiga was engaged to be married. Dvora was married and had many children, I don't know how many, what their names were, or how many were girls or boys. Her husband and all their children perished also.

My father's brother Yankel Moskowitz didn't survive. Neither did his wife Feiga, or their son

Shloyme Moskowitz. His son Bumie survived. Bumie also had two sisters who survived; Getu and Petyu, one is in Florida and one is in Michigan

2

ROUNDUP BY HUNGARIAN POLICE

A day after Pesach (Passover), we had no bread yet, it was a Sunday. They knock on the door, the Hungarian police (Gendermen in Hungarian) say "Get yourself ready, within an hour take whatever you need and come to the following address- to the house across the street".

When they gave us an hour my father took our jewelry and valuables, and buried it underneath his sewing machine in a big five pound jar. He took all the jewelry, and told all the children "Watch where it is". He took away the sewing machine, he dug a hole underneath the sewing machine, and he put jewelry in the ground, and covered it and put the machine on top. We didn't have a bank in Kuzmino. My father used to deposit money in a Munkatch bank. The bank books, he hid them by putting them under the rafters of the wooden ceiling.

There was a very big yard. All of Kuzmino Jews gathered in the yard. We were all scared. The neighbors, goyim came. They asked "Can I have this of yours? Your watches and this...? Where you're going you won't need it anymore".

We thought they were the best neighbors to us. Our neighbors used to baby sit, and even spoke Yiddish. We knew where we were going a little. They knew better. They were very mean to us now.

Then they took us to Kalnick for a night or two. They took us to Kalnick by horse carriage. There were many horse carriages. Everyone went into the horse carriage, no one walked. Old people were in wagons. We stayed in Kalnick for a day, in a school yard. The next day with horse carriage they took us to a ghetto in Munkatch.

ROUNDUP BY HUNGARIAN POLICE

There was a brick factory there, a big building and big yard. We were sleeping on the floors, there were no beds. There was a kitchen. I guess they fed us I don't remember. People were sitting and crying. We were guarded by the Gestapo black shirts. First they told us you're going to a farm in Germany, and you'll work. The children will go to school there. We already knew that wasn't true. They tried to calm people down. No body already believed a word they said.

After being in the ghetto for about four weeks, then they load you into the cattle trains. There were no windows. They packed us in like herring; very crowded you couldn't lay down. There were more than eighty people in one car. There was nothing but screaming and crying the whole journey. They stopped for a while, and said we're going here in the middle of the road somewhere. They were talking on a loudspeaker. They stopped once, and then went to Auschwitz.

3

AUSCHWITZ

We arrived at Auschwitz. The doors open, there were all the SS men. Mengele was there. "Everybody go out". Everyone went out. People from Poland (Jews) in striped suits were there. They were there for three to five years, and they spoke to you in Yiddish.

My mother was with little kids. My younger sister Shoshanna was holding a baby. There were two sides. The ones they wanted to keep (not cremate) the women said you go have a haircut. I was with my sister Leah, and we both went for a haircut. Shoshanna was holding our younger brother, the kids were crying and screaming, and they were holding on to somebody. My

AUSCHWITZ

mother had a baby. My mother and Shoshanna with kids were asked to go there. I later found out that this line was for people to be taken to the gas chambers.

We left them standing. We went to the left. Me and Leah went to the barber. They shaved our heads. I said "oy vey" and we were crying. They give you one dress like a night gown with a string, and then they give you shmatta shoes. The string was a belt. My sister went to a different room, and I was in a different room. When I came out I called "Leah… Leah" and I never saw her.

They put Leah in a different block. I was in that block for six weeks in Auschwitz. We did nothing. There were twelve to a bed; we had one blanket, when one turned twelve people turned. Eating; they give us a piece of bread during lunchtime. It was the size of a brick cut in four. They gave us one square of margarine, a spoon of jam, and a quarter black bread.

In the morning there was something for breakfast. At night in red bowls they gave us spinach. No one ate it. It was so hot and there were flies buzzing around it. It was so hot in Poland. We used to line up five in a row to be counted for tzellappel (roll call). They had a count once a day. Women were separate from men. We were in Birkinau Auschwitz- A Lager, where the crematoria were, and men were in B Lager.

My block was number 13. We were the second block from the crematoria. My sister was in number 19, next block to me, and for six weeks I didn't see her. That block where my sister was, wasn't tattooed. I was tattooed. She wasn't tattooed because they intended to ship her out. I was tattooed because I was going to stay.

My sister when I saw her, I somehow bumped into her, and she said "I have rice for supper", I said "you're lucky". She used to send me once or twice a half a helping of rice. One week later my sister's block got sent out at night. I don't know where. That was the last time I heard about her.

The Jewish Polish women who tattooed us, the people who worked there said if you're not 18 years old they won't keep you. They said to us "We'll put down you are 18". Everyone was put down as being eighteen.

We were tattooed six weeks after we arrived; the ones that they decided would stay in Auschwitz. We didn't know what the crematorium was. At night we could smell a burning smell. Once we went for lunch, we were all pushing each other to get food. The Blochelder (the female Jewish Block supervisor) said "You know you are behaving like animals". First when we arrived they told us they're burning clothes there. Then this Blochelder told us "Your parents and family went into that chimney". So we stopped pushing, and we didn't want lunch that day.

At night it was like hell; the whole sky was red. They were burning only at night. It smelled like burning smoke. At night you saw flame coming through the chimney; it lit up the sky, it looked like hell. We thought we would be next, we never thought we would survive.

We sat in a chair to get tattooed; it hurt each needle. My number was A-7973. We were the first ones, when they ran out of numbers they started with B. The Jewish Polish women's job was to do that. Before they tattooed us they counted us by block number. When we had a number they still counted by block.

While you were tattooed they took down information which included name, number, where you were born, age. They told us all you better be 18, and they wrote it down. They were writing with a pen on paper. No one was typing anything.

I was there from May for about six months (until November). One day some people heard shooting. It must have been Russians. We said maybe they'll shoot us instead of cremate us. Once a day we lined up to go to the bathroom. There was one big bathroom. No one needed to go to the bathroom. We were walking around inside we did nothing. We had no jobs.

If someone got burned skin, they took them away. Anyone was sick was taken away. A lot of people died. We saw on the side they lined up corpses up on top of each other, they looked like wood.

Towards the end of my stay, workers sabotaged the crematorium. They put in an explosion, the crematoria stopped working. They had to ship people to other crematoria. My father worked in the crematorium. I never told this to anyone before. He sent me a letter towards the beginning; he said "Try to leave Auschwitz, you must be strong". I wrote back, and said Leah already left. He wrote back (secretly delivered - see below) and said "Try and get out like Leah".

There were a group of girls, they were wearing white kerchiefs that showed they were working with clothes, whose job was sorting schmattas and looking for gold. They had a job; they took piles of clothes near the train left by each new arrival, and the clothes were sorted by them and then they were sent to Germany. They were looking for jewelry, money and gold in the clothing.

There were about twenty five girls working at this job. One of the girls, we went to school together. Her name was Irene Feldman, she survived. She said *"Your father, and the whole area are working in the crematoria, putting the bodies in the crematorium". She was the one who conveyed letters between me and my father. We wrote to each other in Yiddish (*transliterated using Latin letters*).*

The same area from our transport, all the men went there and worked in the crematoria. My transport came from Munkatch, Kalnick, Kuzmino, Rekutjen, Kadonov, and other little villages. From our transfer they gave the men work in the crematoria. They were talking to the women and said that they worked there for a couple of weeks and they knew they would be put in the crematoria.

They were privileged; they gave them enough food to eat. The Germans told them they were lucky to have that job, because they got more food. Three sisters of Feldman survived.

My father's group sabotaged the crematoria. They dynamited the huge main crematoria. People were working in a munitions factory in

Auschwitz. They transported explosives to give to the crematoria workers. They dynamited the huge brick building with explosives.

After they dynamited the crematoria they tried to run away. They caught them and shot them all. My father was working there in the group, and was shot.

AUSCHWITZ-BIRKENAU: THE REVOLT AT AUSCHWITZ-BIRKENAU (OCTOBER 7, 1944)

"The Sonderkommando were Jewish prisoners who worked the death camps in return for special treatment and privileges. Every few months, the current sonderkommando was liquidated and the first task of their successors was to dispose of the bodies of the previous group. Since a sonderkommando usually comprised men from incoming transports, their second task often consisted of disposing of the bodies of their own families. The sonderkommando did not participate in the actual killing -- that was carried out by the Nazis. The sonderkommando duties included guiding the new arrivals into the gas chambers, removing the bodies afterwards, shaving hair, removing teeth, sorting through possessions (much of which they were given as reward), cremating the bodies, and disposing of the ashes. Their knowledge of the internal workings of the camp marked them for certain death. Someone selected for the sonderkommando had a choice: die then or die in four months' time.

As the time of their execution grew nearer, the members of the 12th Sonderkommando crystallized their plans of revolt and escape. Besides the gunpowder being smuggled by the women, which the men fashioned into crude grenades using sardine tins, there were some small arms that had been slipped through the fence by local partisans. In addition, knives and small axes had been made and hidden throughout the crematoria. Much of the gunpowder was used in creating demolition charges. There was talk of a general uprising that would coincide with the arrival of the approaching Soviet armies, but some sonderkommando were certain that they would not live until that day.

On October 7th, 1944, at about 3 in the afternoon, the Poles in Crematorium 1 begin the revolt.

Hungarians in Crematoria 3 and 4 join in while the sonderkommando of Crematorium 2 break through the wires of the camp. An especially sadistic Nazi guard in Crematorium 1 is disarmed and stuffed into an oven to be burned alive. Small arms fire rattles from the second floor of the crematoria until the Germans bring in heavy machine guns and riddle the wooden roof.

The guards counterattack and penetrate the buildings, indiscriminately shooting at all prisoners they encounter. The sonderkommando in Crematorium 4 drag their demolition charges into the oven rooms and detonate them in a defiant suicide. The revolt is quickly suppressed and the escaped men recaptured with the help of local citizens. Approximately 200 sonderkommando are forced to lie face down outside the crematoria where they are executed with single shots to the back of the head. Some of the men are spared for interrogation, but the bodies of the 12th Sonderkommando are soon disposed of by the 13th Sonderkommando.

The men give up names, including those of some women who were engaged in smuggling gunpowder. Despite months of beatings and rape and electric shocks to their genitals, the only names given up by the women are those of already dead sonderkommando.

On January 5, 1945, the four women are hanged in front of the assembled women's camp. Roza Robota shouts "Be strong and be brave" as the trap door drops.

Crematorium 4 was damaged beyond repair and never used again. On November 7th, 1944, the Nazis destroyed the gas chambers to hide their crimes. Twelve days after the hanging of the four women, the camp personnel forced 56,000 prisoners on a Death March into what remained of the Third Reich; 7,500 prisoners left behind were liberated by advancing Soviet armies on January 27th" (From: The Jewish Virtual Library: https://www.jewishvirtuallibrary.org/jsource/Holocaust/aurevolt.html).

Before we were taken away my father was in forced labor camp (Hungarian), and then he came home a year before from forced labor. He was taken to forced labor (Munkotabor) in 1942. We had a neighbor Sruel Beahr. They took him away, he had a little boy, his wife was pregnant, and they didn't have Hungarian papers. My father was in forced labor and saw him in Poland. They said your family is home. My father found out what they did to him. They took him in Poland made him dig his own grave, and they shot him.

The captain of my father's labor group said "You do what you want I have orders to leave you here". They begged him "Take us over the border to Hungary". His group walked from Poland, they walked for days and there they let them go. He was in forced labor from 1940-1942. He was home for two years before we were taken away. Everyone was envious of us that he came home. He was lucky that the captain was a good guy and escorted them home. They were digging trenches in slave labor. In slave labor we never had any communication with him.

One night he came home, he knocked on the door. She opened the door, my mother, and she thought she saw a ghost. I loved my father. He was charismatic and a joker. When my father wasn't home it was like Tisha B'ov, and when he was home, a lot of people came, even goyim. A rich guy came, brought him news. They called my father Berko.

"You know Berko" he said (years before we were taken away) "I hear they collect Jews and they send them to Germany. You have expensive watches; maybe I can keep them for you".

This man had cancer, and my father joked back and said "I don't think you'll need it either by the time they take us".

Nobody believed a thing like this could happen. Chaym Leib came with stories, no one believed him. The day before they took us, on Shabbas, Chaym Leib in Shul said "You know in Seredna they're already taking the Jews away". They didn't believe him.

After the crematoria was bombed we stayed for a few more weeks. They said we're leaving Auschwitz. They count us at tzellappel; we go to

AUSCHWITZ

an open field. There is a river. Across the river is standing a train. There was a plank across the river. They told us to walk the plank to get on the train to go to Germany. I was thinking they were going to pull the plank from under us; it was for one person at a time.

4

RAVENSBRÜCK

The whole block went into the train (hundreds). We went to Ravensbruck, we were there for a week, the place wasn't ready, they gave us food, a whole brick of bread while we were leaving Auschwitz. That was a suburb of Berlin. There was a big tent; it looked like a circus tent. There was nothing but dirt on the floor. We stayed there for a week. I had a bread brick. I lied down on the dirt. I take the brick of bread under my head like a pillow; in the morning my brick is gone. They fed us nothing. We went outside. When it was raining we drank water from the edges of the tent roof. They gave us another quarter of bread. I ate that one before I laid down.

RAVENSBRÜCK

"The Ravensbrück concentration camp was the largest concentration camp for women in the German Reich. In the concentration camp system, Ravensbrück was second in size only to the women's camp in Auschwitz-Birkenau. German authorities began construction of the camp in November 1938, at a site near the village of Ravensbrück in northern Germany, about 50 miles north of Berlin. In January 1945, the camp had more than 50,000 prisoners, mostly women.

The inmates came from over 30 countries. The greatest numbers came from Poland (36%), Soviet Union (21%), the German Reich (18%, includes Austria), Hungary (8%), France (6%), Czechoslovakia (3%), the Benelux countries (2%), and Yugoslavia (2%)...

Aside from the male SS administrators, the camp staff included only female guards assigned to oversee the prisoners. These female guards were not members of the SS, but were members of the so-called 'female civilian employees of the SS' (weiblichen SS-Gefolges). The main camp contained 18 barracks; By January 1945 the barracks were horribly overcrowded. This overcrowding, aggravated by abominable sanitary conditions, resulted in a typhus epidemic that spread throughout the camp. In early 1945, the SS constructed a gas chamber in Ravensbrück near the camp crematorium. The Germans gassed between 5,000 and 6,000 prisoners at Ravensbrück before Soviet troops liberated the camp in April 1945...

RAVENSBRÜCK SUBCAMPS

The SS required Ravensbrück prisoners to perform forced labor, primarily in agricultural projects and local industry. By 1944, Germany increasingly relied on forced labor for the production of armaments. Ravensbrück became the administrative center of a system of over 40 subcamps with over 70,000 predominantly female prisoners.

These subcamps, many of which were established adjacent to armaments factories, were located throughout the so-called Greater German Reich, from Austria in the south to the Baltic Sea in the north. Several subcamps also provided prisoner labor for construction projects or clearing rubble in cities damaged by Allied air attacks. The SS also built several factories near Ravensbrück for the production of textiles and electrical components. The largest subcamps, which held over 1,000 prisoners, included Rechlin/Retzow, Malchow, Grüneberg, Neubrandenburg, Karlshagen I, Barth, Leipzig-Schönefeld, Magdeburg, Altenburg and Neustadt-Glewe"

(from: The United States Holocaust Museum, Holocaust Encyclopedia :http://www.ushmm.org/wlc/en/article.php?ModuleId=10005199).

One week later we went to Malchow.

5

Malchow

They kept saying Malchow is made for a thousand people. It was built for German soldiers. But they didn't come there anymore; it was coming towards the end.

In Malchow the camp was more human. They had bunk beds, blankets and pillows. There were two to a bunk. I had the bottom. There they gave us jackets and skirts, and a red cross on the back of the jacket that signified you were in a camp; you couldn't run away because you had paint on you. There they had twelve hour shifts day and night. So many people daytime from a week, then they alternated, the next week you had the other shift. They gave us wooden shoes like clogs. When you walked in the thick snow you got stuck. One soldier was nice and said shake off your shoes, be careful of the snow. If you couldn't walk they shot you on the spot, in the meantime he said be careful.

Every day we walked in the snow from Malchow to a munitions factory. It was a three quarters of an hour walk through the snow during winter. The factory was underground. You walk into a cave in the forest. The entrance looked like a cave under the trees. No one would dream there was a munitions factory there. There was an entrance that looked like a door, the rest was forest. The enemy only saw a forest.

We went into the entrance and there was large factory. Everyone was assigned to do work. In the munitions factory there were bullets. Some girls were lucky, they got an easy job; they were sitting at a table, and putting bullets into boxes like chocolates. I had it harder. I had to stand, there was a big wheel and an oven. The bullets were made out of powder. I put the powder for bullets into the oven. I had a wheel and I had to press the bullets. There was a wheel with numbers. I had to turn the wheel to a hundred (degrees), the temperature. When you reached a hundred it was done. It was dangerous. If you went above hundred it would explode and shoot out. It never exploded. They explained it. Other people packed it, took it out. Once the bullets were ready, other people put it in boxes. This was an assembly line.

First step: measure the powder and put in the tray, and partition it. The second step, put it in the oven (not me), the third step was turning wheel, and the fourth step was taking out the bullets and packing them.

Most people lived. You had a decent bed; twenty people at a time went for a shower. In the kitchen you had soup with potato peels and a table like a park with benches and chairs. They gave you bread.

"Malchow concentration camp was one of the numerous sub-camps of Nazi concentration camp: Ravensbrück, located in Germany, which is believed to be first opened in the winter of 1943. It was located in Malchow, in Mecklenburg.

The Malchow camp system consisted of ten barracks on the terrain of the Ravensbrück concentration camp, which each had the capacity to house about 100 women. This meant that the Malchow camp was able to house 1,000 women prisoners. But, by 1945, the camp population had grown to 5,000 women. In the summer of 1943, the camp terrain finally became enclosed by a high fence. The ten barracks that were part of the camp, which was originally used for the construction workers of Ravensbrück, were enclosed by this fence.

Day-to-day conditions in the camp were almost unbearable. The prisoners were forced out of their will to stand at attention for roll call, twice a day, like most regular concentration camp prisoners would have to do. The prisoners were guarded under the watchful eyes of the Schutzstaffel (SS) female guards and their German Shepherd Dogs. The SS were very cruel, but probably one of the harshest female guards at Malchow was the SS wardress by the name of Luise Danz. She was transferred from the main camp of Ravensbrück to Malchow and became commandant of the camp. While stationed at Malchow, she killed a young girl by violently stomping on her.

In Malchow, the prisoners barely received anything to eat and were forced to kneel on sharp gravel stones. Body searches and beatings were routine at Malchow. Although residents of the town of Malchow were not allowed to have any contact with the prisoners of the camp, some townspeople provided the inmates with supplies of food. When they were discovered by the SS, they too were imprisoned in Malchow. Aside from starvation and exhaustion, many prisoners also died during many epidemics of diseases such as tuberculosis and typhus. Some types of forced labor that the prisoners had to do were producing mines, collecting nettles from children's playgrounds, cleaning the factory and town, building canals for the hospital of Malchow, and doing horticultural work.

During 1944, when most of the death marches were taking place across Europe, Malchow served as a transit camp for other prisoners arriving from other concentration camps. Eyewitness reports of many Malchow survivors say that a transport of about 1,000 concentration camp prisoners arrived at the camp on 24 November 1944. They had traveled on a death march for several weeks. There, at Malchow, they were brought to Wismar, and placed on barges that were sunk in the Baltic Sea or a nearby river".

(From: http://en.wikipedia.org/wiki/Malchow_concentration_camp)

6

LIBERATION

One week before liberation, we get no food at all. The Germans started to leave, no one told us. Somebody told me behind the kitchen near a shack there are a lot of potato peels, let's go for potato peels. I walked out of the kitchen and looked out; it was looking like it was raining fire. I look up its like red rain.

We were hiding in the shack next to the kitchen with three other women. Women were running from the kitchen. They found us in the shack and said you could have gotten killed.

The German soldiers were shooting at us because we weren't supposed to go there. The

LIBERATION

only thing that saved us were Jewish women coming out of the kitchen, and walked out and they asked the soldiers, and said stop. They said somebody is looking for potato peels don't shoot. We didn't get potato peels, we didn't need potato peels any more.

That was a week before liberation. We worked and worked. One morning women came in yelling and saying the gates are open. They said maybe nobody should go to the gate; they might shoot us, until further notice. Then they said the German soldiers are not there. We then saw German soldiers with white bands with their arms up. Those were American soldiers. They started giving us spam, crackers. I ate a can and I got very sick. I was in the bathroom night and day for two weeks I thought I would die.

Americans start asking "Where you come from where do you want to go?" We told them we were from Munkatch, I thought my sister Leah survived. I knew the others were dead. They had interpreters. I wanted to go back home.

They said it's now Russia. Then we left there and we had to go to the Russian department. They put us on a train somewhere to go to a Russian village. It took a few hours. We went to a Russian village there was a factory. One person got typhus, and they quarantined the whole place for six months. I stayed there for 6 months in quarantine. We did nothing we hung out. Once they took us out to go shopping.

Here at night, some Russian soldiers came with a flashlight to every bed and they shined a light in our faces. They went to each girl. They shined a light in each face and said, "No not this one, no not this one". One woman was fat (not emaciated) her name was Leah from Ungvar. They took her away they said you come with us. They kept her for two days they all raped her there, she said when she returned "Well that was no picnic".

They said to the skinny ones "No good, no good". I was very skinny. I was 75 pounds. I looked at my legs. They looked like tree branches. I was completely emaciated.

LIBERATION

They schlepped us from Russian town to town. The quarantine lifted. And they said "Where do you want to go?"

"I want to go to Munkatch".

I was hoping Leah would survive. I found a teacher in the market place and I recognized him. I said "You were my teacher". He didn't recognize me. I looked very different.

I asked if I could get a ride to Kuzmino, he was living in Kuzmino. He had a wagon. He took me to Kuzmino. I stayed there for one to two days.

7

Return to Kuzmino

I went to my house, and I see a light is on, and I say gee maybe someone survived. I opened the door. My next door neighbor is in there living there. I knocked on the door. The door opened up, she said "Are you a ghost?" (In Russian ... I was speaking Ukrainian at the time).

I said nothing. She tells me a Jew is living here; Menachem's son, Avrum Feldman. I went to his house, and knocked on the door I said "Can I stay here a night or two?" Avrum said if you want to go someplace "Go to Seredna, a lot of Jews are going there".

I walked to Seredna and met my cousin Bumie. Bumie got married and was on a honeymoon. I don't know where I want to go. I wanted to go to Ungvar because the borders were closed between Czechoslovakia and Ukraine. I went to Ungvar. Someone told me to get there you had to pay them and bribe them to cross border. In Ungvar he said someone is there. My twin mother's sister's husband, Haberman is in the area. I met him, he was nice. He said "Stay in my house as long as you want".

I wanted to go to Czechoslovakia. In order to go to Czech I needed bribe money to smuggle across the border. If you have a table or something in your house can you sell anything. I went to Kuzmino. I sold the roof tiles of my house (like Spanish tile) I sold it for 200 Cronin. I went back and went to Seredna. Bumie says I'd like to go but my wife doesn't wasn't to go. Bumie had a business making tailoring. He was very talented making patterns.

When I was in Kuzmino I had other friends. Phyllis Diamond wanted to go to Czechoslovakia. Phyllis and Seymour came with me to Ungvar. They bought a ticket to get off at Chop. You walk across the forest through the border.

We went to go from Ungvar to Czech across the border. It's closed. One guy knew a way. If you walk through forest you can go. We took a train from Ungvar to Chop. From there we walked a whole night through the forest. Seymour sat down and said I can't walk anymore. He had tickets to go to Prague. They have societies that help you and everything. He got up, he had the tickets for the three of us to go to Prague. We crossed the border in the morning. We see a house with a light. We go looking for a train. We walked. Then we found out Seymour lost the tickets. The conductor said "Oh you come from the camps form Germany?"

"Yeah".

He said "Ok hop on. You want to go to Prague ok, but don't tell anybody anything".

We get to Prague. Phyllis had a brother in Zatec.

She says "You know who is in Zatec? Mrs. Moskowitz and her son Leib".

We came to Prague. The Jewish society in Prague said England is willing to take in 100 kids under 17 who are orphans. I registered for that. Phyllis said we have Mrs. Moskowitz. We went there to meet Mrs. Moskowitz. There was David Mermelstein who had a son who survived; he was 22. He wanted to marry me. I said I want to go to England.

"Why should you go?" He asked.

"I want to go to England because they would rehabilitate you, they said they will send you to school".

In Zatec the police came on a complaint registered. We made so much noise; they took us to the police station. They said we're going to send you back to Russia. David said he'd get me an apartment there in Ash, but I was registered in Prague for England. They said in England it would be temporary, you could not become a British subject.

I went to Ash. I come there and David lives there. I found there a woman with a kid. He told me to come, we live in the kitchen. It's like a suite. "Well you can sleep on the couch" he said. There was a couple with a kid and they rented out the room.

"Where do I sleep? There are two men there."

"So sleep on the couch".

I slept there nobody bothered me. I had nowhere to go.

In the meantime I got a letter from Prague when I registered that I should send them two pictures for a passport to go to England. I go to a photographer.

"How long will it take?" I ask the photographer.

"Two weeks".

They said the transport is leaving in one week. I couldn't go because my pictures weren't ready. So my friend Goldie took my spot. Goldie was my best friend then, and remains my best friend today. Her married name is Schwartz.

They sent me another letter two to three days later and said "You can leave without the picture. Come, we'll fix you up with a photo in Prague".

They took a picture in Prague. It was a Shabbas night. David wasn't home. He was selling cigarettes in Germany, he was smuggling. I told David "I'm going to Prague". David said "Didn't you have enough of the camps?"

Shabbas night I take a train to Prague. I met a guy and he said "If you want to go come with me. A young girl shouldn't go on a train by herself". He was right there were a lot of Russian soldiers.

I went with him. He said "You're smart to go, there's nothing for you here".

I went to Prague; from there I went on February 1946 on kindertransport.

8

KINDERTRANSPORT TO UNITED KINGDOM AND ARRIVAL TO UNITED STATES

We took a plane, fifty people on a plane and landed in Northern Ireland. (See Figures 1-4 documenting stay in Belfast and England). From there a Jewish organization started feeding you, and students were teaching us Hebrew and English. We stayed there for six months. While I was there another survivor, a girl who was skilled, asked me if I wanted a dress. Her name was Miriam. I don't know her last name. She made me a dress out of a checkered blanket cover.

It was like a farm with rooms built up especially for that. The plane, there were no seats; it was like a cargo plane. They gave us a salami sandwich. They gave you a bag to vomit in.

They taught us about Shabbas and Friday night. At that point we forgot about everything (Jewish). We didn't care traveling on Shabbas or not.

After six months we went to Manchester. In Manchester we had a furnished room with four girls in a private house. They told us every day you have to help us with the dishes. They were yekkes (German Jews). *From there we went to Burnly. There they sent us to school to Burnly community college. We stayed by another family, we went to school, and then they took us to a hostel (fifty girls and fifty boys). They kept shifting us all the time. Four girls and me went to Burnly College.*

UNRRA (United Nations Relief and Rehabilitation Administration) took care of us and it was like a Jewish agency. We had a hostel mother taking care of the girls. Every Friday night we got a bar of chocolate. We waited every Friday night for a bar of chocolate. From there they said we cannot stay there too long in England. We have to go to Israel or the United states. A few people went to Israel, most went to America.

People used to think America is like Hollywood. They said either you continue in school or look for a job. They started looking at the school records. They wanted me to go further. I had good records. They were giving lessons to design clothes and cook. Then we went from that hostel to private families. That was the last stage in London. They rented out a room.

They show me the room. There's one double bed, there's a clothes closet, and only one person can go by. So they took me and Goldie. So me and Goldie slept in a double bed for a while.

I said I didn't want to go to school. I wanted a job.

They took us to a factory in London. They told me make a hem, and I didn't do well, so I learned to sew on a machine, I worked there for a while, and I made a few dollars.

In the meantime they said "Do you have relatives in the US? You can never get citizenship in the UK".

"I have an Uncle Abie Moskowitz in the United States".

They tried looking him up in the phone book in NY. There are dozens of Abie Mosowitz' listed.

"We need his address."

Then I remembered the name of my aunt Rose Sprung. I remembered (from when I was young) her address was near Langhorne Pennsylvania. I remember she wrote to my father. She came once a year by boat to visit my grandmother. I gave her address. It said "PA" so I figure it was Pennsylvania. I write in the letter I'm a survivor and my father is so and so, and I said I'm here I'd like to come to the United States if possible.

Within a few weeks they wrote back, and said unfortunately your aunt is no longer here. Her two daughters wrote back and said we'll try to get you here if you want to come, well try to get you here to the United States.

Meantime I had to get someone to prepare papers, and information. I had to get a visa. It took me four years (See Figures 5 and 6 for Visa and Immunization records) *because the US had a quota how many people to take in. I was told that the people in German DP camps were more important and had priority over people in England because we're not suffering as much as them.*

It took four years. They sent me a visa. Meantime a daughter said she has a jewelry business, I could work for her. Every month she sent me a dollar in an envelope (she was married to a goy); the other sister was Florence Kagan. I went through the whole rigmarole; TB test, blood tests, they sent me the visa, and then the two sisters sent me a ticket to come there by boat. It cost $240. Finally I got there right before

Rosh Hashanah 1950. The name of the boat was Queen Mary. I land in New York.

The sisters pick me up. I was sick for five days. I always get motion sickness. They take me to their house in Carney, New Jersey. She had a big house. She said my daughter goes to school; she didn't want me to disturb her daughter or sleep in her daughter's room. She was scared I had a disease. They put a little couch out in the foyer for me to sleep on. I wasn't too happy. Goldie came after me to the USA.

The sisters told me "You know you have to talk to your uncle Abie".

"I don't have his address" I answered.

"Well, I do, and it's about time he does something for you".

They put me on a bus (I spoke English). They told me the number bus to take; they said get off at Port of Authority.

I got up there. I met my uncle. He took me to his apartment. He had borders there. He was in the pocketbook business. I slept there one or two nights.

He said "Let's look for a room for you". We looked for a room. I found a furnished room.

Somebody tells me Mrs. Moskowitz and her son Leib are here. He gave me five dollars the first week to pay for the room. I had $20 on me.

I wrote a letter to Goldie. I said "I'll take a boat back to England. They're finished with me here".

I had to look for a job. I told the woman where I lived that I could sew on a machine.

I take a subway, I go to 37th street and I look for a job. I looked in the newspapers they advertised 'operators needed'.

I went there, they said "First you need to belong to a union before you start a job".

I went from one place to another. They never had a job.

Finally I found a job; he said "I'll pay you 75 cents an hour".

I made $24 a week. Five dollars I payed for the room. They took tax off. Mrs. Gross had a furnished room she was a widow, and renting it out.

She let me use her refrigerator. I got a job, I could pay my room. For food I went to an automat. You take a tray and help yourself. For breakfast I got a container of milk.

There was a bakery; every morning I bought a Danish. Lunchtime I got a cheese sandwich. I worked five days a week. A cheese sandwich was 30 cents.

I saw a sign for blintzes; it was 90 cents. They were very expensive. At night I went back to the cafeteria. I got lettuce, cottage cheese and a hardboiled egg; that was $1.20.

Goldie came here. She had two brothers and two sisters. They bought whatever she needed.

She got a job for a dollar as an operator. She said "Come out here".

I said to my boss "I need at least a dollar an hour".

"No maybe one day" he answered me.

I told the guy "I'm going somewhere else, I got a job offer for a dollar an hour".

"Why didn't you tell me I could have given you a dollar?"

So I left. I worked there for six weeks and they closed and there was no more job.

I went to meet Mrs. Moskowitz and her son. Mrs. Moskowitz is here I went to see her.

I knocked on the door. Her son Leib opened the door. I remembered the last time I saw him, he was small, he was short, my height.

Now he's six foot. I said it can't be him. She invited me over for Shabbas, and made stuffed cabbage. It reminded me of home. That was the first time I ate stuffed cabbage since I left home. I knew very few people and Mrs. Moskowitz was very nice to me. I got married to Leib one year later.

Who could imagine that anyone could survive this? When I was there (in the camps) *I was numb. I didn't care about anything. If anyone finds out that they lose their whole family, under ordinary circumstances they would go crazy. Who could take it? While I was there I felt nothing. All I cared about was if I could eat a meal, I could die happy. Later on things hit me, and you start remembering things slowly. Then you cry alone. No one wants to cry with you. You know what they say "When you laugh, people laugh with you, when you cry, you cry alone".*

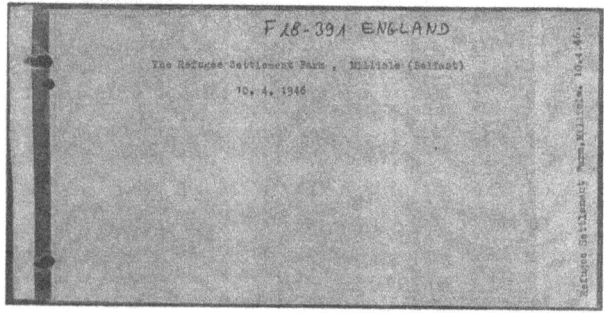

Figure 1A: Cover page of lists of 44 out of 50 people admitted to the Refugee Settlement Farm in Millisle (Belfast) dated April 10, 1946.

KINDERTRANSPORT TO UNITED KINGDOM...

```
                    F 18-391
         THE REFUGEE SETTLEMENT FARM.      3 4
   Phone Millisle 46.                      MILLISLE
                                            (BELFAST)

Name:                     Place of Birth and Residence  Age
MALE:-
ALTER Herman              Polana                         17
BERKOVIC Samuel           Chust                          17
BRANDSTEIN Isak           Bedtina                        17½
CRUCKER Jan               Berehovo                       15
DEUTSCH Ignac             Berehovo                       17
DEUTSCH Zoltan            Berehovo
DIAMANTSTEIN Julius       Seredne                        17
ECKSTEIN David            Brod                           17
FRIEDMANN Alexander       Svaluva        Kobice          17
FRISCHMANN Ladislac       Ushorod                        17
FRISCHMANN Vilem          Ushorod                    new 15
GRUENBERG Vilem           Majdan                         17
GRUENWALD Herman          Kivjaid                        17½
HIML Jan                  Nižni-Veracky                  17
HOFFMAN Adolf             Velki Sevlius                  17
JAKUBOVICZ Chajim Leib    Sandrovo                       17
KLEIN Tomas               Uavorod        Kobice          16
LUGER Herman              Ustčorna                       17
LUGER Mendel              Ustčorna                       15½
LUGER Salamon             Ustčorna                       17
MARKOVIC Moritz           Kopasňo                        17½
ROTHSCHILD Herman         Hamburg,Germany Kobice         17
ROZENBERG Chajim          Neli Peňo                      17½
ROZENBERG Mendel          Neli Peňo                      17½
SALAMON Tibor (Tibor)     Mukačevo                       17
SCHAECHTER David          Ubla                           17
SLOMOVIC Chaskel          Nižni-Apsa                     17
SPIEGEL Eugen             Bardejov       Mukačevo        17½
STEINMETZ Moses           Dubova                         17
FEMALE:-
BRAUNSTEINOVA Blanka      Višni-Bistra   Sevlius         17
DUBOVA Ruzena             Velki Bockov                   17
FRIGOVA Marija            Ganyce                         16
FREILICHOVA Josefa        Višna-Bistra   Chust           17
GALACOVA Zuzanna          Jasina                         16½
ICKOVICOVA Cervenka       Kivjaid                        16
ICKOVICOVA Etelka         Kivjaid                        17
JAKUBOVICOVA Zlata        Veliki Luski                   16
KLEINOVA Marija           Lince                          17
MARKOVICOVA Serena        Kopasňo                        17
MOSKOVICOVA Gizela        Kuzmina                        17
OESTERREICHEROVA Luisa    Strabicovo                     17
PERLOVA Manci             Slatinska-Doly                 17½
RESMOVICOVA Ester         Slatinska-Doly                 17
SABOVA Berta              Višni Apsa                     16½

                                            continued
```

Figure 1B: List of 44 out of 50 people admitted to The Refugee Settlement Farm in Millisle (Belfast) dated April 10, 1946 where Gizela Moskovicova is listed on the fifth line from the bottom. She is noted to be from Kuzmina, and is 17 years old.

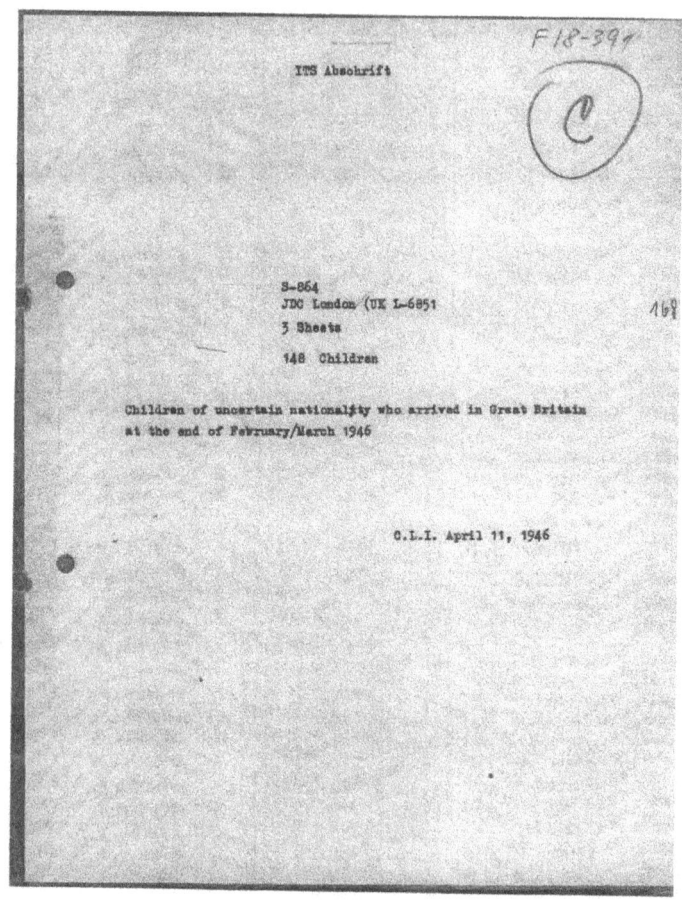

Figure 2A: Cover page of lists 148 children of uncertain nationality who arrived in Great Britain at the end of Feb /March 1946.

KINDERTRANSPORT TO UNITED KINGDOM...

```
LIST OF CHILDREN OF UNCERTAIN NATIONALITY WHO ARRIVED IN GT.BRI
              AT THE END OF FEBRUARY/MARCH 1946.
```

Name and First Name:	Birth Date :	Birth Place
Abis, Sylvia	27. 3.29	Bochov
Abraham, Ruzena	29. 1.29	Nove Klonov
Adler, Arthur	28. 8.29	Berehovo
Alter, Hermann	22.11.29	Poljana
Berkovic, Samuel	5. 8.29	Chust
Berkovic, Sipi	19. 1.29	Velky Bucko
Berman, Bela	2. 1.29	Dubrinic
Blum Julius	6. 4.30	Ushorod
Bognor, Erwin	14. 5.37	Dobrocin
Brandstein, Isak	1. 7.29	Bustina
Braunstein, Blanka	26. 6.29	Majdan
Brody, Simon	23.10.29	Michalovce
Bucci, Andrea	1939	Fiume
Bucci, Liliane	1939	Fiume
Buncel, Erwin	31. 5.31	Zila
Cziment, Aranka	28.10.29	Szuerte
Chaimovic, Fratiska	30. 9.30	Zadno
Chaimovic, Karel	19.11.31	Zadno
Czucker, Jan	7.11.31	Berehovo
Diamantstein, Julius	1. 2.29	Sorednc
Deutsch, Ignac	5. 5.29	Geca
Deutsch, Zoltan	12. 6.30	Geca
Dub, Ruzena	1. 3.29	Velky Bocko
Eckstein, David	20. 2.29	Brod
Emer, Manfred	20. 5.30	Hamborn
Ehrman, Alzbeta	12. 2.30	Csop
Farkas, Efraim	1.10.29	Horinoovo
Farkas, Jakob	30. 7.29	Slctinske
Farkas, Arnold	22. 1.37	Bratislava
Farkas, Eva	14. 1.34	Bratislava
Farkas, Salomon	4. 5.30	Bockov
Feig, Marie	10. 5.30	Genice
Fischer, Marketa	12. 4.29	Rochov
Fischer, Berta	10. 5.29	Rachov
Fischer, Cecilie	17. 7.31	Rachov
Fixler, Adolf	24. 8.30	Isko
Fried, Desider	27. 9.30	Mukacovo
Friedman, Hedvika	21. 1.31	Michalovac
Friedmann, Arnost	20.12.29	Hakasin
Friedmann, Bedrich	8. 8.39	Flosivec
Friedmann, Hedvika	20. 7.37	Flosivec
Friedmann, Alexander	22. 2.29	Svalava
Trischmann, Ladislav	16. 9.29	Ushorod
Trischmann, Vilem	27.1. 31	Ushorod
Frydmann, Simon	28.12.29	Backing

Figure 2B: List of children on the page preceding the page with Gittel.

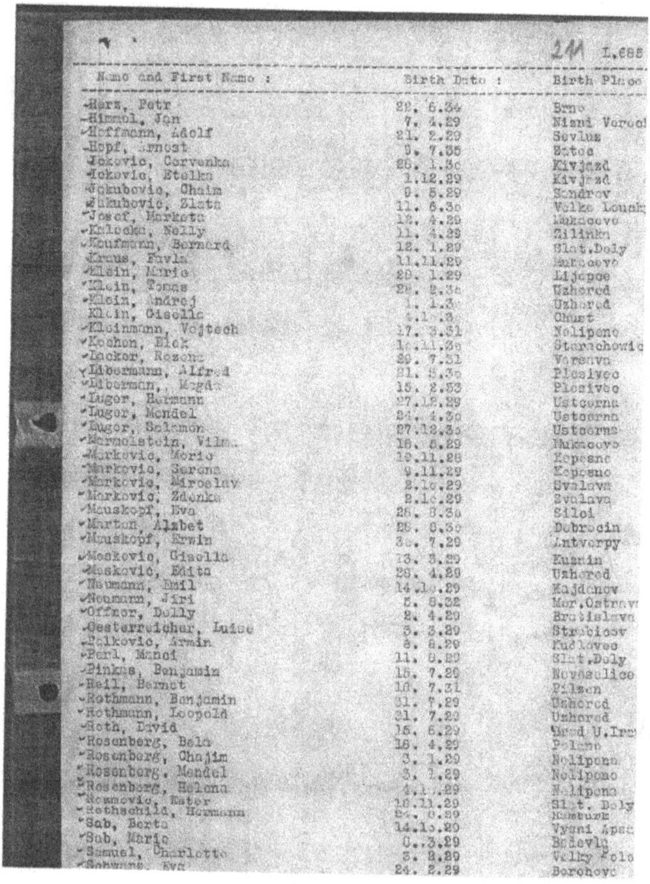

2M L.685

Name and First Name :	Birth Date :	Birth Place
Herz, Petr	22. 6.34	Brno
Himmel, Jan	7. 4.29	Nizni Verec[illegible]
Hoffmann, Adolf	21. 2.29	Sevlus
Hopf, Ernest	9. 7.35	Zatec
Jokovic, Cervenka	26. 1.3o	Kivjazd
Jokovic, Etelka	1.12.29	Kivjazd
Jakubovic, Chaim	9. 5.29	Sandrov
Jakubovic, Zlata	11. 6.3o	Velke Louck[illegible]
Josef, Marketa	12. 4.29	Mukacevo
Kalocka, Nelly	11. 4.29	Zilinka
Kaufmann, Bernard	12. 1.29	Slat.Doly
Kraus, Pavla	11.11.29	Mukacevo
Klein, Marie	29. 1.29	Lijepce
Klein, Tomas	28. 2.3o	Uzhorod
Klein, Andrej	1. 1.3[illegible]	Uzhorod
Klein, Gisella	4.1[illegible].3[illegible]	Chust
Kleinmann, Vojtech	17. 3.31	Nelipeno
Kochen, Eick	1[illegible].11.3[illegible]	Starachowic[illegible]
Lacker, Rezena	29. 7.31	Varsava
Libermann, Alfred	21. 5.3o	Plesivec
Liberman, Magda	15. 2.33	Plesivec
Luger, Hermann	27.12.29	Ustcorna
Luger, Mendel	24. 4.3o	Ustcorna
Luger, Salomon	27.12.3o	Ustcorna
Mermelstein, Vilma	16. 5.29	Mukacevo
Markovic, Maria	19.11.28	Kopesno
Markovic, Serena	9.11.29	Kopesno
Markovic, Miroslav	2.1o.29	Svalava
Markovic, Zdenka	2.1o.29	Svalava
Mauskopf, Eva	25. 8.3o	Siloi
Marton, Alzbet	28. 6.3o	Debrecin
Mauskopf, Erwin	3o. 7.29	Antverpy
Moskovic, Gisella	13. 3.29	Kuznin
Moskovic, Edita	29. 4.29	Uzhorod
Naumann, Emil	14.1o.29	Kajdanov
Neumann, Jiri	5. 8.32	Mor.Ostrav[illegible]
Offner, Dolly	2. 4.29	Bratislava
Oesterreicher, Luise	5. 3.29	Strabicov
Palkovic, Armin	8. 8.29	Kudlovec
Perl, Manci	11. 8.29	Slat.Doly
Pinkas, Benjamin	15. 7.29	Novoselice
Reil, Bernat	18. 7.31	Pilsen
Rothmann, Benjamin	31. 7.29	Uzhorod
Rothmann, Leopold	31. 7.29	Uzhorod
Roth, David	15. 6.29	Brod U.Ir[illegible]
Rosenberg, Bela	18. 4.29	Polana
Rosenberg, Chajim	3. 1.29	Nelipeno
Rosenberg, Mendel	3. 1.29	Nelipeno
Rosenberg, Helena	4.1[illegible].29	Nelipeno
Romanovic, Ester	18.11.29	Slat. Doly
Rothschild, Hermann	24. 8.29	Hamburk
Sab, Berta	14.1o.29	Vysni Aps[illegible]
Sab, Marie	[illegible].3.29	Bodovlg
Samuel, Charlotte	3. 2.29	Velky Pole
Schwarz, Eva	24. 2.29	Borohov[illegible]

Figure 2C: Lists 148 children of uncertain nationality who arrived in Great Britain at the end of
Feb /March. Refer to 23rd line from the bottom where
Gisella Moskovic from Kuznin is listed.

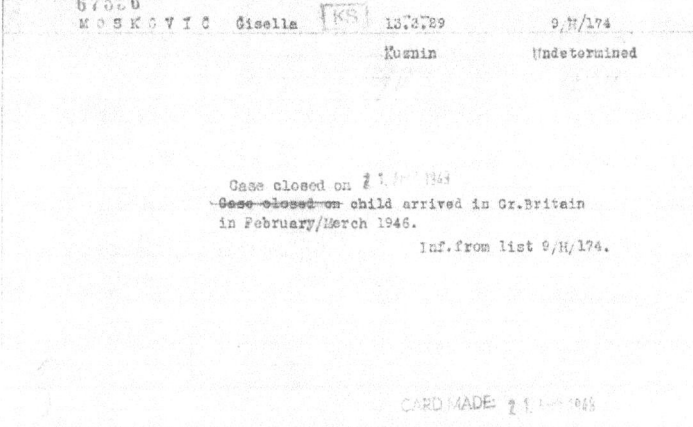

Figure 3: Name index card created by the child tracing service in 1949 documenting Gisella Moskovic's arrival in Great Britain in Feb/March 1946. The card was created on April 21, 1949.

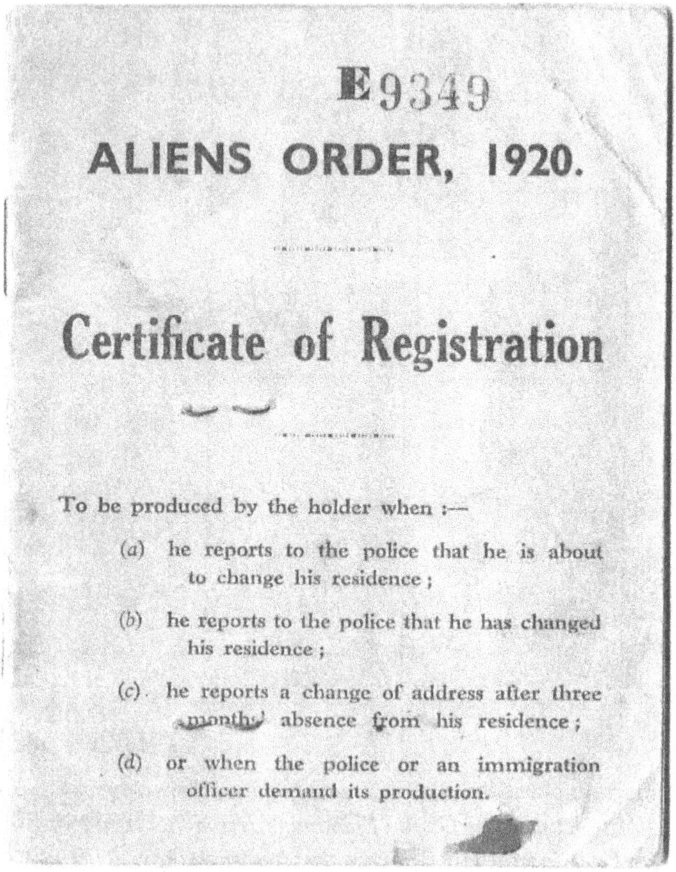

E9349

ALIENS ORDER, 1920.

Certificate of Registration

To be produced by the holder when :—

(a) he reports to the police that he is about to change his residence;

(b) he reports to the police that he has changed his residence;

(c) he reports a change of address after three months' absence from his residence;

(d) or when the police or an immigration officer demand its production.

Figure 4.1: Certificate of registration for Gizela Moskovicova stamped on April 4, 1946. It was also later stamped on September 21, 1946 by the Lanashire Constabulary. This notes that the day of her arrival to the United Kingdom was on February 24, 1946. Her registration certificate number is E9349.

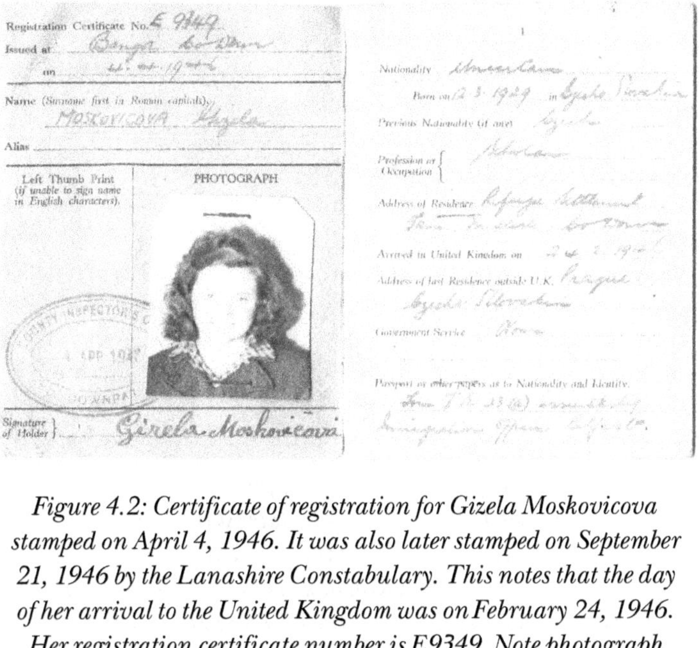

Registration Certificate No. E 9349
Issued at Bangor Co. Down
on 4. 4. 1946
Name (Surname first in Roman capitals) MOSKOVICOVA Gizela
Alias
Left Thumb Print (if unable to sign name in English characters).
PHOTOGRAPH
Signature of Holder Gizela Moskovicova

1
Nationality
Born on
Previous Nationality (if any)
Profession or Occupation
Address of Residence
Arrived in United Kingdom on
Address of last Residence outside U.K. Prague
Government Service None
Passport or other papers as to Nationality and Identity.

Figure 4.2: Certificate of registration for Gizela Moskovicova stamped on April 4, 1946. It was also later stamped on September 21, 1946 by the Lanashire Constabulary. This notes that the day of her arrival to the United Kingdom was on February 24, 1946. Her registration certificate number is E9349. Note photograph and signature on the page preceding page 1 of certificate.

KUZMINO CHRONICLES

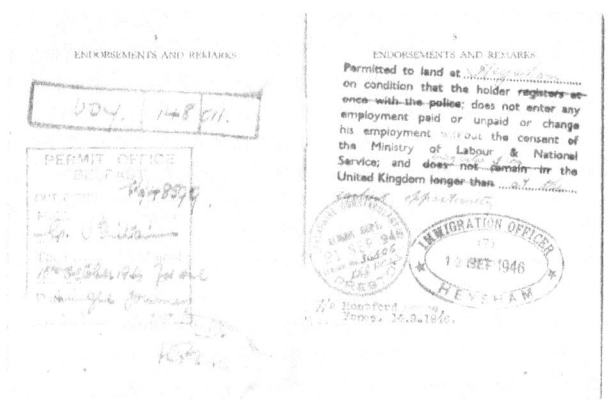

Figure 4.3: Certificate of registration for Gizela Moskovicova stamped on April 4, 1946. It was also later stamped on September 21, 1946 by the Lanashire Constabulary. This notes that the day of her arrival to the United Kingdom was on February 24, 1946. Her registration certificate number is E9349 (pages 4 and 5).

KINDERTRANSPORT TO UNITED KINGDOM...

> **NOTICE TO THE HOLDER OF THIS CERTIFICATE**
>
> 1. Before you effect a *permanent* change of residence (from the last address shown in this Certificate) you must give the Police of the district in which you reside your new address and the date on which you intend to move.
> 2. If your new residence is in another Police district you must within 48 hours of your arrival there, report to the Police of the new district.
> 3. A *temporary* absence of less than 14 days from your permanent residence need not be reported, but if such absence exceeds 14 days you must report your temporary address and all subsequent changes of address (including your return home) to the Police of the district where you are registered. *This may be done by letter.*
> 4. If you stay at an hotel, lodging-house, boarding-house, or other place where lodging is provided for payment, you must, *on arrival*, write your name, nationality, the number of this Certificate, and the address from which you have come, and, *before leaving*, must write the address to which you intend to go on the form provided for the purpose.
> 5. You must report to the Police of the district where you are registered, within 48 hours, any change in any of the personal particulars given within (including profession or occupation), also marriage, divorce, or death of husband or wife.
> 6. Your children, if not British, must have separate Certificates when they reach the age of 16.
>
> Failure to comply with any of the above requirements, making any false statement with regard to registration or with regard to this certificate, altering this certificate or any entry upon it, refusing to produce this certificate when legally required to do so, or having in possession or using without lawful authority any forged, altered, or irregular certificate, passport, or other document concerned with registration, will render the offender liable to be detained in custody and to a fine of £100 or six months' imprisonment.

Figure 4.4: Certificate of registration for Gizela Moskovicova stamped on April 4, 1946. It was also later stamped on September 21, 1946 by the Lanashire Constabulary. This notes that the day of her arrival to the United Kingdom was on February 24, 1946. Her registration certificate number is E9349 (Notice to the holder of this certificate).

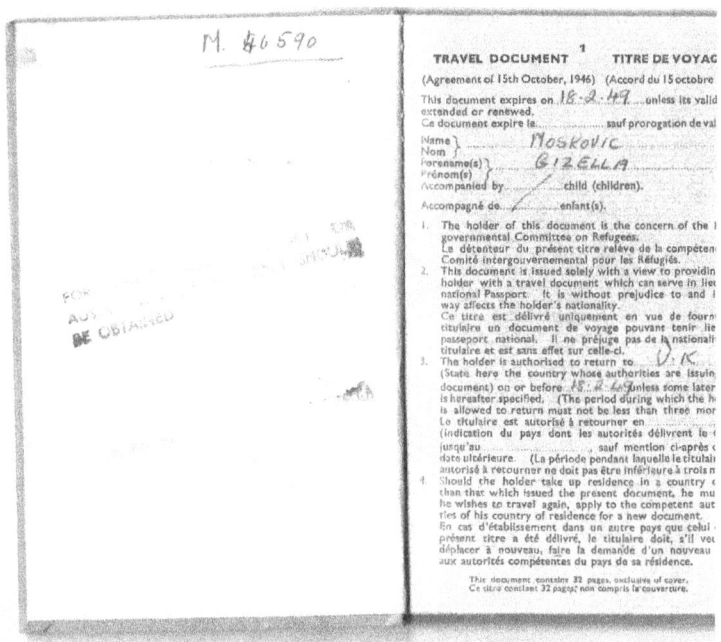

Figure 5.1: Visa (page 1) issued to Gizella Moskovic residing in London SW2.

KINDERTRANSPORT TO UNITED KINGDOM...

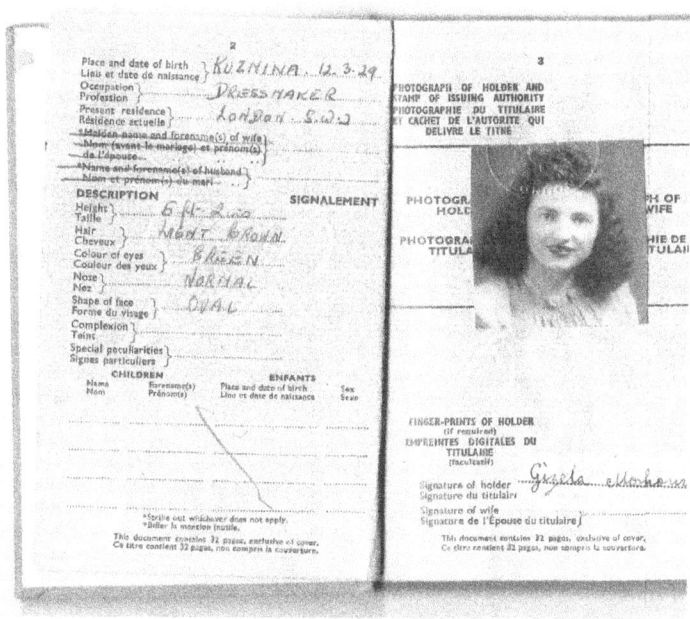

Figure 5.2: Visa (pages 2 and 3 with photograph) issued to Gizella Moskovic residing in London SW2. Her occupation is dressmaker.

Figure 5.3: Visa (pages 4 and 5) issued to Gizella Moskovic residing in London SW2.

KINDERTRANSPORT TO UNITED KINGDOM...

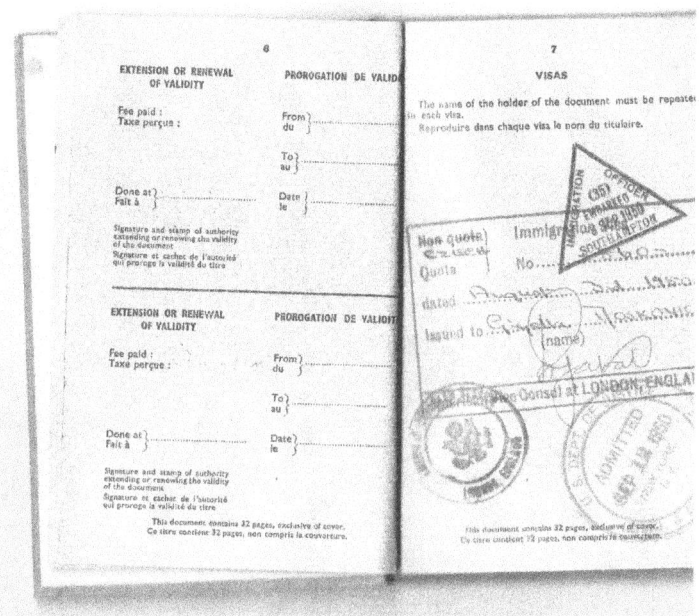

Figure 5.4: Visa (pages 6 and 7) issued to Gizella Moskovic residing in London SW2. Her occupation is dressmaker. Note triangular stamp on page 7 by an Immigration Officer in Southampton documenting her embarking on September 8, 1950. A circular stamp on the same page by the US department of Justice documents that she was admitted on Sep 12, 1950 to New York, NY.

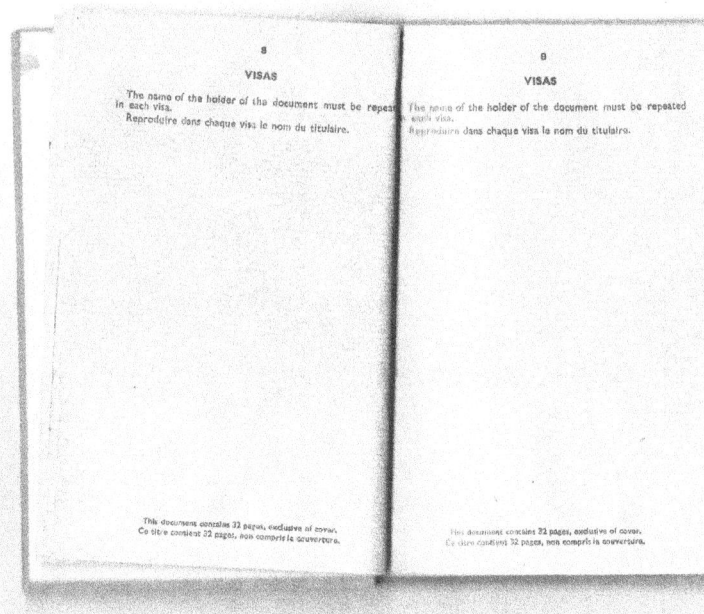

Figure 5.5: Visa (pages 8 and 9) issued to Gizella Moskovic residing in London SW2.

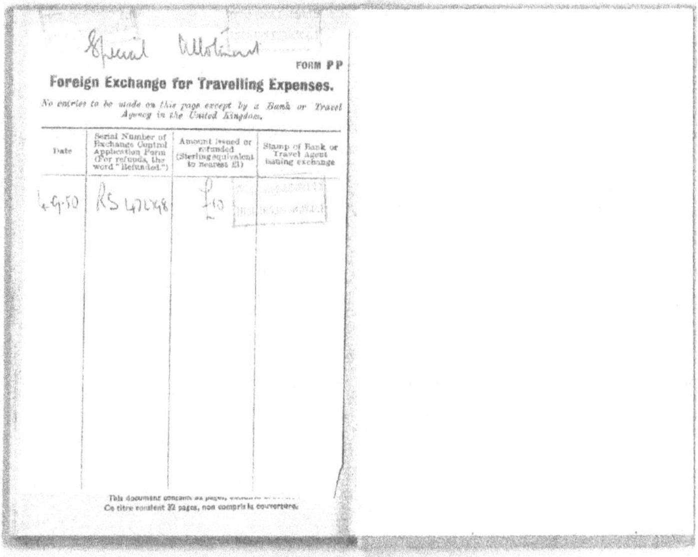

Special Allotment

FORM PP

Foreign Exchange for Travelling Expenses.

No entries to be made on this page except by a Bank or Travel Agency in the United Kingdom.

Date	Serial Number of Exchange Control Application Form (For refunds, the word "Refunded.")	Amount issued or refunded (Sterling equivalent to nearest £1)	Stamp of Bank or Travel Agent issuing exchange
4.9.50	RS 472298	£10	[illegible]

This document contains 32 pages, [illegible]

Ce titre contient 32 pages, non compris la couverture.

Figure 5.6: Visa (last page) issued to Gizella Moskovic residing in London SW2.

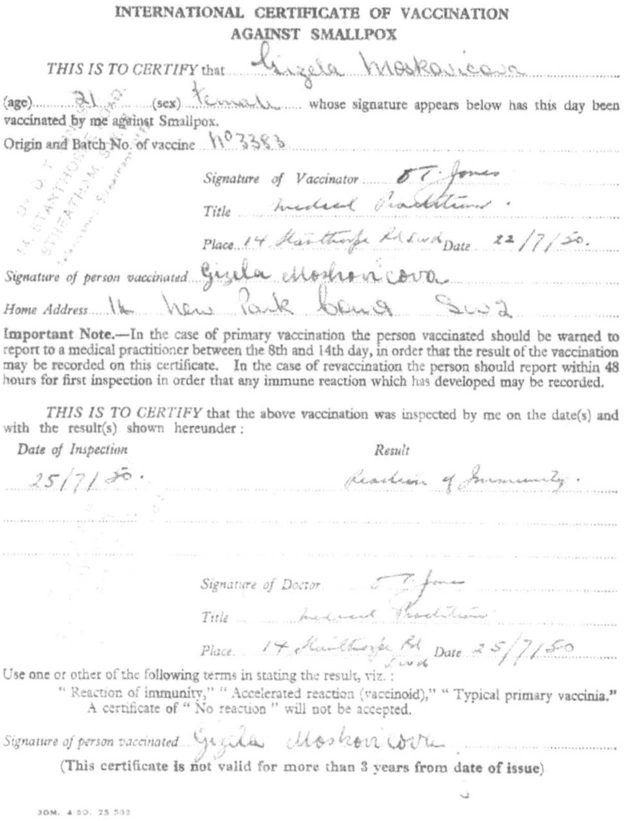

INTERNATIONAL CERTIFICATE OF VACCINATION
AGAINST SMALLPOX

THIS IS TO CERTIFY that Gizela Moskovicova

(age) 21 (sex) Female whose signature appears below has this day been vaccinated by me against Smallpox.

Origin and Batch No. of vaccine N° 3383

Signature of Vaccinator D. T. Jones

Title Medical Practitioner.

Place 14 Hawthorpe Rd SW16 *Date* 22/7/50.

Signature of person vaccinated Gizela Moskovicova

Home Address 14 New Park Lane SW2

Important Note.—In the case of primary vaccination the person vaccinated should be warned to report to a medical practitioner between the 8th and 14th day, in order that the result of the vaccination may be recorded on this certificate. In the case of revaccination the person should report within 48 hours for first inspection in order that any immune reaction which has developed may be recorded.

THIS IS TO CERTIFY that the above vaccination was inspected by me on the date(s) and with the result(s) shown hereunder:

Date of Inspection	*Result*
25/7/50.	Reaction of Immunity.

Signature of Doctor D. T. Jones

Title Medical Practitioner

Place 14 Hawthorpe Rd SW16 *Date* 25/7/50

Use one or other of the following terms in stating the result, viz.:
" Reaction of immunity," " Accelerated reaction (vaccinoid)," " Typical primary vaccinia."
A certificate of " No reaction " will not be accepted.

Signature of person vaccinated Gizela Moskovicova

(This certificate is not valid for more than 3 years from date of issue)

30M. 4-50. 25 502

Figure 6: International certificate of vaccination against smallpox for Gizela Moskovicova dated July 25, 1950 prior traveling to US.

Postscript

LEIB AND GITTEL married in 1951 and currently reside in Bronx, New York. They have children, grandchildren and great grandchildren.

A photo of Leib and Gittel after their engagement. Prospect Avenue, Bronx, New York, 1951.

POSTSCRIPT

A photo of Leib and Gittel in their home in Bronx, New York, 2014.

About the Editor

Nathan C. Moskowitz, MD, PhD, FACS, FICS is a visionary painter, neurosurgeon, neuroscientist, and inventor. He authored a neuroscience book entitled "Molecular Modulation of Chemical Presynaptic Neurotransmission" (Praeger Press), and a Biblical- Art book entitled "The Color of Prophecy: Visualizing the Bible in a new light" (Gefen Publishing House). He published over thirty scientific articles related to neuroscience and neurosurgery, multiple articles on biblical analysis for the Jewish Bible Quarterly, as well as forty patents/ patent pendings of medical device designs and applications. He has exhibited his paintings either in solo or group exhibitions in the United States, Europe, and Australia, and one of his paintings is in the permanent collection of the Yad Vashem Art Museum in Israel. He is currently Assistant Professor of Neurosurgery at the Johns Hopkins Medical

School, a member of the Arts and Letters Council of the David S. Wyman Institute for Holocaust Studies, and President and Founder of the Shoah Forensics Art Institute.

www.ingramcontent.com/pod-product-compliance
Lightning Source LLC
Chambersburg PA
CBHW051813090426
42736CB00011B/1458